MEMORIES BEYOND MOSCOW

Mereo Books

2nd Floor, 6-8 Dyer Street, Cirencester, Gloucestershire, GL7 2PF
An imprint of Memoirs Books. www.mereobooks.com
and www.memoirsbooks.co.uk

MEMORIES BEYOND MOSCOW

ISBN: 978-1-86151-841-5

First published in Great Britain in 2024
by Mereo Books, an imprint of Memoirs Books.,
in association with Pectopah Press

Copyright ©2024

Harald Lipman has asserted his right under the Copyright Designs and
Patents Act 1988 to be identified as the author of this work.

A CIP catalogue record for this book is available from the British Library.
This book is sold subject to the condition that it shall not by way of trade or otherwise be lent,
resold, hired out or otherwise circulated without the publisher's prior consent in any form
of binding or cover, other than that in which it is published and without a similar condition,
including this condition being imposed on the subsequent purchaser.

The address for Memoirs Books can be
found at www.mereobooks.com

Mereo Books Ltd. Reg. No. 12157152

Typeset in 12/15pt Garamond
by Wiltshire Associates.
Printed and bound in Great Britain

MEMORIES BEYOND
MOSCOW

Memoirs Of A Benevolent Lepidopterist

HARALD LIPMAN

To my darling wife Nahid

I am a rose that grows on hills of love
I am a soul that learns the drills of love
I am a heart in agony and joy
From fire and chills and woes and thrills of love

- Baba Tahir Oryan, 11th century Persian poet

Acknowledgements

Our youngest, granddaughter Bella, although studying English in her final year at Bristol University, found time to advise me and achieved a First Class degree.

My beloved wife, Nahid, has been a great support to me during the sometimes arduous task of writing these memoirs and on many occasions has corrected my recollection of events.

Martin Dewhurst, an acknowledged expert in Russian affairs and Russian language, has being invaluable in his considered amendments and translation of my letters to Vladimir Putin.

Marc, our son, a chest physician, although extremely busy during the Covid pandemic, found time to advise me on aspects of the book.

I wish also to mention Bente Fasmer and her excellent photos.

My publishing team, for supportive and helpful undertaking the task of preparing the manuscript for publication

Many thanks to Mereo Books for their excellent front cover.

CONTENTS

Introduction
Prologue

Chapter 1	Return to London	1
Chapter 2	Tushinskaya Trust	6
Chapter 3	Russian economy	20
Chapter 4	South Pacific	27
Chapter 5	Princess Diana	54
Chapter 6	Constitutional crisis	60
Chapter 7	Problems in Tushinskaya	66
Chapter 8	Further developments Tushinskaya	81
Chapter 9	Princess Diana's Moscow visit	87
Chapter 10	Where do we go from here	100
Chapter 11	Our varied life	110
Chapter 12	Princess Diana's death	117
Chapter 13	A change of tack	124
Chapter 14	Balkans and eastern Europe	132
Chapter 15	Scholarships and visits	138
Chapter 16	Tushinskaya Hospital	144
Chapter 17	Scholars	155
Chapter 18	Balkan visits	160
Chapter 19	Politics and war	167
Chapter 20	A dreadful year	173
Chapter 21	ICHARM	181
Chapter 22	ICHARM pilot project	192
Chapter 23	Great Recession	207
Chapter 24	Fortuitous events for the Tushinskaya Trust	213
Chapter 25	Russian Bill Gates	224
Chapter 26	Amanda	228
Chapter 27	Life goes on	238
Chapter 28	Sequelae 2012	243
Chapter 29	Problems and pleasures	250
Chapter 30	Progress	256
Chapter 31	A preventable war	264

Chapter 32	Kazakhstan	271
Chapter 33	The last Tsar	278
Chapter 34	Red star over Russia	287
Chapter 35	Our Trust and Russia	295
	Finale	302
	Epilogue	312
	Index Alphabetical	316

Introduction

2000, Arkhangelsk Oblast

Vologda, Totma, Kargopal

Kathy and Geoff Murrell had arranged, in 2000, a trip to Arkhangelsk Oblast and invited several old Moscow hands. It would be the beginning of the "White Nights", when the sun sets only for a short while.

Kathy, Geoff, Jill Braithwaite, Nahid and I flew together to Moscow where, following a short tour of the city, we checked into the Leningradskaya Hotel. That evening we invited Galina, Sergei, Olga and Sasha to join us for supper, and later caught the overnight train from Yaroslavsky Voksal to Vologda, spending a very disturbed night in a four-berth compartment.

At the station prior to departure, we had met up with the other ten members of the group, some Russian and some English, some we knew such as Kate Cook and Rodric Braithwaite, and others who we were meeting for the first time.

We all stayed in the Spasskaya Hotel in Vologda in comfortable suites and took a previously arranged coach tour to the local Kremlin and then visited the Belozersky Monastery and the Ferapontevo Monastery in Krillov, where we viewed the Dionysiou frescos.

Vologda, situated on the Vologda River, a tributary of the Dvina, was a major transport centre as it was a junction for north–south Moscow-Archangel and east–west Trans-Siberian railway lines.

In 1918, for several months, after the Bolshevik revolution, it had become the diplomatic capital of Russia when several of the foreign Embassies, incuding United States, Great Britain, France, China, Italy, Japan, Serbia, Brazil and Siam moved there from Moscow. Initially, until accommodation could be found, they lived on the railway train on platform 5, taking their food from the station restaurant. *"There was a fair assortment of food to offer: big jars of dill pickles, black bread chorney kleb, kvass, a non-alcoholic beer and hard- boiled eggs."*

When they moved into a large clubhouse, the US Ambassador's valet described their *"living in grand style"*. The American historian George Kennan described *"the wood fires crackling cosily in the big brick ovens, whilst outside they heard the sound of distant church bells and the creaking of sledge runners on the snow-covered street."*

Arthur Ransome, correspondent for the Manchester Guardian, described winter in Vologda thus: *"There's hardly a brick building in the place, but little log houses of one or two stories, broad untidy squares and street markets, with churches in every open space, white churches against the blue winter sky, churches capped with towers of every kind of intricate design, showing the great bronze bells hanging in their airy belfries beside domes of gold and green, plain grey lead and of violent deep blue, thickly sown with golden stars."*

There had recently been an abortive anti-Lenin coup d'état, in large part initiated by countries who opposed the Communist state.

The Russian-born British agent Sidney Reilly, and Robert Bruce Lockhart, Consul general in the British Embassy in Moscow, who had been assigned by the British government to meet and parley with the Bolshevik authorities, met with them and separately met with others who had conceived the anti-Lenin plot, in Vologda. Coincidentally, a failed assassination attempt on Lenin was made by an anarchist, Fanny Kaplan. Bruce Lockhart was subsequently imprisoned in the *Lubyanka*, the headquarters of the *Cheka*, the secret police, and later deported in exchange for Maxim Litvinov, our erstwhile Russian teacher, Vera Chalidze's grandfather.

By chance, I had an aunt called Fanny Caplan, my mother's youngest sister, but she was not related to the similarly named anarchist.

Several foreign Embassies, now based in Vologda, agreed to advise their governments that multinational military expeditions should be sent in attempts to re-establish the Eastern front, the front line between Germany and Russia, and also to assist in overthrowing the newly established Bolshevik regime.

In 1919, French, British, American, Italian and Canadian troops were sent to Archangel in the north and Vladivostok in the east, where they were later joined by the Japanese. In southern Russia, French troops went to Odessa and Sebastopol, British troops to the Caucasus. The following year most of these expeditionary forces were withdrawn.

Next day, following a visit to the undecorated Spaso Prilutsky Monastery to attend and view the service in the cellars, we boarded a hydrofoil on the river. It was a very beautiful river with several small villages along its banks, and apart from the mosquitoes, a most enjoyable journey. In the evening after supper on board the boat, a pianist played and sang Russian melodies, including, by request, *"Moskovskaya Vechera"* which translates as Moscow Evenings.

The boat moored in a small town called Totma, and after breakfast a coach took us to visit the town museum with its fascinating historical, geographic and ethnographic records. It was there where, in the 18th century, Ivan Kuskov, the first Administrator of Fort Ross in California, which we had visited several years previously, was born.

The name Totma originates from a Finno-Ugrik word meaning "swampy lowlands". In the 13th century on the banks of the Kovda river, salt deposits were discovered. Over subsequent centuries the salt industry brought considerable wealth to those who owned the salt mines.

In the 18th century, Vitus Bering, a Danish cartographer and explorer in Russian service and an officer in the Russian Navy, travelled from St Petersburg via Vologda and Totma to the Kamchatka Peninsula in Eastern Siberia. He crossed the straits now named after him and travelled on into Alaska, thus expediting Russian colonisation of the western coast of North America.

Kathy told us over supper that night in Vologda, which we had returned to after our visit to Totma, a most interesting story about her previous visit with a friend to Totma, several years earlier. They were both fluent Russian speakers and, due to the idiosyncrasies of the transport system, whilst travelling in the region they had unexpectedly arrived in Totma and were told by the local inhabitants that they were the first English people ever to have visited the town.

Later, on her return to Moscow, Kathy wrote an article for a Russian newspaper about the journey, and was surprised, sometime later, to receive a letter from an unknown Russian man. He informed her that in fact they were not the first English people to visit Totma. Apparently, when Thomas Randolph had been sent by Queen Elizabeth I as an envoy to Ivan the Terrible, en route to Moscow, he had passed through and spent the night in Totma. Touché!

Our next port of call was Kargopol, which entailed a train and coach journey.

In the 16th century, Kargopol, lying on the route between Moscow and Archangel, at that time the only Russian port, was very prosperous. Unfortunately, when we arrived there, it seemed to have fallen on hard times. The Hotel Kargoplochka had no baths or showers, and only communal loos.

We found a local banya, public bath, where we performed our ablutions.

We visited the cathedral complex, saw several wooden churches and then the toy museum full of moulded painted clay figures of people and animals.

Lunch had been arranged for us with a Russian family, Galina Sergeiva, in the village of Lyadina. They told us that many small villages in the region had now become depopulated as there was no work for young people, and they had all moved to larger towns. In several of the villages we visited there would be only a handful of aged men and women to be seen.

The following day, after a visit by coach to Oshevensk, we caught an overnight train from Nyandoma to Moscow.

This had been a most interesting and instructive trip, and we had had the opportunity of viewing many aspects of rural Russia previously unknown to us.

Prologue

Henry IV part 2

I was in the sixth form of the City of London School, studying Henry IV part 2 for the Higher School Certificate examination. That year, in the annual school play, I played the role of Archibald, Earl of Douglas. *"Know then, my name is Douglas; And I do haunt thee in the battle thus."*

In one scene, Archibald marches aggressively on to the stage to battle with Henry. The reviews of the play in the school magazine mentioned that Lipman played the part of Archibald, Earl of Douglas and, with sword raised in his hand, wandered on to the stage, looking like a benevolent lepidopterist. I thought that this might be an appropriate subtitle for *Memories beyond Moscow*.

The author as Archibald, Earl of Douglas

Following Nahid and my years spent in Moscow, living and working in the British Embassy as Medical Attaché during the 1980s, we had developed a close attachment to Russia and Russians.

What an eventful decade it had been.

Although by the end of 1991 the Soviet Union had ceased to exist, and a very different country, the Russian Federation, was slowly feeling its way with the assistance of Western countries to evolving into a democratic country with a capitalist economy, the future remained very uncertain.

Sadly, the United States and Western Europe had little understanding of Russian thought processes, or of the proud nationalistic nature of the Russian people. The West felt that it knew all the answers and merely had to graft their political and economic systems onto Russia, and set about this task in a rather "ham-fisted" way.

Knowing many Russians as close friends, and having lived in Russia for over five years, it was obvious to Nahid and me that the West's approach would not be acceptable to many Russian politicians or people.

Over 20 million Russians had died during the Second World War, and, not surprisingly, looked at it through Russian eyes, they were suspicious and fearful of Western desires to encircle them by admitting the Eastern European satellite states to membership of Western organisations, such as NATO and the European Union.

The world had turned upside down for Russians following the dissolution of the Soviet Union in December 1991.

Russians, a very proud people, felt absolutely deflated. They had ceased to be a world power and had lost their position of influence, and their dignity.

Swamped by foreigners trying to graft their beliefs and their ways of life onto them, they became suspicious that all "do-gooders" had ulterior motives.

Often, we felt that some of our Russian contacts thought we must have some ulterior motive for wishing to help them resolve some of their health care problems.

Nevertheless, we found, in general, the Russian people warm and welcoming, and at a personal level, relatively easy to get on with. Gradually, however, over the course of the future years, as there was little understanding of Russian views by the West, and of Western views by Russia, a complete lack of trust developed in both parties.

In future chapters, as you will see, misunderstandings, or misinterpretations, could destabilise Russia and the West's mutual relationships.

The next three decades would turn out personally, nationally and internationally to be, in many ways, even more eventful than the previous decade.

How could anyone, other than a reliable clairvoyant, know what the future would bring? Unfortunately, I have mislaid Mme Arcati's phone number, but if any "table tappers" amongst my readers are in touch with her, perhaps they could let me know.

You may recollect, Mme Arcati was the clairvoyant in Noel Coward's *Blithe Spirit*. Margaret Rutherford, in the 1941 stage production, and later in 1945 in David Lean's screen version, played a memorable representation of her.

Those who have seen photos of Margaret Rutherford may recollect that she had a very prominent chin. Theatre critic, Kenneth Tynan, once said of her performances: *"The unique thing about Margaret Rutherford is that she can act with her chin alone."*

Chapter 1

Return to London

Return to London, Iraq invasion Kuwait, IRA, Russian lessons, Health of expatriates, EETMAS, August putsch, UK recession, Breaking the Code, Gorbachev resigns

Return to London

When we returned to London in 1991 after our trip to Madras, Kuala Lumpur, Singapore, Australia and New Zealand, our Hampstead house was still rented out. Marc had been living in the Wimpole Street flat but then moved to a flat in Holloway, so we resided in, and I consulted from Wimpole Street for the next three years. The flat also became the office of Tushinskaya Trust.

I had contacted many of my previous patients informing them that I was back and practising in London, and, perhaps surprisingly, quite a significant number of them began to consult me again.

*

Gulf War

Saddam Hussein had invaded Kuwait in August 1990, and in January 1991 a UN coalition, led by the United States, commenced a military operation to force out the Iraqis from Kuwait.

Chris Lee, one of the Medical Advisers to the Foreign Office, was a British army reservist and was called up at that time, leaving them short-staffed. David Snashall contacted me and asked if I would be prepared to step in and help the health and welfare department out.

This fitted in with my plans, and I was able to undertake this on a part-time basis with immediate effect. I was happy to be back again working with colleagues in the Office.

*

IRA Downing Street mortar attack

The Provisional Irish Republican Army (IRA) launched a mortar attack on 10 Downing Street in an attempt to assassinate Prime Minister John Major and his War Cabinet. One mortar shell exploded in the back garden but none of the Cabinet were hurt.

*

Russian lessons

Nahid and I had decided that we should continue to study Russian, as otherwise we would rapidly forget it.

We found that Russian language classes were being held in the evening in an Institute not too far from us, close to Primrose Hill, and enrolled there.

Our teacher was a lovely Russian woman, Nataly Duddington, who was married to a half-British/half-Russian psychiatrist called Sasha. In Moscow, she had worked with Yevgeny Primakov, in the International Relations department of the USSR Academy of Sciences. He, Primakov, later entered politics and became the Minister of Foreign Affairs, and briefly Prime Minister of the Russian Federation.

Quite quickly we became close friends and Nataly became involved with the Trust. Her daughter Masha and son-in-law Sergei still lived in Moscow and were very helpful in many ways when we visited there.

*

Going Abroad course

I had been asked to speak at a Going Abroad course, as part of the RAF diploma course in aviation medicine, held at RAF Halton. The letter of invitation contained a typographical error and the request was for me to speak on the "Health of Ex-patriots", not as I had expected "Health of Expatriates."

As a preamble to my talk, I showed a slide of Guy Burgess and Donald Maclean, who were certainly both ex-patriots and also, after decamping to Moscow in 1951, expatriates. They were both sick men, and, so far as we know, had not had the benefit of advice regarding preparations for living abroad in the USSR, other than possibly from their KGB masters.

EETMAS

Paul Arnisson-Newgass, Medical Adviser in Warsaw, and I felt that we should apply some of the knowledge we had obtained during our overseas postings to assisting travellers to Eastern Europe and the former Soviet Union, FSU.

Thus, the Eastern European Travellers Medical Advisory Service, EETMAS, was developed and incorporated as a limited company.

Its geographical scope covered all eleven of the former Soviet satellite states and all the Republics of the FSU.

We set up a database for each country, listing recommended English-speaking doctors, dentists, hospitals, laboratories, radiologists, pharmacists, opticians, nurses, physiotherapists and ambulance services.

Subscribers would be given details of local health risks, recommended protective procedures such as immunisations, risks from water pollution and national natural hazards, and details of the available health care in the locality to which they would be travelling. Each subscriber would be supplied with a standardised record form detailing their medical history, allergies and so on, plus a glossary of medical terms in the local language with their phonetic pronunciation.

All advice would be tailored for specific requirements such as the geographical location and specific occupational hazards.

Membership would be available to major industrial Western European companies, small Western European companies, individual Western European travellers and governmental and non-governmental organisations.

It was an excellent idea, and we both put a lot of hard work into developing the database and seeking potential subscribers, but sadly, we ultimately found that we had "bitten off more than we could chew".

You may recollect the lines from Frank Sinatra's song "My Way": "*Yes there were times, I'm sure you knew, when I bit off more than I could chew. But through it all when there was doubt, I ate it up and spat it out.*"

*

August putsch

Members of the Government of the USSR who were hard-line members of the Communist Party of the Soviet Union were opposed to Gorbachev's reform programme and the new union treaty and attempted to take control of the country.

Mikhail Gorbachev, holidaying in the Crimea, was incarcerated in his house.

They were opposed, mainly in Moscow, by a short but effective campaign of civil resistance led by the President of the Russian Republic, Boris Yeltsin, who had been both an ally and a critic of Gorbachev. Although the coup collapsed in only two days, and Gorbachev returned to power, the event destabilised the USSR and is widely considered to have contributed to both the demise of the CPSU, Communist Party of the Soviet Union, and the dissolution of the USSR.

You may recollect the photograph of Yeltsin standing on top of a tank haranguing the crowds outside the White House, the Russian Parliament. Jill Braithwaite and a few members of the embassy staff bravely joined the crowds.

On Gorbachev's return to Moscow, Russia was a "different country", and according to a report in *Izvestiya*, *"he did not seem to recognise it."*

*

UK recession

The UK recession of 1991 was primarily caused by high interest rates, falling house prices and an overvalued exchange rate. Membership of the Exchange Rate Mechanism, ERM (1990–1992) was a key factor in keeping interest rates higher than desirable.

The recession followed the late 1980s economic boom – a period of high economic growth and rising inflation.

One of the effects of the recession was that it reduced advertising by businesses. This seriously affected Amanda's free listing paper, *The Good Times*, as it depended on the revenue from advertisements. Although we tried to find ways to continue publication, it was eventually, sadly, put into receivership. A dreadful blow for her.

*

Breaking the Code

We all went to see Breaking the Code, a play by Hugh Whitemore about the British mathematician Alan Turing who was a key player in the breaking of the German Enigma code at Bletchley Park during World War II, and a pioneer of computer science. The play thematically links Turing's cryptographic activities with his attempts to grapple with his homosexuality.

Gorbachev resigns

Mikhail Gorbachev resigned the Presidency of the Soviet Union on December 25, 1991. That same day, the Soviet Union ceased to exist. It was replaced by the Commonwealth of Independent States (CIS), a free association of sovereign states founded by the elected leaders of Russia, Ukraine and Belarus (Belorussia).

CHAPTER 2

Tushinskaya Trust

Tushinskaya Trust GOSH assessment, The Charity, British Embassy residence, Enku Kebede, Patron, Modern Children's Hospital, Visits to and from London, Moskovskya Pravda, Trust's objectives, Master & Margarita, BESO, Specialist teams, Russian Booker Prize, With a doctor's bag in Russia, Skiing in Heavenly Valley, IAPOS, Christine's wedding, Dublin, Tsewang visit

Tushinskaya Trust GOSH assessment

David Hatch, Susan MacQueen, both from GOSH, and Ray Morgan from SIMS Pharmaceutical had prepared a very comprehensive report assessing the problems as they saw them in Tushino Hospital, then known as Moscow City Children's Hospital No 7.

They felt that the major problem was the lack of trained paediatric nursing staff and that the Trust, with the advice and assistance of Great Ormond Street Hospital, GOSH, should concentrate on that aspect of Tushino's problems, with the objective of improving nursing status and standards. All this would be subject to obtaining the agreement of GOSH, Tushino Hospital, Moscow city authorities and of course Mossoviet.

Following protracted and sometimes difficult discussions with all the organisations that would be involved, it was decided that a formal charitable trust should be incorporated, which could then formally start trying to assist Tushino Hospital.

*

1991 The Charity

The Charity, to be known as Friends of Tushino Hospital, was registered in March 1991, and the trustees were Sir Bryan Cartledge, then Principal of Linacre College Oxford, who agreed to be Chairman, Dr Michael Nicholls, Dean British Postgraduate Medical Federation, and myself, Dr Harald Lipman.

The objectives of the Trust were to relieve the sickness, and preserve and protect the health, of children in the Soviet Union, particularly by the provisional of medical equipment and supplies for the Tushino Hospital in Moscow, and to advance education and training through the exchange of Russian medical specialists with British hospitals.

In 1993, the Trust's name was formally changed to Tushinskaya Children's Hospital Charitable Trust. The significance of this name change was that in Russian it meant "Children's Hospital of the district called Tushino", thus directly linking it to the area it served.

Donations had been received from the Wellcome Foundation, Vickers Medical, Smith Kline Beauchamp and Boots.

Sir Bryan approached The Baroness Cox of Queensbury MSc FRCN, who kindly agreed to become President of the Trust.

Baroness Caroline Cox, at that time Deputy Speaker of the House of Lords, had studied Sociology at University and campaigned for many humanitarian causes. She was also honorary Vice President of the Royal College of Nursing. Her specific interests related to the plight of the South Sudanese people and assisting Armenians in Nagorno-Karabakh, a disputed territory on the border of Armenia and Azerbaijan, in their struggle for self-determination. She later founded the Humanitarian Aid Relief Trust, HART.

*

Colonel Violet Williams of the Salvation Army was ascertaining whether the Queen Mother would consider giving her patronage to the Charity. However, she was advised that the Queen Mother was not undertaking any additional patronages.

In November 1991, Sir Bryan Cartledge agreed to make inquiries with the Princess of Wales's private secretary to ascertain if the Princess would become Patron of the Trust.

Meanwhile, it had been agreed with Tushino Hospital that the Trust should aim to establish a School of Paediatric Nursing in conjunction with the hospital. This would be the first dedicated School of Paediatric Nursing in the Soviet Union and the Eastern bloc satellite states.

*

British Embassy residence

To mark the 100th anniversary of the completion of the British Embassy building in Moscow, Kathy Murrell launched her excellent book *The British Embassy Moscow,* containing many evocative photos taken by John Freeman, and it was translated into Russian by Sergei Romanyuk.

*

1992

In January 1992, Yuri Pavlov proposed that training of paediatric nurses should only be part of a radical restructuring of the hospital. This should involve changes in the system of management, the organisation of labour and a review of the workload, with the aim of developing the hospital as a model of a modern children's hospital.

We all agreed that the ultimate objective should be to make the ill child the focus and centre of the hospital, and the welfare of the child was paramount. The aim should be to achieve holistic childcare. Under the still existing Soviet system, too often hospitals appeared to be run primarily in order to give employment to the staff.

Quite quickly, it was realised that each part of the hospital is interdependent on all other parts. Merely improving the nursing in isolation, even if that were possible, would have disturbed the balance between doctors/nurses/ancillary staff.

The Trust needed now to widen its knowledge base, and King's Fund College agreed to cooperate with us in this project, with Dr David Knowles of the Leadership Development department representing them.

*

In May 1992, Nahid and I, for the first time since we had left post, returned to Moscow. Kathy and Geoff Murrell had invited us to stay with them in their flat in Sad Sam. We visited Peredelkino with Olga and her husband Sasha, and it felt just like old times, when we lived and worked in Moscow.

*

Enku Kebede

Whilst Nahid and I were walking in one of the Moscow streets, we heard a voice from a person walking behind us calling out "Nahid", "Harald". Surprised, we turned round and who should it be but Enku, our friend from the Australian Embassy, in whose house in Canberra we had spent Christmas in 1990.

She told us that she had recently been in the United States during the Presidential election campaigning on behalf of the third candidate Ross Perot, who managed to attract almost 19 per cent of the vote. Bill Clinton defeated George H W Bush and the rest was history.

Over several long discussions with Yuri and Nelli in Tushino, we all felt that although it would be long and arduous, subject to agreement by all the relevant Russian authorities, it should be possible to achieve the aims of creating a modern children's hospital.

Yuri introduced us to Dr Olga Skorobogatova, the Director of Medical School No 12, a school for training nurses and paramedics, and she was very interested in the possibility of opening a School of Paediatric Nursing. As an aside, her surname translates in English into "soon rich", but let me hasten to say that in no way did she collaborate with us in order to enhance her personal wealth.

Meetings were also held with Moscow Department of Health, our Embassy where I spoke with my successor Hugh Carpenter, the British Council, and Minzdrav, where I had arranged to meet Professor Bella Denisenko, deputy Minister of Health, but she didn't turn up.

In August 1992, we invited Yuri Pavlov, Ivan Leshkevitch, the deputy Head of Glavk, and Nelli Naigovzina, with Dr Vadim Ivanov, deputy Head of Infectious Diseases department, acting as interpreter, to visit us in London. This gave us the opportunity not only to show them London and a different style of life, but also to see Great Ormond Street Hospital and discuss the manner in which we could help Tushino Hospital to develop.

We put them up in a hotel in Southampton Row, within easy walking distance of Great Ormond Street Hospital, took them around and showed them the sights and entertained them at our home and in restaurants.

*

The following month, David Knowles, Fellow of King's Fund College, Sheila McKenzie, consultant Paediatrician at the Queen Elizabeth Hospital for Children, London, Olga Kurtianyk, Director of Nursing Queen Elizabeth Hospital for Children, Michael Kidd, Planning Officer Borough of Hackney, a fluent Russian speaker, Gordon Peters, representing the King's Fund College and Nahid and I flew out in an Aeroflot Ilyushin to Moscow. For several members of our team, this was their first taste of the still-existing Soviet-style organisations.

The hospital had organised a busy and comprehensive programme for us, including a visit to Zagorsk and the Bolshoi where we saw a production of the ballet *Korsar*, loosely based on Byron's poem *"The Corsair."*

We were shown many of the departments in the hospital and had numerous, long, detailed discussions with Yuri Pavlov and his team, as well as a meeting attended by sixty or seventy members of the hospital staff. Some of the meetings were held in the hospital banya – steam bath.

In Glavk, the Moscow Health department, we met Dr Anatoly Soloviev and Dr Ivan Leshkevitch, and in Minzdrav, the State Ministry of Health, Dr Dina Zelinskaya. Following a final meeting in Starya Ploschad with Yuri Cherepov, I signed, on behalf of the Trust, with Cherepov, Soloviev and Yuri Pavlov, a letter granting a considerable degree of autonomy to Tushino Hospital and the change of its name to Tushinskaya Hospital. The Trust's name was then formally changed to Tushinskaya Children's Hospital Charitable Trust.

We agreed that the Trust and the hospital should, on an experimental basis, jointly work together to develop aspects of the existing hospital, in particular by applying the principles of Family Centred Care and control of Hospital-Acquired Infections.

This was a remarkable achievement; remember, only eight months previously the all-powerful and all-knowledgeable Communist Party ruled the State.

Effectively, the Trust had been given carte blanche to advise and assist the hospital in a pilot scheme, and eventually, if successful, extend the new principles that would be introduced in Tushinskaya to hospitals throughout Moscow and the Russian Federation. A very successful visit.

*

The *British Medical Journal* published an article called "Advice to a Moscow Children's Hospital", from which I quote: *"Western endeavours to advise Russians have been severely criticised. Interest in the Russian predicament has not altogether been altruistic, and it has been emphasised that Westerners should listen to what the Russians want. The doctors at Tushino Hospital had asked for advice. A recommendation to introduce family centred care was accepted by the Moscow authorities and Tushino was granted financial autonomy."*

*

Moskovskya Pravda

An October edition of the Russian newspaper *Moskovskya Pravda* in 1992 published L Arinicheva's interview with Yuri Pavlov, Nelli Naigovzina, Ivan Leshkevitch and me. The article was titled "Speak with me Mama". The gist of it was that the existing health service which had been created was for the convenience of the doctors, and this should be changed so that the interest of the child was the prime objective.

The essence of the agreement which had just been signed was that the structure and working principles of British children's hospitals should be borrowed and copied. The Russians were particularly impressed that health care in Great Britain was funded by the State, rather than by medical insurance. The hospital would now be able to independently allocate nurses' pay from their budget and decide how many nurses and doctors were required.

Leshkevitch stated, *"We were lucky to have got the agreement of the government to developing Tushino as an experimental basis for a modern multidiscipline children's hospital. There's a play therapist in every ward of English children's hospitals and they enlist the support of the parents and encourage a positive emotional frame of mind. It has been proven that the more the parental content the quicker the sick child will recover from his illness. Every London hospital has a room where the parents who are looking after their child can snatch some sleep in a bed, make a cup of coffee or a sandwich for themselves or some tasty titbit for their child."*

Nelli Naigovzina felt that probably the principal thing about the care of sick children as inpatients in English hospitals is the real professionalism of the nurses. *"We have decided to use in our training school English types of programmes for training nurses at various levels and it is these staff who will ensure success in the reorganisation of our hospital."*

Some doubt was expressed about the question of security of the hospital buildings and staff, and when there should be free access for parents. *"Who will ensure that gangs won't enter?"*

Yuri Pavlov explained that they were organising their own internal security services. Already they had started daycare facilities in ten specialities, so children could have medical attention at the hospital but go home to sleep and then return the next morning to the hospital.

At the reception marking the signing of the agreement between the Russian and British parties, Dr Lipman, who was representing the Tushinskaya Children's Hospital Charitable Trust, said, *"We are convinced that together we're going to create a better children's hospital because the doctors working here are so highly qualified and we have met people who understand that children also have rights and it is up to the adults to take account of these rights."*

*

Trust's objectives

On return to the UK, we asked all those who had visited Moscow to let us have their views. David felt that changes to the management structure in the hospital were necessary and that it should further develop daycare and the hospital polyclinic.

Sheila expressed the opinion that the hospital was underutilised and overstaffed. Michael suggested that it was necessary to obtain more information about the healthcare needs of the population in northwest Moscow, as following the breakup of the former Soviet Union the hospital had now become a district hospital. Olga had concentrated on improving nursing education and the role of nurses in the ward. Gordon had recently visited several cities in the Urals and was of the opinion that they were more prepared to initiate change than the Moscow authorities were.

By the time we had absorbed all the various views and discussed them, Yuri Pavlov was on a visit to China, and unfortunately, Nelli was ill.

Galina Romanyuk was meanwhile trying to establish, with considerable difficulty, a Russian voluntary fund in Moscow which would assist the hospital with its material requirements and establish a liaison between the hospital, parents and the community.

She wrote in a report: *"When I was asked by my friends to set up a charitable fund to help transform Children's Hospital No 7, I was frightened to start it. I knew nothing about charities, I was absolutely inexperienced. It was not easy to find proper information about establishing charitable funds in the regulations as none existed at that time, so some friends and I prepared documents for registration in accordance with the rules which are used for trading company registrations."*

Galina ended her report with a final paragraph: *"Lastly I learnt the motto which best expresses what I gained from visiting your country. 'A charity name is precious.' It is the means by which the charity is known and by which its reputation will be judged. It is precisely towards this end I intend to work in future."*

The Trust now had a formal committee, and Ken Lovett, previously in the guise of Air Attaché in Moscow, had agreed to become the Treasurer.

Subsequently, it was mutually agreed that the initial steps should concentrate on the following areas – holistic care of children, Family Centred Care, hospital management to replace the old existing command structure, improvement in the standards of existing hospital nurses and training of new paediatric nurses, reduction of hospital-acquired infection, change of the bias from inpatient to day and community care, and introduction of English language classes for hospital staff.

By the end of 1992, parental visiting had been started in three wards in Tushinskaya.

*

Down the line, during the coming year, the Trust would be introducing further new projects.

We would assess ways of assisting the medical staff to raise their standards and improve their working methods, improve estate management and hospital maintenance, initiate improvement of the organisation of the ITU, intensive treatment unit, help with maintaining the excellent standards of the neonatal unit, and assist the hospital to become self-financing, whilst remaining within the framework of the Moscow City health care system.

*

All these ambitious plans, agreed both with the hospital and the Russian authorities, would cost substantial sums of money and we would need to source further funding.

We decided to approach the Know How Fund (KHF), a UK government agency set up to provide technical assistance to the countries of Eastern Europe and the former Soviet Union in transforming themselves into market economies after the collapse of central planning.

The KHF had, understandably, very strict requirements and it was quite a complex business submitting applications, which eventually were successful. We also sought funding amongst the increasing numbers of British firms which were embarking on trade with the post-communist Russian Federation.

*

Over 70 per cent of medical conferences and journals worldwide are spoken or written in the English language. If the Russian health care service was to be modernised it was essential doctors and nurses were able to understand and speak English. Teaching English to the medical staff in Tushinskaya Hospital was therefore a very high priority.

The hospital agreed that medical staff members could attend English language classes during their working hours. We then found a British woman to undertake this task and teach classes of about twenty individuals for an hour twice weekly. Our first language teacher was Sarah Collyer, who worked with Kingsmill Bond in BESO, and subsequently I understand became his wife. When she was returning to the UK, she was succeeded by a Russian man, Max Chursin.

Later during Kingsmill's posting in Moscow, he became the Trust's representative and in later life achieved considerable success working with Russian financial organisations.

*

Master & Margarita

The Four Corners Theatre Company staged a theatrical adaptation of Bulgakov's classic novel *Master & Margarita* in the Almeida theatre in London. Possibly not as interesting an adaptation as we had seen in Moscow, but certainly worth seeing.

*

BESO

BESO, British Executive Services Overseas, was a charitable organisation set up by a group of businessmen in the early 1970s with the aim of arranging for volunteers to undertake short advisory, consultancy and training assignments in many overseas countries.

*

Specialist teams

Between 1991 and 1996, the Trust arranged for specialist teams in the fields of hospital management, surgical care, hospital acquired infection, holistic childcare, family centred care and management of the pharmacy to visit Tushinskaya Hospital and assess and advise the departments in ways of improving their services.

This entailed me making frequent visits to Moscow, either by myself, but, often with Nahid to introduce the adviser or advisers, to arrange the accommodation, to arrange interpreters and generally ensure that the advisers were comfortable and happy.

The hospital had three flats in nearby blocks, which they were permitted by Glavk to use, and which they allowed us to stay in during our visits.

*

Travel was by no means in one direction only as several of the hospital medical and nursing staff were invited by the Trust to visit the UK for specialised training in their fields of interest. Amongst others, Dr Ivanov, Infectious Diseases department, Dr Kalinina, Microbiologist, and Dr Garkusha, Neonatal unit all visited for periods of 10 to 14 days.

Although our main objective was to transfer knowledge, from time to time, due to shortages of medication or equipment, we had to arrange for these to be sent out to Tushinskaya.

In the latter part of 1993, the Trust organised a very large donation of drugs and medication for the hospital, valued at £250,000. Baroness Cox and Sir Bryan Cartledge attended the ceremony in Moscow when the donation was formally handed over to the hospital.

In 1994, the Trust arranged for a year's supply of dried milk to be donated to the hospital by Nutricia. On the recommendation of the British Embassy Moscow, the AUS fund of the FCO, Assistant Undersecretary Fund, purchased a blood gas analyser for the Neonatal unit at a cost of £5,000. The supplier had to deliver and install the equipment, train the users and maintain it.

Supplies of asthma drugs worth US$10,000 had been received from the British firm Fisons. A Russian donor donated 1.5 million roubles to make purchases for the children in the hospital. Ansell, an Australian UK-based firm, donated 80,000 pairs of disposable surgical gloves. Dekomed donated a sterile washer unit for the microbiology laboratory, as well as a supply of antiseptic soap solution and dispensers for hand washing.

Tushinskaya Children's Hospital

Chancellor Freight offered to transport all the above goods from the UK to the hospital and placed a 38-tonne lorry at our disposal.

The International Woman's Club Moscow donated a TV/video recorder to the Trauma ward of the hospital for the use of the children. Five large cartons of bed quilts, toys and handknitted babywear had been donated by a group of British helpers, headed by children's nurse Anne Talbot, who was a very active associate of the Trust.

*

Russian Booker Prize

The first Russian Booker Prize was awarded to Mark Kharitonov for his novel, *Lines of Fate* – Линии судьбы, *Linii sudby*.

A philosophical mystery novel populated with artists, criminals and drug-addicts, *Lines of Fate* is one of the most extraordinary novels to emerge from the last years of the Soviet Union. Written at the height of Gorbachev's power in 1985 but not published in Russian until 1992, the novel is a profound meditation on Russia's past and present, and a subtle examination of the crippling effects of Soviet power on the nation and on the Russian psyche.

*

With a doctor's bag in Russia

Contemporaries of mine had arranged a reunion of graduates from UCH Medical School who had qualified in 1954, 1955 and 1956. I was invited to speak about my experiences as a doctor practising in Moscow. I entitled it "With a doctor's bag in Russia."

I concentrated solely on the Soviet health care system and did not show it in a particularly good light.

Hospitals were mainly old, poorly maintained buildings, equipment was minimal and often Heath Robinson in appearance, hygiene was absent, toilets were filthy and in-patients' food was very basic and often barely edible.

In contrast, Research Institutes were lodged in "marble palaces" and they were well run and well equipped. So-called, exceptionally equipped and staffed Kremlin clinics were reserved for the nomenklatura. A very hierarchical health care system.

In the USSR there were a vast number of doctors, over 40 per 10,000 of the population, which compared with 12 per 10,000 in the UK. The status and salaries of doctors was low and that of nurses even lower.

There were an excessive number of bureaucratic regulations, and Soviet patients were very conscious of their rights.

Medication was in short supply. In 1989/90 only 70 per cent of national requirements were available and it was anticipated that in 1990/91 only 17 per cent would be available. Thus, traditional remedies such as herbal medicines, cupping, leeches and hypnosis were widely used. Hyperbaric oxygen was often used for a variety of conditions.

The main medical problems I had encountered and had to deal with were much the same as in other parts of the world. Namely road traffic accidents, sports injuries, hypothermia in winter, pollution-related problems, overindulgence in alcohol and tobacco, psychological stress and infections including unusual ones such as diphtheria.

Nevertheless, my wife Nahid and I had certainly enjoyed, in sometimes difficult circumstances, our years in the Soviet Union.

*

Skiing in Heavenly Valley

Our time wasn't solely taken up with the Trust, and Nahid and I with our daughter Amanda made a visit to Los Angeles to see Nahid's family and some of our friends.

We left Pectopah, our Siberian Forest cat who we had brought back from Moscow, in the care of Airpets.

Nahid and I arranged to drive to Palm Springs in the desert and Manda visited her friend Dorna, who lived with her parents in Salt Lake City, the capital of Utah and the centre of The Church of Jesus Christ of Latter-day Saints, known as the Mormon faith.

On our return to LA, Parviz, Nahid's brother, accompanied us all to Lake Taho, near Reno, where we enjoyed some good skiing in Heavenly Valley.

*

IAPOS

I had been a member of IAPOS, International Association of Physicians in Overseas Services, since returning from Moscow.

Twice yearly meetings were held in London, and most years one of the members would also organise an overseas meeting. As we had several members from Holland, Norway and Sweden as well as in the UK, one of them would arrange a meeting in their own country.

The first overseas meeting Nahid and I attended was in Amsterdam, in May 1992.

Following an early morning in King's Fund College, discussing aid to the former Soviet Union, FSU, we caught a train from Victoria to Gatwick and then flew to Amsterdam. There we met up with Robin Cox, the IAPOS chairman, and the other 15 members of our group.

We had been booked into the very comfortable and well-located Krasnapolsky

Hotel, facing the Royal Palace, with its renowned Wintertuin restaurant, where in long-past days Victorian ladies and gentlemen sipped wine and nibbled pancakes.

After a good night's sleep, we didn't receive the alarm wake-up call we had requested and so missed breakfast, and we hurriedly rushed out to catch the coach to the conference hall where four talks on very varied subjects had been arranged – Basra, planes, HIV and Beriberi.

That evening our hosts, Heineken, had arranged a dinner in a private room in the Museum van Loon, beside one of the numerous canals in Amsterdam. The beautiful house, built in 1672, containing many portraits, antique furniture, silverware and fine porcelain, was first occupied by Ferdinand Bol, a pupil of Rembrandt.

Next day a coach took us to view the wonderful tulip blooms in Keukenhof, an hour's drive away. I personally felt that having seen them once it became rather boring seeing row after row. However, the boredom was alleviated by meeting Ingmarie and Lars Lidstrom from Sweden, who became close friends.

No visit to Amsterdam is complete without a visit to the Rijksmuseum to view Rembrandt's Nightwatch, Vermeer's miniatures and numerous works of Frans Hals. This is one of the most impressive collections of Old Masters in the world.

A most enjoyable and unforgettable trip.

*

Christine's wedding

Shortly after our return from Amsterdam we drove up to Oakham, the county town of Rutland, the smallest county in the UK, for the wedding of Christine Evans. Christine had been my nurse in Moscow for a couple of years and it was lovely to see her again on such a happy occasion.

Later she, her husband Clive, their two daughters Imogen and Lauren and their son Jethro went to live in rural Wales where they learnt the Welsh language and had a smallholding farm. We still hear from her regularly and occasionally manage to meet up. Happy memories.

*

Dublin

Nahid and I decided to take a short break in Dublin, which I had last visited as a student with my good friend Tsewang thirty-five years ago.

We flew Air Lingus to Dublin Airport, *Aerfort Bhaile Átha Cliath,* caught the hotel minibus to Fitzpatrik Castle Hotel, located in the fashionable suburbs of Killiney and Dalkey, overlooking Dublin Bay, and only 30 minutes from Dublin city centre.

During our stay in Ireland, we visited Trinity College Dublin which was holding an exhibition called *Treasures of the Mind,* and also viewed the *Book of Kells.*

The *Book of Kells* contains the four Gospels in Latin based on the *Vulgate* text which St Jerome completed in 384 AD, intermixed with readings from the earlier Old Latin translation.

The book is written on vellum (prepared calfskin) in a bold and expert version of the script known as "insular majuscule."

Trinity College (Irish: *Coláiste na Tríonóide),* officially the College of the Holy and Undivided Trinity of Queen Elizabeth, near Dublin, is the sole constituent College of the University of Dublin. Queen Elizabeth I founded the College in 1592, modelled after the collegiate Universities of Oxford and Cambridge.

Trinity College is widely considered one of Europe's elite Universities and is Ireland's most prestigious University.

The University has educated many of Ireland's most successful poets, playwrights and authors, including Oscar Wilde, Jonathan Swift, Bram Stoker, Oliver Goldsmith, William Congreve, Nobel Laureate Samuel Beckett, and philosophers George Berkeley and Edmund Burke.

*

Tsewang visit

My very close Tibetan friend Tsewang Pemba, who I had known from our first meeting in the Medical school, UCL, in 1949, having been teaching medical students in the USA and en route to Darjeeling, visited us and stayed with us in Hampstead for five days.

We reminisced, lunched in the Royal Society of Medicine with two other colleagues from our student days, Michael Nicholls and Dicky Boyde, and had a most enjoyable time.

Dicky Boyde had visited us whilst we were in Moscow following the sad death of his wife Shirley after a minor operation in a Hong Kong Hospital, where Dicky, at that time, was a consultant professor of biochemistry.

Chapter 3

Russian economy

Russian economy, Trust's methods, Western-style democracy and market economy, Galina and Sergei Romanyuk, Russian Tushinskaya Fund, Problems in Tushinskaya, Dhaka, Burma

Russian economy

There was hyperinflation in Russia in the early 1990s, in part due to lifting of price controls and in part to the State printing money. This was worsened by the privatisation of State enterprises, which entailed the Russian government selling vouchers for a nominal price to every member of the Russian population, giving them a minute share in these inefficient organisations.

Over a period of quite a short time, these vouchers were purchased from individuals by a small number of farsighted Russians, many of whom became future oligarchs. Shades of Gogol's 19th century novel *Dead Souls*.

All pre-1993 banknotes were withdrawn, and as few Russians used banks and kept their savings at home, many were left "pennyless."

*

Trust's methods

There is a Russian proverb, Тише едешь, дальше будешь, which roughly equates to *festina lente* – make haste slowly. This was the adage that determined the Trust's policies. We knew that in the UK introduction of Family Health Care had taken several decades to be generally accepted.

We also had a quite good understanding of Russia and the Russian people, possibly better than many of the Western "advisers" who descended upon Russia with the objectives of introducing simultaneously Western-style "democracy" and a market economy.

Russia had no experience of Western-style democracy or of a modern market economy in either Tsarist or Communist times, and following the demise of the Soviet Union and the loss of their International status, many Russians were completely demoralised.

This was a time for trying to understand their situation and helping them to gradually adjust to the new circumstances. The West, for both political and commercial reasons, was overhasty.

The Trust members understood this, and only helped to try to introduce changes in the hospital after they had been fully discussed with and agreed by Yuri Pavlov and his team.

*

On my arrival in Moscow in January 1993, I was met at the airport by Yuri Pavlov, Nelli and Vadim who had come in an ambulance to collect me as the hospital car had been written off in an accident.

Snow lay on the ground, and the temperature was -6°C. They drove me to Galina and Sergei Romanyuk's flat where I would be staying.

They, Galina and Sergei, lived in a small flat near the University and across the road from the new circus. Their living room was full of English books, piles of old British newspapers, maps of England and on the walls there were scenes of London.

Galina prepared some tasty dishes accompanied by a glass of vodka or cognac. They had converted the couch in the living room into a bed for me. I made a point of giving Sergei the copy of the English newspaper which I had been offered by the stewardess on the plane.

After breakfast, the hospital ambulance took Galina and me to the hospital where I met the Trustees of the Russian Tushinskaya Fund, Volodya, Khima and Mikhail, and for the rest of the day held long and detailed discussions with Yuri, Nelli, Vadim and Galina.

Over the next couple of days, we had many further detailed discussions. The outside temperature had fallen to -20°C, but fortunately it was pleasantly warm in the hospital.

*

I needed to make a short visit again to Moscow in June, and Galina and Serge kindly once again offered me hospitality. There was only one problem: at that time, there was no hot water in their apartment.

When I spoke with Kathy Murrell, I discovered that there were bigger and much more serious problems in Tushinskaya. From a series of discussions with Yuri, Nelli and other members of the hospital staff, it appeared that they were mainly concerned about the proposed restructuring of the management system.

Following meetings with Heads of departments in the hospital, and Leshkevitch in Glavk, eventually we came to an agreement. But I was left with the feeling that I really couldn't depend 100 per cent on anyone in the hospital.

I knew that almost all the Russians we were collaborating with couldn't understand why we were spending our time and money assisting them with their problems. Some doubtless felt that we had ulterior motives and others were merely nonplussed. Of course, there is a universal fear of change and many people regard the prospect of change as a threat to themselves.

On the lighter side, Nelli invited me to lunch in her flat with Dimi, her husband, and then we all went for a cycle ride in a nearby park where there was a pure water spring known as *Ishak* which apparently had medicinal benefits.

*

Dhaka and Burma

Our friend from Moscow, Sandra Johnson, with whom we had visited Armenia and Georgia in the early 1980s whilst posted in Moscow, was now PA to the Ambassador, Nicholas Fenn, in Rangoon Burma, as Myanmar was then called. Interestingly, although the name of the country was formally changed in 1989, the United States continues to use the name Burma.

Sandra had invited us to visit her and stay with her, and we felt this was an opportunity we could not miss.

Following a 10-hour overnight flight in a Burma Airways DC 10, we arrived in Dhaka in Bangladesh. The Foreign Office was considering basing a Medical Adviser there and had asked me to discuss this with the High Commission.

Dhaka

We booked into the Sonargaon Hotel, which had armed guards on each floor of the hotel, rang Michael Peart, the Head of Chancery, and he sent a car and driver to show us the very busy city and the Old Fort. Later the car took us to dinner at Michael's flat where we discussed establishing a Medical Adviser in Dhaka.

Michael told us an interesting tale highlighting some of the difficulties the post was experiencing. Some items of essential equipment had been sent from London several months previously, and they still awaited customs clearance.

The High Commission contacted customs every few days to inquire why there was such a long delay in clearing them, and were advised that this was due to the bureaucratic regulations introduced by the Brits in the days of the Raj, when Bangladesh was part of India. Touché

The following morning, after breakfast, a ramshackle taxi drove us to the airport. Halfway there, a tyre blew. The driver pulled over to the side of the road and replaced it with an even more worn tyre.

Rangoon

We sat at the airport for a couple of hours, had some lunch, and a Boeing 707 flew us to Rangoon, where a chaotic customs and immigration took two hours to clear us. An Embassy car drove us to Sandra's bungalow.

Sandra had arranged a welcome party where we met several members of the embassy staff and an old friend from Moscow, Simon Butt, who several years later was appointed Ambassador to Lithuania.

Burma

The name Burma means "the first inhabitants of the world."

The first kings of the country 2,500 years ago were thought to be descendants of the Buddha's family.

In 1498 a Portuguese seafarer discovered the sea route from Europe to India, and later Portugal acquired Burma. In 1886 the British annexed Burma and it became a province of British India. After the First World War, Burma was granted a degree of self-government.

During the Second World War, Japanese troops invaded Burma, and following bloody, often hand-to-hand, fighting in the jungle, were defeated. Some of you may have seen David Lean's 1957 film *The Bridge on the River Kwai,* starring Alec Guinness.

Burma, led by Thakin Aung San, the father of Aung San Suu Kyi, the renowned politician and diplomat, gained independence in 1948.

In a bloodless coup, General Ne Win swept into power and ruled by decree for 12 years.

"The country casts a kind of spell over its friends, which they cannot break if they could" – John Cady, *A History of Modern Burma.*

No one visits Rangoon without viewing the great gilded 20-metre high Shwedagon Pagoda, within which are said to be eight hairs of the last Buddha.

Palmistry

We had been advised that we must visit a renowned palmist who lived in the suburbs of Rangoon.

The best way to get there was by hiring a "tik tok" rickshaw. The driver didn't appear to know the way, but pedalled us through the busy streets until we came to a small bungalow surrounded by a veranda and a sign by the front door showing two palms.

Nahid and I entered the building and found a middle-aged Burmese woman sitting cross-legged on the floor, as if she was expecting us.

We told her nothing about ourselves or our relationship, but when she read Nahid's palm she began to tell her about her past, which was largely accurate, and her future. I took brief notes of all she said.

The palmist then asked if I wished to have my palm read, and although I was in two minds, in light of the accuracy of much of her commentary, I somewhat reluctantly agreed.

Of course, she expressed herself in terms determined by her Burmese way of life, but most of her comments could easily be understood. However, we are still waiting for our third child, which she stated we had!

Truly a most interesting experience.

Our tour of Burma

There was so much to see and do in Burma, and the Burmese friends we were introduced to by Sandra were all very friendly and courteous. We wished, however, to see other parts of the country as well as Rangoon, and with some difficulty the Embassy arranged permission for us to visit Pagan, Mandalay, Heho and Inle Lake.

Foreigners were forbidden to visit other parts of the country, as several areas, particularly adjacent to the Thai border in the east, were held by insurgent Shan forces who wished to establish their own state.

Burma Airways Corporation would fly us in a de Havilland Twin Otter on the round trip to Moulmein and back to Rangoon. We were fortunate to have relatively uneventful flights, other than long delays in departures and arrivals.

We later heard that the plane for the flight after ours had burst a tyre on landing in Moulmein and passengers had had to wait three days before a replacement tyre could be flown out from Rangoon.

Pagan

Our first stop was the ancient religious city of Pagan.

Sir James Scott, a colonial officer, had written in 1882, *"Pagan is in many respects the most remarkable religious city in the world. No other city can boast the multitude of temples and the lavishness of design and ornament that make marvellous the deserted capital on the Irrawaddy river."*

There is perhaps nowhere in the world a sight so striking as the view across the plain of Pagan – one red-brick pagoda after another.

Many temples had been damaged by an earthquake in 1975, but reconstruction had been completed by 1981.

The best way to get around the city was by horse-drawn carriage.

Mandalay

The Golden City was largely destroyed in 1945 when British troops shelled the city which was defended by a handful of Japanese and Burmese soldiers.

In the poem "Mandalay", Rudyard Kipling had immortalised the city: *"For the wind is in the palm trees and the temple bells they say. Come back, you British soldiers, come back to Mandalay."*

We had been advised to visit the temples on Mandalay Hill – two-thirds of the way up stands a gold-plated statue of the Shweyarraw Buddha.

Returning to Mandalay city, we had an interesting adventure. The coach was full and we could not find a seat; however, the driver of a Jeep offered to take us down the narrow steep winding road. We wondered how safe this journey would be, but when we saw a Buddhist monk was one of the passengers, we felt that this was a good omen.

Inle Lake

Flying up to Heho Airport, a Jeep took us to the shores of Inle Lake to see the fishermen. Perched precariously on one foot on the boat's stern, the fisherman twists his free leg around a single long oar and manoeuvres through the shallow lake water. He captures the fish in a long conical trap containing a gill net.

Pindaya

Several kilometres north of the lake in the village of Pindaya, we visited the Pindaya caves, where countless images of the Buddha are stored.

Burmese language

The Burmese language is a Tibeto-Burman language. Burmese script derives from the Pali language of south India. It contains 44 letters and is written and read from left to right, top to bottom. The Burmese numerical system is based upon the Arabic and decimal systems in common use in the West.

Chapter 4

South Pacific

South Pacific, Japan, Singapore, New Guinea, Solomon Islands, Nauru, Tawara, Fiji, Vanuatu, Tonga, Auckland, Brisbane, Honolulu, International Date Line South Pacific

Rodgers and Hammerstein's 1949 musical *South Pacific* contained many memorable songs including "Some Enchanted Evening". Andrew Lloyd Webber considered this to be *"the greatest song ever written for a musical".*

> "Some enchanted evening
> Someone may be laughing
> You may hear her laughing
> Across a crowded room
> And night after night
> As strange as it seems
> The sound of her laughter
> Will sing in your dreams"

During our five-week visit to the South Pacific, Nahid and I would meet many strangers and have many enchanted evenings.

*

On behalf of the Foreign Office, I had arranged to make a five-week medical inspection tour of several of our Embassies and High Commissions in the South Pacific, including Singapore, Papua New Guinea, the Solomon Islands, Fiji, Kiribati, Vanuatu and Tonga.

Nahid had arranged to meet me in Fiji, on the day of her birthday, accompany me for part of the trip, and then we would both fly back together via Auckland, Hawaii and Los Angeles.

*

The day before I was due to depart, Pectopah, our Siberian Forest cat, had disappeared. Nahid and Amanda had placed reward notices on lampposts near our house, and after a few days were informed by a local vet that someone had brought Pectopah into their surgery.

When they went to collect her, initially, Pectopah refused to recognise Nahid, but, eventually, she was brought safely home.

I was greatly relieved when, 10,000 miles away, I heard the good news.

*

Japan

Our previous visit to the Pacific had been in 1988 when, whilst posted in Moscow, we had visited Japan.

I was reminded of two interesting anecdotes relating to that visit.

Shopping in Ginza, the main thoroughfare in Tokyo, Nahid was looking for a dress. Nahid, who is petite, found, when we entered one of the stores, that Japanese women are ultra-petite. There were very few customers in the store, and on each side of the aisle were glass-fronted counters with a young female assistant standing behind them. As we passed, each one in turn bowed their heads and said *"Hai"*, the Japanese greeting.

We explained that we wished to see some dresses. They looked at Nahid and said, very politely, that they had larger sizes on the first floor. Taking the lift to the first floor, their response was exactly the same as the initial one.

Going up a further floor, we were told the same story, and eventually arriving at the top floor, they had to admit that none of their dresses in stock would be large enough for petite Nahid.

Later, during our visit, we travelled to Lake Ashi in the Imperial coach, took a boat trip on the lake and the cable car to the top of Mount Fuji. Unfortunately, weather conditions had changed and there was no visibility.

On arrival at our hotel, Prince Hakone, there was a notice in our bedroom requesting guests who would be dining in their restaurant to dress in Japanese kimonos. These were supplied by the hotel, and they offered assistance with dressing us in them.

On entering the restaurant, we found that our table was at the far end of the long room. We were the only foreign guests and all the Japanese in the restaurant, who were sitting on cushions on the floor in front of low tables, were dressed in European suits and dresses. We enjoyed an excellent sukiyaki dinner served by very attentive waitresses.

There must be some moral to this little story, if only we could think of it.

Singapore

Nahid and Amanda drove me to Heathrow where, late in the evening, I caught a Singapore Airlines Boeing 747 for the 13-hour flight.

I now held the rank of Counsellor in the Foreign Office, equivalent to Major General in the army, and thus was entitled to fly comfortably in the Raffles Business class. I had chosen a non-smoking window seat and, in fact, had a reasonably comfortable night.

Originally my flight had been booked to fly via Bombay, but I had managed to persuade the booking clerk in the Office to change this to a non-stop flight.

Singapore time was seven hours ahead of British summer time, and arriving in the early evening, at hot and humid Changi Airport, I took a taxi to the Hilton Hotel.

I had previously visited Singapore on a couple of occasions, once to attend a medical conference, and on the other occasion en route to Thailand.

On this occasion I had arranged to meet the New Guinea Senior Medical Adviser of Asia Emergency Assistance (ASEAS), who organised medevacuation, on behalf of the FCO, from the South Pacific islands.

I knew many people in Singapore, as by chance my medical partner Fred Kampfner had lived and practised in Singapore for many years before he and his family returned to the UK and he joined my practice, and we became the Medical Advisers to the Singapore, Malaysian and Indonesian Diplomatic Missions.

Singapore is a sovereign island city lying off the southern tip of the Malay Peninsula with a population of more than 5 million; it occupies a total area of 280 sq miles, and thus is very overcrowded. There are four official languages spoken there: English, Malay, Chinese and Tamil, but English is the *lingua franca*.

Having been, at various times, controlled by the Portuguese and then the Dutch, in 1819 Sir Stamford Raffles established it as a trading post for the British Empire.

In the Second World War, it was occupied by the Japanese army and there they built the infamous Changi prison camp, which held captured British troops.

Singapore became self-governing in 1959 and, following numerous initial problems, eventually, on the basis of its strength in International finance and shipping, and thus the strength of its economy, it became one of the four "Asian Tigers". Churchill called it "The Gibraltar of the East."

Although a democracy, in fact the People's Action Party, led by Lee Kwan Yu, their first Prime Minister, had held power since the inauguration of independence until 1990. I had met him on a couple of occasions in London, when he consulted me with medical problems.

Russian–Singapore relations

In 1890, the First Consul of Tsar Nicholas II visited the island, and the following year Tsar Nicholas II visited it during a world tour and diplomatic relations were established. In 1968 Singapore and the Soviet Union established diplomatic relations.

When we were posted in Moscow, we were very friendly with the Singapore Ambassador, Chiang Hai Ding and his family.

Asia Emergency Assistance, ASEAS, was based in Singapore, and Dr Stanley Quek acted as our contact there.

The day after my arrival on the island, I spoke with the Management Officer in the British High Commission, Colin Lane, who somewhat surprisingly had not been informed I would be visiting the island.

I lunched in the Pine Tree Club with Stanley Quek. He and his colleague, Dr Ian Lee, looked after the members of the British High Commission and they felt that most medical problems in expats were related to the "good life" that expats led – overindulgence in alcohol, excessive smoking of cigarettes and cigars and overeating rich food, with a high incidence of liver disease, type II diabetes and lung cancer. They told me that 100 cases of AIDS had been diagnosed in Singapore and preoperatively all inpatients were tested for HIV.

In later chapters you can read more about my work to modify these lifestyle causative factors in the development of heart disease amongst Russian men and women.

The following day I was due to leave for Port Moresby in Papua New Guinea, and as it was hot and humid I spent the morning reading by the pool, and after lunch arranged a tour to a Buddhist temple, Changi prison, the Air Force Museum and a crocodile farm. I followed this with a cream tea in the Hilton Hotel. Was I becoming an archetypal expat!

A taxi took me to the airport, and I caught the six-hour Air Niugini Airbus flight in the late evening to Jackson's Airport Port Moresby in Papua New Guinea, crossing two time zones and arriving in the early hours of the morning, local time. Port Moresby is usually called either Pom or simply Moresby.

New Guinea

On arrival I was met by the Management Officer from the High Commission, Rufus Legge, and taken to the Travelodge, where I would be staying.

He had arranged a picnic lunch in Varirata Park and we all played with frisbees, which they had brought with them.

*

New Guinea, called in the local language *Tok Pisin,* is situated in Niugini, the second largest island in the world, and the largest in the southern hemisphere, lying 150 km north of Australia, in the region known as Melanesia.

Prior to 1919, it was part-controlled by the Netherlands, having been discovered by Dutch explorers, and was a part of the Dutch East Indies. Other parts of the island were controlled by the Germans, and the British, who later transferred them to Australia. In the Second World War the Japanese invaded, and after they were driven out it became known as Papua New Guinea, and Indonesia acquired the Dutch region. In 1975 New Guinea gained its independence.

*

Pidgin is the term applied to a mixture of two languages which have been grammatically simplified. If it has a fully developed vocabulary and grammar, it is known as Creole. In the 19th century, many English words used in trading in Southeast Asia and the Pacific, spoken with a Chinese pronunciation, became pidgin words. Examples of pidgin are *Tank yu trule,* meaning "Thank you very much", and *plis,* meaning "please".

Over forty Papuan languages are spoken in PNG, but the official languages are English, Tok Pisin and Motu.

*

I was feeling quite fatigued and jetlagged, had a somewhat restless night and woke up late next morning.

After lunch I visited a couple of dental practices, both run by Australians. They seemed to be well run and had acceptable standards of hygiene. Their patients were mainly middle-class locals and expats. Anecdotally, I was told by a member of the High Commission, who had had a wisdom tooth extracted, that the results were satisfactory. Complex dental problems, such as crowns and bridge work, were transferred to Brisbane.

One of the practices was located in Johnson Pharmacy and I took the opportunity of visiting it. Over-the-counter medication and toiletries were in good supply, but some prescription medicines were sold over the counter without a prescription – potentially a rather risky practice.

My first port of call was to the 700-bed Port Moresby General Hospital, which had recently been built by the Japanese and opened only a few months previously. There had been many problems during commissioning.

There were four medical consultant teams including surgery, gynaecology and obstetrics, medical and research. In many instances, expat Australian doctors were being replaced by locally trained doctors. There was, however, a shortage of nurses, and their standards were variable, so that relatives were required to assist with the care and feeding of patients.

The hospital had a microbiology department, but, at the time when I visited, no haematologist. They found that power and water supply cuts caused problems, and they had their own generator. The X-ray department could undertake limited studies, but had an ultrasound. For some diagnostic investigations it was necessary to send samples to Australia. Samples were taken with disposable needles, using glass syringes which required repeated sterilisation.

The air-conditioned wards appeared clean and not overcrowded. However, some drugs were in short supply. Apparently adequate numbers of donors supplied blood.

For unexplained reasons, possibly because they were in use, I did not have the opportunity of visiting the operating theatres. I did however view the ITU, intensive treatment unit, which seemed reasonably well equipped with modern equipment and used disposable catheters.

Anecdotally, I was told that the staff was dissatisfied, and there were problems with supplies of medication.

My overall impression was that the hospital was probably adequate, for the services it supplied, but although modern, not dissimilar to some I had seen in Eastern Europe.

*

I then visited three general practices. Two of the General Practitioners had qualified in Australia and one in PNG.

Stephen Webber ran his own prIvate clinic with three other doctors and six nurses, one of whom was a midwife. They performed minor surgery and all their equipment was disposable. When necessary, they would make domiciliary visits to see patients.

The members of the High Commission, who used the clinic, all spoke highly of him and felt they were well looked after. In fact, one of the wives had been delivered of her first baby in the clinic.

The other Australian GP also ran a small clinic with four doctors and nine nurses. No surgery was undertaken, but he was Medical Officer to Air Niugini and Quantas. His first name was James, and he was known by all and sundry as "Jim the Jab."

There was a small laboratory and a treatment room containing three beds, which were used for day cases. He appeared very pleasant and businesslike in his approach.

I had been invited to lunch in the Galley restaurant, following a short tour of the Aviation/Yatch club. Other guests included a doctor from the POM General Hospital and a visiting delegation from the EC Commission.

*

Crime was a serious problem in PNG, particularly in urban centres where bands of unemployed and poorly educated youths, known as *Raskol* gangs, rascals, who lived in squatter settlements and chewed betel nut and smoked marijuana, committed both petty and more serious crimes.

One of their rather bizarre customs was to tie the laces of a pair of boots or shoes together and throw them high in the air so that they landed on the telephone lines. As one drove through the streets of Port Moresby, one could see pairs of boots festooning the lines.

Members of the local population, who could afford it, and expats, lived in comfortable houses but with a tight security. Surrounded by high security walls, all doors and windows were fitted with grilles, and each house had a high-security room where the occupants could lock themselves in if anybody broke into the house. Twenty-four-hour security guards, with guard dogs, patrolled the grounds.

Little refuse was collected from the streets, and one could see the dead bodies of animals lying on the roads. Untreated sewage was discharged directly into the sea.

In the evening it had been arranged for me to dine with Bryan Baldwin, the acting High Commissioner, and his wife, Liz. A doctor and his wife from the Health Department and several members of the VSO who were working in Port Moresby were also there.

The Voluntary Service Overseas, VSO, was founded in 1958 as a not-for-profit International development charitable organisation.

The volunteers, who came from several countries, assisted with developing conditions for positive social change in the communities in which they were engaged to work, including education, health and livelihood. They were required to have had at least two years' experience in their fields of expertise, and engaged for two-year stints, and were given basic accommodation and small sums of pocket money.

Having slept badly, I was tired all day, and after breakfast I checked out from the hotel and was taken to visit a pharmacy, City Pharmacy. It had good supplies of over-the-counter medication and toiletries. Then I visited a supermarket, which appeared to be well stocked.

In the early evening, I was driven to Jackson's Airport and flew the short one-and-a-half-hour flight in a crowded Air Niugini Fokker 48 plane to Cairns, where I was due to stay for the night.

*

Cairns

Nahid and I had visited Cairns together as tourists during a visit to Australia and New Zealand after finally leaving our Moscow posting, and on that occasion had viewed the Great Barrier Reef, one of the great natural wonders of the world. This time I would merely be staying overnight and catching a flight next morning to Honiara in the Solomon Islands.

On arrival at the airport, I arranged to spend the night in the Tropical Beach Suite, which was quite close by, and had a somewhat disturbed night, possibly due to the rain.

I rang Nahid, who was leaving London for LA later that day.

Qantas, in a Boeing 737, flew me comfortably, in just over two hours, to Honiara's airport, Henderson Fields.

*

Honiara

On arrival, I was met by Colin Bedwell, Second Secretary in the High Commission, and driven to the Mendana Hotel.

In the evening, a reception had been arranged in the grounds of the residency to introduce me to the ODA and VSO members who worked in Honiara. A very interesting and varied collection of people.

*

ODA

The Foreign and Commonwealth Office uses ODA, Official Development Assistance, known as overseas aid budget, to support the government's aid strategy in developing countries.

*

The 900 islands known as the Solomon Islands form a double-strand necklace which trickles across the Western Pacific. There are six main islands, and Honiara, the capital, is located on the largest, Guadalcanal.

In the 16th century the Spanish navigator Alvaro de Mendana was the first European to visit the islands. At the end of the 19th century, traders and missionaries began to arrive.

In 1893 Britain declared them a British protectorate. During World War Two there was intense, prolonged fighting between the US and Commonwealth troops and the invading Japanese. The islands gained independence in 1975 but remained a constitutional monarchy, where Elizabeth II is represented by a Governor General.

At the time of my visit there had been long-standing tensions between the Solomons and PNG, centred around the status of the island of Bougainville.

Honiara has an interesting Chinatown, which has the flavour of the old American Wild West.

The weather was hot and humid next day, and after breakfast I was taken to visit the General Hospital, with 280 beds of which only 50–60 per cent were occupied. The wards were overcrowded, had mixed-sex patients and standards of hygiene were poor with no handwashing, no soap and dirty towels. I felt I was back in the Soviet Union.

In theory there were 20 doctors on the staff, but probably in fact only about 15, and trained nurses also were in short supply. Their laboratories could undertake haematology, microbiology and biochemistry tests, but at that time, as several of the culture plates had been found to be contaminated, investigations were limited.

The X-ray department could undertake limited studies, and medical drugs were in short supply or out of date. The operating theatres were only equipped with basic equipment and there was no ITU.

They told me that it was difficult to find blood donors, and usually relatives had to supply blood when required.

Taiwan was planning to build a new hospital adjacent to the existing one.

Following medical consultations with two members of the High Commission, I visited a dental practice. The dentist was a young woman who had qualified in Fiji and was very pleasant, but the quality of the equipment was basic and her hygienic standards questionable.

On returning to the hotel, I went to my room to start preparing my report, and whilst sitting at a small table, a fluorescent light fell from the ceiling, but fortunately missed me. Later, after that somewhat eventful afternoon, I supped on the hotel terrace with several of the HC staff and their families.

There was a small Methodist Missionary hospital on the island of New Georgia in the town of Munda, which was the main hospital for the Western Province, and arrangements had been made for me to visit it.

This entailed an early morning flight in a small propeller-driven DHC3 Otter plane, which required only a short take-off and landing strip. There was a one-and-a-half-hour stopover on a small island, Vila.

The plane could take up to 10 passengers, but on this occasion there were only five or six, who all disembarked at Vila. I engaged in a conversation with a young woman who was one of the passengers, and to my surprise discovered that she was a doctor who had worked for some time in the Royal Brompton Chest Hospital in London with my son Marc. What a small world!

On the final two-hour leg of the flight, flying over several forested islands with surrounding atolls, we landed on a small airstrip built by the Japanese in the Second World War, from where I caught a speedboat to the hospital.

The Medical Director, Dr Charles McMillan, who had been at post for six years, was very welcoming. He was a very engaging, considerate and thinking person, who in addition to running the hospital had developed two small industries for the local population. One entailed producing impregnated mosquito nets, and the other, rather surprisingly, was manufacturing toilets, as it was the common practice to defaecate in the fields and thus spread infection.

The 54-bed private hospital called G120, or Helena Goldie Hospital, practised general medicine, general surgery, paediatrics and obstetrics. It was very well organised and well run, and adequately staffed.

Following lunch with several members of the hospital staff, the speedboat took me back to the airstrip from which I flew back in the DHC3 Otter to Honiara.

*

In 1943, a Patrol Torpedo boat, commanded by future President John F Kennedy, was bombed and sunk by a Japanese plane in Blackett Strait off the coast of New Georgia.

*

A very long and interesting day which left me dog-tired, and I collapsed into my hotel bed.

The next morning, I visited an adequately stocked pharmacy and then was taken on a tour of the town, which included a side-trip to view the wreck of a sunken WW2 US battleship.

Following the final "washup" session with the High Commissioner, I was driven to the airport where an Air Solomon Boeing 737 plane took me on the four-hour flight to Nadi, pronounced "Nandy", in Fiji.

*

There I overnighted in the Travelodge, from where next morning I flew in an Air Nauru Boeing 707, which was only a third full, the two-and-a-half-hour flight to Bonriki Airport, Tawara.

*

Nauru

Nauru, formerly known as Pleasant Island, is the third smallest country in the world with an area of 21 m^2 and a population of approximately ten thousand.

In the 19th century, it was a colony of the German Empire, and during World War Two it was invaded by Japanese troops, subsequently becoming a UN trustee and gaining independence in 1968.

It was rich in phosphates from migrating birds' "droppings" and as there was a worldwide demand for phosphates used in the food production industry, pharmaceuticals, high-tech electronics and agricultural fertilisers, it became very rich and acquired a national airline. In the 1990s the deposits were exhausted and thus Nauru lost its main source of income.

The population is obese, and this is associated with a high incidence of type II diabetes and heart disease.

*

Tarawa

Until 1976 the Gilbert and Ellice Islands were a British colony; they are now independent, separate states and have new names. The Gilberts are now called Kiribati, pronounced Kiribas, and the Ellice Islands are called Tuvalu. Most Kiribati people call their republic Tungaru. It is situated around the point where the dateline cuts the equator, and the islands are scattered over more than 2 million sq miles of ocean.

Tarawa is the capital of Kiribati. All the islands are no more than 12 feet above sea level, and all are coral atoll lagoons with areas of coral sand. They are devoid of hills or streams, but covered in towering palms.

The seas around the islands swarm with fish, and the islanders' main diet consists of taro, bananas, uncultivated coconuts, breadfruit and seafood.

The islands were first sighted by Europeans in 1765, but not until almost a century later, with the coming of the missionaries, was there any real European contact. They became a British protectorate in 1892 and remained so until the Japanese invaded in 1941.

Robert Louis Stevenson travelled to the Gilbert Islands with his wife, Fanny, and family, on a ship called the *Equator*, in 1888–89.

RLS felt he had unique material for a book: *"such wild stories, such beautiful scenes, such singular intimacies, such manners and traditions, so incredible a mixture of the beautiful and horrible, the savage and civilised. I propose to call the book The South Seas."*

*

I was met by Frank McDermott, British High Commissioner to Kiribati and HM Ambassador to the Federated States of Micronesia and to the Republic of the Marshall Islands. He drove me to Otintaai Hotel, then took me by his boat to a small sandbank in the lagoon where we swam and picnicked.

The next morning, we visited Tungaru Central Hospital which had been built by the Japanese and opened in 1991. It had 140 beds and 20 beds for mentally disturbed patients. In addition to the medical and surgical departments, there was also attached a School of Nursing and a dental department.

As with so many hospitals in the South Pacific, which the Japanese had built in an attempt to atone for their criminal acts during the Second World War, these modern well-equipped hospitals, in the majority of cases, were "marble palaces", as it was difficult to obtain medical and nursing staff, and they were far too expensive for the impoverished island governments to run.

My overall impression was that the hospital was adequate for patient admission, when necessary, but standards of hygiene were only fair, as was the quality of medical care and nursing.

Later in the day, I visited a small psychiatric hospital. The male ward had 23 patients, sleeping on palliasses on the floor of a long dormitory. In the female ward there were only five patients. I discussed the situation with Dr Ashok Singh, an Indian Psychiatrist, who also doubled as a general Physician, and was seconded by the UNDP, the United Nations Development Programme.

That evening a reception had been arranged in the High Commission for me to meet 15 of the ODAs and VSOs. Most of them felt that there were limited supplies of food, and, rather surprisingly, it was particularly difficult for vegetarians. They also felt that they had been inadequately briefed before taking up their postings.

Following a good night's sleep, I saw two patients in the High Commission and then was taken by car to Betio, near the seaport, to visit the food and general store, which was very crowded.

Most food and general supplies had to be imported, and the ferry boat would arrive every few months but was often delayed. At this time, possibly due to adverse weather conditions, there had been no boat for several months and supplies were running very low. Now finally the boat had arrived, the cargo was unloaded and was in the process of being put on the shelves in the general store. Rapidly, the news had got around, and everybody who could had rushed to replenish their supplies.

I lunched in the residency of the High Commissioner. It was a two-storey building and, apparently, had termites attacking the upper floor, which made the whole building potentially unsafe. Understandably this was a matter of great concern to the High Commissioner and his wife.

During lunch I heard that the Air Nauru flight to Nadi, which I was due to catch on Thursday 9 September, two days hence, had been cancelled.

Apparently, the Air Nauru flight from Nauru to Christmas Island had not been permitted to refuel unless the pilot paid for the fuel in hard cash. It would take several days for the cash-strapped Nauru government to raise the money and send it to him.

Fortunately, I was able to book a flight, via Tuvalu, for 10 September with Air Marshall. That was the day Nahid was due to meet with me at Nadi, in Fiji, having flown from LA via Honolulu in Hawaii – enabling us to be together on her birthday.

After lunch and sorting out the flights, I was driven to Golden Beach to view the Church of God and in the evening had supper with several of the expats.

As I now had an extra day on the island, I decided to make the most of the free time available.

It had rained in the night and was hot and humid, so I decided to get a small boat to take me across the lagoon to the sandy strip, took some fruit and bottled water with me and had a swim and relaxed on the beach.

Every village in Kiribati has a *Mwaneaba* – "meeting place." It is located in the middle of the village and is convenient for all people throughout the island. Like the traditional houses, it is built in a rectangular shape with the two ends differing somewhat. There is a pitched roof, thatched with palm leaves, supported by poles at the four corners and no walls. The *Mwaneaba* is a symbol of local authority; a place where elders, *unimane,* meet and make decisions for their community. I arranged to visit and view one.

Then I visited the Australian High Commissioner and found that he knew well our friends in Moscow, Neil Fraser and Enku Kebede, who were attached to the Australian Embassy there.

As I would be leaving for Nadi next day, I had a final "wash up" in the High Commission with Frank and his deputy Jimmy.

I didn't know at that time that Frank, the fourth British High Commissioner to Kiribati since their independence, would be the last. A year later, in 1994, the HC was closed and the British Embassy in Fiji became responsible for our representation in Kiribati.

They had arranged a farewell barbecue for me in the residency grounds, and I bade farewell to my many new friends.

I would truly miss Kiribati and could understand why one of Frank's predecessors as High Commissioner, Charles Thompson, had requested that after his death, his ashes should be scattered on the lagoon in Tarawa.

On the day of departure, Frank accompanied me to the airport and we waited in the VIP lounge until the Air Marshall Boeing 748 departed for Tuvalu, where there was due to be a half-hour stopover.

The small airport in Tuvalu was very basic, and air traffic control, passenger arrival and departure and immigration and customs all took place in a building which basically resembled the *Mwaneaba* in Kiribati, which I had recently visited.

*

Fiji

Following a reasonably comfortable three-hour flight, we landed in Nadi and a coach took me to the Travelodge, where I met up with Nahid.

It was really lovely to see her again after a 17-day separation, and we sat with a drink by the pool and later had a buffet supper in the open air.

She, poor thing, having arrived the previous day, had woken up in the morning to find several insect bites on her legs. When she spoke with the hotel receptionist, she was told, *"Oh don't worry, those are just the bed bugs."*

Suva

After breakfast by the pool, we caught a taxi to the airport, and then the fun began. They told us there was no seat booked for Nahid in the eight-seater single-engine Islander B-N 2 Fiji Airplane.

I explained that we were flying on an official visit to Suva, and that it was essential that we must both be on the same flight. They asked us to go away for half an hour or so, have a coffee, and they would try to see what they could do to sort out the problem.

On our return, they informed us that they had discussed the matter with the pilot, and subject to Nahid's agreement, he was happy to have her sitting on his lap in the cockpit during the 45-minute flight. Having no other choice, we agreed to this arrangement.

In fact, flying low over the island, one could see the deep-blue sea, atolls and the densely forested land, and we both, separately, had an interesting and enjoyable flight.

The Islander, requiring only a short take-off and landing, was, and still is, widely used in many parts of the world where only small airstrips are available.

We would be staying at the Travelodge for three nights, and Bob Hunter, the vice Consul, met us at Nausori Airport and drove us there.

After lunch, Nahid went to the hairdresser and I started to write my report. We had been invited to dine that evening with the Ambassador, Tim David, and David Noble, deputy Head of Mission, and his wife Yvonne and small daughter.

*

In the 17th century, the Dutch explorer Tasman sighted the islands and reefs in the Fiji group. A century later, Captain James Cook and, separately, in 1789, Captain William Bligh sailed through the group after surviving the HMS *Bounty* mutiny.

The 19th-century European contact increased steadily, with traders in search of sandalwood, settlers in search of land and missionaries in search of souls. A British Consul was appointed to Fiji in 1857, and 17 years later the islands were voluntarily ceded to Great Britain.

Many people from India were brought to Fiji to work as "coolies" on the island, and their descendants form the majority in towns and dominate commercial and professional life. They are the nation's shopkeepers, taxi drivers, importers, lawyers and doctors. Only 44 per cent of the population is of Fijian descent.

Following independence in 1970, a Fijian Alliance government was formed. In 1987 a largely Indian coalition government was elected, but shortly afterwards a Fijian army Lieutenant Colonel led a troupe of armed and masked soldiers into Parliament House. After a second coup d'état, Fiji was declared a republic, the constitution was abolished and the former Governor General appointed as President.

Fiji lies 1,000 miles south of the equator and consists of 300 islands with a total land area of 7,000 sq miles, equivalent in size to Wales. The International airport, Nadi, on the west side of the island, and the capital, Suva, on the east, are both on the largest island, Viti Levu, with a mountainous interior and lush forest vegetation. The highest point is Mount Tomanivi with a height of 4,300 feet. There is a road around the perimeter of the almost circular island.

It is largely an agricultural country, which grows sugarcane both for home use and export.

The national flag of Fiji displays a Union Jack and the national Coat of Arms on a blue background. It, perhaps, seems rather odd that a republic should continue to use the UK's national flag, but this apparently is in recognition of the past close associations of the two countries and their admiration for Great Britain.

Kava, made from the crushed roots of a pepper, and known in the Fijian language as yaqoma, pronounced "yong goma", is presented in complex rituals to guests of honour on ceremonial occasions, and at meke, performances, when there is Fijian dancing and singing.

Firewalking is a fascinating ceremony, practised by both island cultures. Fijians believe that a legendary spirit God passed on knowledge of firewalking to the Sawau tribespeople, who live on Beqa Island off Viti Levu. Sawau walk barefoot over stones heated by an enormous log fire on special occasions. Indians of the Hindu Madrasis sect practise firewalking as a means of cleansing the spirit.

Thanks to the influence of the Brits, sport plays a large part in life in Fiji. In winter they play rugby football and in summer cricket.

On our final day in Suva, we visited Dr David Phillips, Regional Health Adviser to the Pacific Regional Advisory Group, PRAG, and had a long and interesting discussion. He told us that little family planning was undertaken by the population, as they looked upon it as a form of "white man's genocide."

There is no malaria on the island, but dengue fever, which is spread by mosquitoes, was a serious problem. Sufferers develop a cough, fever, general muscular aches, headache and vomiting. There is no specific treatment, and the initial infection resolves spontaneously. However, repeat infections can cause serious haemorrhagic fever, with bleeding into many of the body's organs.

One risk of deep-sea scuba diving, which was commonly practiced on many of the Pacific islands, is a condition known as the "bends", which can occur when divers surface too quickly from deep water. The cause of the bends is nitrogen gas coming out of solution in the diver's blood and forming bubbles in the muscles, causing severe cramp.

Treatment requires putting the patient in a decompression chamber filled with 100 per cent oxygen, which effectively pushes the nitrogen out of the sufferer's tissues.

*

The University of the South Pacific was located in Suva but, apparently, many of the graduates went to either New Zealand or Australia for postgraduate studies and didn't return to the islands. To reduce the loss of graduates, there were proposals that Fijian medical degrees should only be recognised on the Pacific Islands and not in any other countries.

We visited the Colonial War Memorial Hospital, built in 1923 and known as CWM. The Japanese were building the first phase of a new wing which was due to open in December 1993.

The 400-bedded hospital had surgical, medical, obstetric and paediatric departments. There were four operating theatres, but we did not have the opportunity of seeing them, and a small ITU – intensive treatment unit and CCU – coronary care unit. Most wards were bright and airy but overcrowded with patients.

Anecdotal reports said, *"clinical acumen and diagnostic skill was poor, nurses performed their duties but did not understand the rationale behind them."*

Our impression was that standards of hygiene were reasonable and that the hospital was probably adequate for dealing with non-acute problems. However, apparently, locally it was known as "the house of death."

A meeting had been arranged for us to speak with 16 ODA and VSO members who worked in Suva. They confirmed most of what we had already heard regarding health care facilities, but expressed satisfaction with dental treatment, and one had had root canal treatment and a crown, which she was very pleased with – perhaps partly because it was very cheap. Physiotherapy for sports injuries in CWM was highly spoken of, and the International school ran a free immunisation programme for children.

We also had the opportunity to visit a general practice, where we met Dr Rosemary Mitchell who trained in Adelaide and was assisted by her Fijian husband Robert. Apparently, there were monthly specialist visits by medical teams from Australia, who undertook a variety of medical procedures in their small operating theatre. She seemed to offer a good service and had a daycare surgery facility.

*

After returning to our hotel, in preparation for an early morning start to the airport for the flight to Nadi, we packed our suitcases.

With little sleep and no breakfast, we were driven to the airport to catch the Air Honolulu flight. This time they had allocated Nahid a seat and the pilot had the cockpit to himself.

The Air Pacific Boeing 737 to Vanuatu was due to depart one hour after our arrival in Nadi, but we managed to catch it by the skin of our teeth.

A comfortable flight, and with some much-appreciated breakfast, after just under two hours we arrived at Bauerfield Airport in Port Vila, Vanuatu.

*

Vanuatu

In 1772, Captain Cook sighted the 80 islands spread over 900 km of the South Pacific and named them New Hebrides. They had first been sighted and colonised 160 years earlier by the Portuguese navigator, Pedro Fernandez de Quiros, whilst looking for land and gold for his sponsor, King Phillip III of Spain.

A mixed bag of missionaries, whalers and sandalwooders followed Cook in increasing numbers.

A hundred years later, John Higgins, an Irish-born trader, but a naturalised French citizen, urged the French government to take over the New Hebrides islands. This was met with cries of outrage from the well-established British missions and Australia.

In response to the increasing show of interest by the Germans in acquiring the islands to extend their influence in that part of the Pacific, the French and British governments set up a Franco-British condominium.

This jointly controlled administration, known in the Pacific as the "Pandemonium" with its two sets of laws, two education systems and two official languages plus pidgin, was clumsy and expensive to run.

In the Second World War, the French administration of the New Hebrides was amongst the first of France's overseas territories to rally to de Gaulle. Independence was granted by Britain and France to the elected government of the New Hebrides in 1980 and the new state was christened Vanuatu, meaning "Our land."

The people are sturdy, proud and independent with a strongly developed sense of fair play. An early missionary asked an islander, *"Why do you put that paint on your faces?" "Why do you put those clothes on?" asked the islander. "This is our way of clothing, that is yours."*

*

We were met at the airport by the deputy High Commissioner and driven to Le Lagon Hotel, a series of thatched-roofed chalets situated by a pretty bay.

We were quite tired but had to visit the High Commissioner, Tom Duggan, and after a rather poor lunch in the hotel, visited three general practices.

One of the GPs was from PNG, one Australian and one French. According to anecdotal reports, one, no names mentioned, was too attentive to female patients, one good but didn't wish to be responsible for the care of patients with difficult problems, and one rather concerned about possible litigation.

Following a short rest on our bed, we had supper in a local restaurant.

Port Vila

The capital, Port Vila, a pleasant small tropical town with a population of 15,000, is located on the island of Efate. Life ambles on in the same lazy way it has for nearly a century. A colourful open-air market sells artifacts, clothing and food stuffs, and one sees many warm-hearted, eccentric, generous and hospitable locals.

*

One of the dentists we visited practised in a surgery in his own house on the outskirts of the town, surrounded by a rose garden. Reportedly, his work was good and we felt that his services were adequate. The other, who had qualified in Louvain in France, worked in the centre of the town in a modern building. He spoke good English and French, and again, reportedly anecdotally, he gave a good service, and we felt the practice was very adequate for routine work.

A visit to meet the Australian High Commissioner, Andrew Goledzinowski, had been arranged, and I discovered that he knew and had been posted with Neal Fraser and Enku Kebede, our friends from Moscow.

At a meeting with ODA spouses, we discussed many social, educational and health care matters.

The HC had invited us to dinner in the residency, where we met Dr George Cuboni, the WHO representative, and several local doctors.

Next day we called on Dr Ajayi, acting Superintendent of Vila Central Hospital who had qualified in Abadan in Nigeria. This was followed by a tour of the hospital. Our impression was that the hospital was adequate for surgery up to the level of appendicectomy and stabilisation for serious medical problems pre-medevacuation to Sydney or Brisbane.

A cocktail reception had kindly been arranged for us in the evening by David Miller, the deputy HC, and his wife Gill at their house.

The following day, our last day in Vanuatu, we had a most interesting experience. We hired a Toyota Corolla from Thrifty Car Rental for the princely sum of 4,400 vata, equivalent to 44 US dollars, and set out on the narrow coastal road around the island, taking a picnic and some beer with us. We had been advised the trip would take about four hours, which would get us back in time for supper.

In Vanuatu, cars drive on the right side of the road, and Nahid, a very experienced driver, was driving. On the left-hand side of the unasphalted and potholed road was a narrow strip of land and some low scrub, beyond which was the blue sea.

At fairly frequent intervals on this strip of land were open stalls, with either varieties of food stuffs or small ornaments and clothing. None of them had any attendants, but each had an "honesty box" where buyers could leave their money. Quite remarkable – there must be few places in the world where one would find this.

Driving down a steepish narrow part of the road, with a sharp right bend at the bottom, we both felt the drive was getting very bumpy. Having turned the corner, Nahid pulled into the right-hand forested side of the road, and on getting out of the car we realised that the offside rear tyre had a puncture and was completely flat.

Rummaging in the car boot, we found a rather threadbare spare tyre, but no jack. This was a problem as in those days no mobile phones existed, so all we could do was wait and hope that a car came along. In fact, we had so far seen no other vehicles on the road since leaving Vila.

Suddenly, two young men dressed in torn T-shirts and shorts came out of the bushes, looked at the flat tyre and said in pidgin, *"Man bilong nambis stret long taim soon,"* and disappeared into the forest.

After about ten minutes they returned with half a dozen other young men. Three of them lifted up the offside side of the car, and another two unscrewed the wheel nuts with their bare fingers, removed the wheel with the flat tyre, replaced it with the spare, and tightened up the wheel nuts.

We, naturally, were delighted and thanked them in French, which they appeared to understand. We had a few vala in our pockets and offered them to them, but they wouldn't accept them so we gave them our picnic lunch and bottles of beer, which they happily received and disappeared again into the forest.

On our return, eventually, to our hotel, we told the receptionist about our adventure, and she informed us that the previous week a young couple visiting from abroad had crashed their car on the bend in the road and been seriously injured.

Nahid phoned Amanda in London, who mentioned that there had been an unsuccessful attempt to break in to our London house. It all seemed a long way away in another life!

Surprisingly, we slept well that night, went to the local market to buy some fruit which we ate by the hotel pool, and after lunch were driven to the airport for our Air Solomon flight back to Nadi.

*

A taxi took us to the very lovely deluxe beach resort Regent Hotel, only 20 minutes away from Nadi Airport. We had originally arranged to take a couple of days' rest in the Regent to celebrate Nahid's birthday, but had had to postpone that following my delayed return from Kiribati.

The hotel was situated on the man-made Denauru Island, and although the beach was pebbly, the hotel had wonderful grounds, full of palm trees, tropical flowers and several small lakes and bridges.

Whenever we wandered through the gardens, on meeting a hotel staff member, they greeted us with the words *Bula, Bula* – "Welcome, Welcome."

Most of the following day, Sunday, was spent by the pool reading, talking and playing Scrabble.

Next morning, feeling refreshed, settling our bill, the equivalent of £110, very reasonable for two nights' stay, a taxi took us back to the airport. An Air Solomon plane flew us in just over one hour to Nuku'alofa, the capital of Tonga.

*

Tonga

Most people in the UK knew very little about Tonga, other than that it had a first-class rugby football team, and those with long memories could recollect Queen Salote's memorable drive in an open carriage during a downpour of rain on the occasion of Elizabeth II's coronation in 1953.

In fact, Tonga, which had never been colonised, is the only sovereign monarchy in the Pacific, with its unique constitution, and membership of the Commonwealth.

Its first contact with foreigners was in 1616 when Dutch navigators arrived on its shores. Captain James Cook visited Tonga in 1777 and named it the "Friendly Island." Christian missionary influences have remained very strong since the 19th century.

The present king, when we visited, was HM Taufa'ahau Tupou IV, the son of Queen Salote, who could trace his origins back to the chiefs who reigned 1,000 years previously.

There are no political parties, but Parliament, the legislative assembly, consists of nine noble's representatives and nine people's representatives. The people are poor but proud. Women are skilled at mat weaving, basket weaving and producing tapa cloth. Men and women wear the skirt-like *tapanu,* men to the knee and women to the ankle.

There is a fragile agricultural economy, growing copra, bananas and coconuts.

The Kingdom of Tonga consists of four scattered groups of volcanic and coral islands lying southeast of Fiji and north of New Zealand. There are 170 islands of which only 40 are inhabited, with a total land area of 700 km². The largest island is Tongatapu, on which is the capital Nuku'alofa.

*

No one was at the airport to meet us, so we took a taxi to the Pacific Royale Hotel. Later, we discovered that there had been a mix-up in the High Commission as they had not received the message informing them of our change of itinerary due to the unfortunate delay of my return from Kiribati.

An HC member had gone to the airport to meet us the day before and found we were not on the flight.

Our original itinerary had included a reception for 60 guests, mainly from the medical community, and a full programme of appointments, arranged by the Ministry of Health. They had also arranged tours for us on Sunday.

Cancellation of all these arrangements had caused considerable embarrassment, and unnecessary expenditure of time and money.

Our hotel was reasonably comfortable, but on entering or leaving it one had to pass through the bar, which invariably was full of somewhat scantily clad young women of questionable moral values.

*

We heard on the radio that evening that Yeltsin had dissolved the Duma, Russian Parliament. In a later chapter, I shall enlarge upon this matter.

*

After visiting the High Commission, I met the HC Bill Cordiner and his deputy and then had a meeting with Dr Helga, who ran the German clinic which was used by most expatriates. Approximately 50 per cent of her patients were Tongans. She seemed very pleasant and a reasonable person, although anecdotal reports were that she tended to over-dramatise problems and possibly over-treat.

The following day was very busy, with visits to the Kalavale Clinic and the Mission Clinic and then the Vaiola Hospital.

Kalavale Clinic was run by a British nurse who was married to an OSA judge. They required a sphygmomanometer, which the British HC offered to donate.

The Mission Clinic depended largely on donations from voluntary groups and charged minimal fees for consultations, but could only afford to be open on a part-time basis.

Vaiola Hospital had 200 beds and two operating theatres.

Reportedly, there were poor standards of nursing care, and out-of-hours cover was very limited. There was a good radiologist, and a Japanese doctor supervised the laboratory.

The building was poorly maintained, standards of hygiene were poor and toilets and showers were in a state of disrepair. I felt that it was adequate for stabilisation of seriously ill patients, prior to medevacuation to Auckland, and, in terms of skills, for operations up to appendicectomy.

The High Commission staff more than adequately looked after us, lunching and dining us and taking us to the local market and supermarket. There were seasonal shortages of food and necessities, particularly during the cyclone season.

Tongan, the official language of the Kingdom of Tonga, is a Polynesian language which includes borrowed words from English, Fijian and Samoan, and is spoken by about 130,000 people. "Hello" is *Malo e lelei,* and "goodbye" is *Alu'a.*

The Tongan currency is the *pa'anga,* unofficially known as Tongan $. It has no fixed rate of exchange and is totally worthless outside Tonga. At that time, for 1 US dollar you got about T$ 1.45

There was little violent crime, but increasing theft and occasional "Peeping Toms."

Cultural facilities for expats consisted of occasional concerts. The residency had a tennis court, two hotels had swimming pools and boats could be hired. Most people played bridge.

There was a government primary school, which taught a New Zealand syllabus by rote, and was not suitable for children older than eight or nine.

On our last morning, we were woken at 5 a.m. by loud raucous drunken singing from the bar.

Following further discussions with a Public Health specialist from the WHO, Dr Ian Welch, and a meeting with Dr Laumeesi Malolo, Medical Superintendent of Vaiola Hospital, and after debriefing by the HC, we were driven to the airport.

Having paid our departure tax of T$ 10 each, we boarded the Air New Zealand Boeing 767, and three and a half hours later we landed at Auckland Airport.

*

Auckland

Nahid and I had last visited Auckland in December 1990 as tourists, but on this occasion we were making a short official visit to view the air ambulance facilities which were used for medical evacuation from Tonga, and, sometimes, from other South Pacific islands.

At that time, it was run by Air BP Air Ambulance, a Charitable Trust, and when I spoke with Dr Lyndon Novak, their Medical Director, he sent a car to bring us to their 24-hour control centre where we discussed the mechanics of medevacuation.

They arranged admission for patients to Middlemore Hospital, and cardiac cases to Greenlane Clinical Centre. Diving-related problems were admitted to the Navalbase hospital. He offered to take us in their Westpac BK 117 helicopter to the airport to view their fleet of planes.

It was fascinating to view Auckland from above, situated on the edge of the Hauraki Gulf.

Following lunch in the hotel, a taxi took us to the airport for our Air New Zealand/Quantas flight to Brisbane. The flight departure, for unexplained reasons, was delayed for two hours. After arrival, following the comfortable three-hour flight, a taxi took us to the Travelodge.

Brisbane

The main reason for our visit to Brisbane, the capital of Queensland, named by Queen Victoria, was to assess the ability of local hospitals to cope with medical evacuations from the islands.

A taxi dove us to the Royal Brisbane Hospital, through the beautifully landscaped city with jacarandas, tulip trees, flame trees, coral trees, oleanders, frangipani and bougainvillea lining the pavements.

Of primary interest to us was the A&E department of the 2,000-bed modern hospital, which received 65,000 patients annually, 50 per cent of whom required admission. This was an enormously demanding task, and they had introduced a triage system, at that time almost unheard of in the UK.

Trained nurses assessed each attendant to determine the gravity of their medical problem and decide whether or not further investigation or admission was necessary. They were then referred to the relevant department in the hospital. We were welcomed by the Head of the Department, Dr Michael Chang, and had a most instructive discussion with him.

After lunch we made a visit to the Princess Alexandra Hospital and concentrated on their psychiatric unit and infectious diseases department.

The British Consul General, John Durham, and his wife Sheila, had invited us to dine with them in the Brisbane Club, where we spent a pleasant evening with them and their guests.

Another late night for us, and following breakfast in the hotel we watched on television the film *Henry V*, with Laurence Olivier playing the main role.

Then we went by taxi to the airport, where Ansett in a Boeing 737 flew us to Sydney. We had time to sit by the pool in the airport Hilton before boarding a Continental DC-10 for the eight-and-a-half-hour flight to Honolulu, in Hawaii.

*

Honolulu

During the flight we crossed both the equator and the International Date Line, thus nominally adding a day to our journey. When Nahid had flown from LA, via Hawaii, to meet me in Fiji, she had crossed the line from east to west, and thus nominally subtracted a day from her journey.

*

International Date Line

The IDL, International Date Line, established in 1884, is an imaginary line on the Earth's surface defining the border between east and west, which roughly approximates to 180° east or west of Greenwich.

Thus, travellers journeying from east to west subtract a day, and those from west to east add a day.

However, countries can choose the date and time zone in their own territory. For example, in 1994, Kiribati, as some of its islands were on one side of the IDL and some on the other, decided to bend the line and keep all their islands nominally on the same eastern side of the IDL. To achieve this, they decided to skip the date 1 January 1995, and therefore they are now the first country worldwide to enter a New Year.

Remarkably, the Arab geographer Abulfeda, in the 13th century, had predicted that circumnavigators of the world would experience a one-day offset to the local date.

*

We had now completed the official part of our journey and were on our way home to London, and so were free to relax for a few days.

We had arranged to stay in the Sheraton Royale Hotel on Waikiki beach, ate that evening at an excellent fish restaurant and collapsed into bed.

The following day was a Sunday, and after a good night's sleep we felt refreshed and had a late breakfast. We swam in the mild waters of the Pacific, walked around the town, bought a few presents, played Scrabble on our balcony and ate a tasty supper in a restaurant.

*

Honolulu is situated in the Polynesian part of the Pacific, 2,000 miles from the US mainland, and is the capital of the US state of Hawaii.

Surprisingly, its flag includes in its design the Union Jack, in recognition of early British influence following its discovery by James Cook in 1778. It became an independent kingdom in 1810, and was annexed by the United States in 1898.

Barack Obama, a future President of the United States, was born and raised in Honolulu.

The island's motto is *Ua Mau Ke EA o ka Ainu I ka Pono* – "The Life of the Land is Perpetuated in Righteousness."

*

We breakfasted in the nearby Reef Hotel, took a taxi to the airport, caught the Air New Zealand Boeing 767 flight, watched *Much Ado About Nothing* on the inflight TV and, on arrival in LA four hours later, were met by Nahid's sister, Parvin, and brother, Parviz, who drove us to Nahid's parents' house in Beverley Hills.

There we spent three most enjoyable days being spoilt by many members of Nahid's family. I played tennis on a couple of occasions with Parviz, and we ate excellent very tasty Persian food in several family homes and Persian restaurants.

On 30 September, following numerous fond farewells, United Airlines flew us comfortably in a Boeing 747 for the 10-hour flight to Heathrow, where we arrived early the next morning.

During my 38-day journey, I had flown around the world, a total distance of approximately 25,000 miles, taken 18 flights with 15 different airlines, some of them accompanied by Nahid, and visited 12 different countries.

*

Although, probably, not quite such a renowned event as Jason's quest for the Golden Fleece, he had, so we are told, visited only four or five islands including Lemnos, Doliones, Colchis, Crete and Thrace, and travelled with the Argonauts, probably the equivalent of 1,500 miles. Please believe me, I am in no way trying to belittle his epic voyage.

Chapter 5

Princess Diana

Princess Diana reception, The Worshipful Society of Apothecaries, The Fugitive, Diana's continuing interest in the Trust, Lord Mayor's Banquet

Princess Diana reception

In April 1993, Patrick Jephson, Private Secretary to HRH Diana, Princess of Wales, informed us that the Princess had graciously accepted the patronage of the Trust. A press release, translated into Russian, was prepared. Copies were sent to Patrick Jephson, the Palace press office, the FCO and British Embassy Moscow, the Russian Ambassador to the UK and our President, Baroness Cox.

The release announced that the Princess of Wales had graciously given her patronage to a British charity, the Tushinskaya Children's Hospital Trust, which was dedicated to the support and development of a children's hospital in Moscow.

"The Princess of Wales is known the world over for her love of children and for her concern for the sick and handicapped. By agreeing to be Patron of the Tushinskaya Children's Hospital Trust she has contributed immeasurably to improved care for the sick children of Russia now and in the future."

*

In June 1993, Princess Diana wrote: *"Now that the Cold War is behind us there are new opportunities for us to share with Russians the experience which we have built up in many fields, in the framework of a free society. In some areas of medical science, we can learn from them: in those of paediatric medicine, hospital management and patient care it is we who have a great deal to give."*

*

We decided to hold a reception, hosted by Baroness Cox, to welcome HRH Princess Diana as our Patron.

Initially, we considered holding it in the Durbar Court in the Foreign Office, but as it was not heated it was not used from October onwards, and it was so vast that 100 people would be lost in it. The other possible locations in the FCO that we considered were the Grand Locarno room and the Council Chamber of the India Office, both of which were available for 18 October.

*

As a Liveryman of the Worshipful Society of Apothecaries, I was able to arrange that a reception could be held in the Apothecaries Hall in the City of London, hosted by Baroness Cox and attended by HRH.

The Hall is the oldest extant livery hall in the City of London, with an impressive Great Hall with its stained-glass windows and walls hung with portraits of past masters of the Society. The total cost, including room hire, staff, catering and wine, would be £1,600.

In conjunction with Patrick Jephson, guest lists had to be agreed and arrangements made with the Apothecaries as well as with Kensington Palace. Representatives from all major UK firms involved in trade with Russia were invited, as of course was the Russian Ambassador, HE Boris Pankin, and some staff members from the Russian Embassy. Approximately 150 invitations were sent out and 95 guests attended the reception.

The reception was scheduled to run from 6 p.m. to 8 p.m. on Monday 18 October. At about 4.30 p.m., just as Nahid and I were about to set out for the Hall in Blackfriars Lane, the phone rang and it was a rather concerned Clerk of the Apothecaries who had just realised that members of the Royal Family entering the City of London had to be met at the gates in Temple Bar by the Lord Mayor of London, welcomed and invited to enter the confines of the City. Somehow or other this had been overlooked.

Urgent phone calls were made to the Lord Mayor, Sir Francis McWilliams, a Liveryman of the Company of Loriners, who was at that time attending some other official function, and he hurriedly arranged to meet Her Royal Highness at Temple Bar and welcome her to the City.

Traditionally, Loriners were the makers of iron bits for horses' bridles, spurs and stirrups.

Guests were requested to arrive no later than 6.15 p.m., as HRH was due to arrive at 6.30 p.m., and they were informed that they would not be able to leave the reception before HRH's departure.

We arranged for Dr Yuri Pavlov, Dr Nelli Naigovzina, Dr Olga Skorobogatova, Dr Margarita Kosigina and Galina Romanyuk to attend the reception as guests of the Trust. Journalists from several newspapers, including the *Daily Mail, Daily*

Express and *The Times* attended, and several thousand pounds was raised to assist the Charity.

Ten years later I invited the then Russian Ambassador, His Excellency Alexander Yakovenko, to dine as my guest at a livery dinner in the Apothecaries Hall.

*

The Worshipful Society of Apothecaries

The Worshipful Society of Apothecaries of London was incorporated by Royal Charter on 6 December 1617. The Apothecaries, originally vendors of wines, spices and herbs, had become the equivalent of present-day pharmacists.

A wealthy and influential Huguenot, Gideon de Laune, Apothecary to Anne of Denmark, wife of James I, played a very significant role in establishing the Society. The Society's Hall, formerly the guesthouse of the Dominican priory of the Blackfriars, was acquired in 1632, and later rebuilt following destruction in the Great Fire of London.

*

The Fugitive

In 1993, the new Warner West End cinema, following two years' closure for refurbishment as a modern nine-screen cinema, reopened in Leicester Square.

Warners chose the tense suspense thriller *The Fugitive,* starring Harrison Ford as a man wrongly convicted for killing his wife who escapes en route to prison and becomes the object of an intense manhunt, as the opening film.

Princess Diana had graciously agreed to be present at the premiere, held on Thursday 23 September 1993, and donated to the Trust the proceeds of the film, totalling approximately £66,000. Sir Bryan and Lady Cartledge attended the premiere representing the Trust.

The official brochure contained both a full-page photograph of Princess Diana and a full-page detailing Tushinskaya Children's Hospital Trust's work in Moscow, with a large photograph of an endearing young patient in the hospital.

There was a line-up of stars at the premiere including Gary Glitter, Sting, Stephen Fry, Paula Yates and Bob Geldof, and Simon and Yasmin Le Bon.

The Princess, wearing a dark blue dress split to the thigh, which provoked wolf whistles as she stepped from her Jag, met one of her favourite film stars, Clint Eastwood, at the premiere, and later they travelled together to a private dinner, with 18 other guests, at the Savoy Hotel.

*

Following the separation of Princess Diana and Prince Charles in 1992, several political figures, including the prime minister, John Major, had resolved to find Diana a role as an International "Ambassador."

According to reports in the *Daily Mail*, *The Times* and *The Sunday Times* and the *Daily Express*, John Major was working behind the scenes to secure a new role for the Princess of Wales, an International icon and mother of a future King, to make high-profile overseas trips. All the newspaper reports highlighted the work Tushinslaya Trust was undertaking in Russia.

Apparently, following Diana's acceptance of the role of Patron to Tushinskaya Trust, John Major had met with her in Kensington Palace to discuss a possible visit by her to Moscow in November 1993, to support the Trust's work with Tushinskaya Hospital.

*

On 3 December 1993, we received a signed letter from the Princess regarding her decision to *"find the space, the time and space necessary to acquire deeper understanding of a more specialised range of interests. This means that I will sadly be unable to accept any of your invitations for the forthcoming programme period, nor for the foreseeable future thereafter."*

The letter continued: *"However, if it is your wish, I would feel honoured and grateful to be able to continue our association, albeit at an essentially nominal level. I would certainly value being kept informed of developments and will always follow your progress with the closest interest."* It was signed in her hand: *"Yours sincerely, Diana."*

Naturally, we fully understood how problems in the Princess's private life must have impinged upon her public undertakings, but the loss of our Patron would be a major blow to the Charity. We were in the process of arranging, with the impresario Victor Hochhauser, a gala performance of the Moscow City Ballet, which would be visiting London in January 1994. We were hoping Her Royal Highness would attend, and there was also a proposed visit by HRH to Tushinskaya Hospital in the same month.

Sir Bryan, the Chairman of the Trustees, wrote on behalf of the Trust to HRH thanking her for her kind words and telling her that we would be honoured if she would be prepared to continue in the role of Patron.

In fact, she was to play a major role in the future development and progress of the Trust.

*

The Trust committee had been strengthened by the inclusion of Bente Fasmer, a professional photographer as Press Officer, David Knowles, representing the King's Fund College, and Dr Harvey Markovitch, a Paediatrician.

*

In July, a team including Sir Bryan Cartledge, Dr Michael Nicholls, Susan MacQueen, Olga Kurtianyuk, Bente Fasmer and me had visited Tushinskaya to assess hospital infection, ITU and general problems. We all stayed in the hospital flats.

Sir Bryan and I met our Ambassador Brian Fall in the British Embassy in order to keep him in the picture with developments, and we had a meeting with Leshkevitch in Minzdrav, the Department of Health. We all felt this had been a useful trip and things at long last were moving forwards.

*

Lord Mayor's Banquet

The Lord Mayor Elect, Alderman Paul Newall, the Sheriffs of London and Alderman John Chalstrey requested the honour of our company at a banquet at the Guildhall on Monday 15 November 1993 to observe Lord Mayor's Day.

John, a Gastrological Surgeon attached to St Bartholomew's Hospital, was a good friend of ours, and he was in line to be the second medical Lord Mayor of London in a couple of years' time.

We would be seated at table two in places eight and seven, with the other 3-400 guests including politicians such as Michael Heseltine, Chief of the General Staff Gen Sir Peter Inge, the Earl and Countess of Airlie, the Master of the Apothecaries, the Headmaster of Harrow School, Nicholas Bomford, the Archbishop of Canterbury, the Most Reverend Carey, Judge Denison, Robert Fellowes, Private Secretary to the Queen, several Ambassadors including Raymond Seitz, the Ambassador of the United States, and amongst many others, Lord Palumbo who I had known as a neighbour in my teens.

The excellent menu consisted of Thames salmon, smoked venison, roast pheasant, autumn berries, Lord Mayor's fusillade, coffee, truffles and mints. Each course was accompanied by an appropriate matching wine.

Numerous toasts were drunk: the Queen, the Queen Mother, Prince Philip of Edinburgh, the Prince and Princess of Wales and other members of the Royal Family, Her Majesty's Ministers, the Late Lord Mayor and the Court of Aldermen, and finally the Lord Mayor and Sheriffs, the hosts.

Music was provided by the Duke of Kent's Band, and there were Trumpeters of the Lifeguards and Choristers of St Paul's Cathedral.

Chapter 6

Constitutional crisis

Russian constitutional crisis, Encyclopaedia of Russia and the FSU, Family centred care, Paediatric Nursing School, Textbook of Paediatric Nursing, Funding PNS, Ham & High, Solzhenitsyn

Russian constitutional crisis

Relations between the Russian President and the Parliament had been deteriorating for some time.

The power struggle reached its crisis on 21 September 1993, when President Yeltsin intended to dissolve the country's highest body, Congress of People's Deputies, and Parliament, the Duma, although the constitution did not give the President the power to do so.

Parliament declared the President's decision null and void, impeached Yeltsin and proclaimed Vice President Aleksandr Rutskoy to be acting President.

Ten days later, demonstrators removed police cordons around the Parliament and, urged by their leaders, took over the Mayor's offices and tried to storm the Ostankino television centre. On Yeltsin's orders, the army, which had initially declared its neutrality, stormed the White House, the Russian Republic Parliament building, and arrested the leaders of the resistance.

The ten-day conflict became the deadliest single event of street fighting in Moscow's history since the Russian Revolution. According to the General Prosecutor's Office, 147 people were killed and 437 wounded.

*

Encyclopaedia of Russia and the FSU

I was invited by the Cambridge University Press to contribute a chapter on Soviet medicine to the second edition of the *Encyclopaedia of Russia and the Former Soviet Union*. This entailed contacting Ivan Leshkevitch in Moscow and spending several hours in the reading room of the British Museum.

As the social upheaval of the 1917 revolution resolved, the authorities developed a centralised health care system, offering comprehensive medical care to the widely dispersed war and famine-devastated population. Most significantly, they largely controlled infections, although unfortunately in recent years there had been a resurgence of some of these illnesses, as medical facilities had deteriorated.

After many years of isolation from the West, in some instances because of political policies, there was often duplication of research occurring outside the USSR and development of original ideas only at a relatively low technological level.

Developments in anaesthesia, neurosurgery, plastic surgery and orthopaedics were largely stimulated by treatment of casualties during the Second World War.

Under the auspices of the Academies of Science and Medical Sciences, much basic and clinical research had been undertaken in many fields, including molecular biology and genetics, basic physiology, mechanisms of illness and recovery, reconstructive surgery and microsurgery.

In some areas such as surgical treatment of short sight, traumatic surgery, sporting injuries and space medicine, they were way ahead of facilities in the West.

In recent years international contacts had expanded and formal agreements for cooperation in research and health care were made with the UK, USA, France, Finland and Italy, in addition to Eastern European countries. The USSR actively participated in the WHO, World Health Organisation, and in 1978 hosted in Alma Ata, an International conference on primary health care.

Yevgeny Chazov, Minister of Health, 1987–1990, expressed the hope that by the year 2000, health care in the USSR would have achieved a level comparable with that of other developed countries.

*

Family centred care

In September, a team led by Michael Kidd including Dr Sheila McKenzie, Dr Susan Vas Dias, a specialist in Family Centred Care, and Olga Kurtianyuk had visited Tushinskaya to hold seminars on Family Centred Care and discuss hospital management.

In the UK, following the Second World War, two children's Psychiatrists attached to the Tavistock Clinic, Bowlby and Robertson, had recognised the psychological trauma experienced by children in hospitals and devised the concept of Family Centred Care, FCC.

A young child in a hospital had stated, *"Well there was nobody there [meaning no one who was human] to ... I might have just been a lump of meat, you know, but don't forget that I was only four and a half, five, but I never saw my parents. And I was terrified of what they [the nurses and doctors] were going to do."*

FCC would permit the parents of the children in the hospital not only to visit on a regular basis, and, when necessary, stay overnight, but also to assist with the care of their child with simple measures such as helping them with washing and eating. Psychologically the children's spirits would be raised, their fears allayed and their recovery speeded up.

It had taken several decades before this became accepted practice in the UK. It was hardly surprising that we could not expect its introduction in Russia overnight.

Of course, introduction of Family Centred Care into the hospital was not welcomed by many of the staff who believed in restricting parental visiting because, in their view, parents brought in infection, parents would not comply with the children's special diets, parents were a nuisance and children would be upset when the parents left.

*

1993 Paediatric Nursing School

In the field of nurse training, Tushinskaya would be opening a School of Paediatric Nursing in 1994 – the first in Russia.

Discussions were held with Miss Betty Barchard, Director of Nursing at Great Ormond Street Hospital, and she arranged to visit Moscow in January/February 1992 with a view to selecting six to eight children's nurses for a six-month course of further training to teach them to act as Paediatric Nurse-trainers. The initial part of the course would be held in London, the subsequent part in Moscow. The British course tutors would accompany the nurses throughout the whole period.

In October 1993, Dr Yuri Pavlov, Dr Nelli Naigovzina, Dr Olga Skorobogatova, Director of Moscow Medical School No 24, a school for training nurses which was located in a building in the grounds of Tushinskaya Hospital, and Dr Margarita Kosygina, Head of the School of Postgraduate Nursing Education Moscow, accompanied by Galina Romanyuk acting as interpreter, came to visit London and stay with us for a week in our house. In GOSH they studied hospital management, clinical management, voluntary organisations and further discussed the details of the paediatric nurse training course.

Following many discussions between the Trust, Betty Barchard, Olga Kurtianyk, Tom Bolger of the Royal College of Nursing, Olga Skorobogatova and Margarita

Kosygina, it was agreed that 17-year-old Russian school leavers would be trained in the new school. Much of the discussion concentrated on whether the input of young women to be trained in paediatric nursing should be school leavers or those who had already had general nursing training. In fact, similar discussions were taking place in the UK at that time.

The curriculum would be based on a modified Charles West School of Paediatric Nursing – the Great Ormond Street Hospital curriculum – and the course would last for three years with two annual entries of 15 students.

The training course at GOSH was due to commence in January 1994. Candidates would be drawn from the Tushinskaya, Filatov and Rusakov Children's Hospitals in Moscow.

Teachers for teaching in the new school would be sourced from general trained Russian nurses who had received a course of advanced training in Moscow in Medical Academy No 1. Three of those nurses already worked in the Tushinskaya Hospital, one as Senior Theatre Sister, Svetlana Chapla, and two, Olga Troshina and Lydmilla Bederdinova as Clinical Tutors, and the rest were teaching in Medical School No 24. All of them were receiving intensive language training in English from a British teacher who the Trust had sent out to Moscow and a Russian teacher of English, Marina Minina, who would accompany them to London to act as interpreter.

Very sadly, Marina, several years later, went to one of the Gulf States to work as an interpreter and an English and Russian language teacher, and was murdered in her apartment by an intruder.

The first two months of the course would be held in London at the Hospital for Sick Children Great Ormond Street and at Queen Elizabeth Hospital, Hackney. The subsequent four months of the course would be held in Moscow at Tushinskaya Children's Hospital.

Both the principal course tutor Sheila Barlow, Director of Nursing Education GOSH, and the deputy course tutor, Linda Dale, Senior Clinical Nurse Tutor Queen Elizabeth Hospital would accompany the nurses back to Moscow to continue the second part of the course.

Sheila Barlow commented: *"The philosophy that the Trust is endeavouring to introduce to doctors and nurses, put simply, is that the sick child should be their central concern and parents should be involved in caring for the child in the hospital. They are stressing the importance of infection control and teaching that good nursing requires an understanding of the child's psychological development."*

The prime objective of the first part of the course would be to demonstrate and teach the philosophy of paediatric nursing as practised in the United Kingdom. This would be developed practically, in light of Russian requirements, during the second part of the course.

Five of the course participants would teach in the new school and three would work in Tushinskaya Hospital upgrading existing children's nurses.

During the first two years, three UK-trained British nursing tutors would be seconded to the new school by the Trust. They would also assist with further training of the present existing nurses in the hospital, initially concentrating on the Trauma ward and Intensive Care Unit.

*

Textbook of Paediatric Nursing

Sheila Barlow and Barbara Weller had written a *Textbook of Paediatric Nursing*, published by Bailliere Tindall in 1991, in the Nurses Aids series. Sheila had agreed that I could try to secure the foreign rights for publication in a Russian translation.

Following a series of discussions with Christine Morton, foreign rights manager of Harcourt Brace, which was a subsidiary of the original publisher, it was agreed that we could translate and publish the book into Russian. Sergei Rezayev, Nataly Duddington's son-in-law, kindly offered to seek a Russian publisher.

Translation and editing of *Textbook of Paediatric Nursing* had now been completed, but the publication date had been delayed. Drs Margarita Kalina and Olga Skorobogatova had been asked to write a foreword.

*

Funding Paediatric Nursing School

The Wellcome Foundation, Smiths Industries Medical Systems, the Know How Fund, TACL and the Department of Health UK would all be supporting the project.

The Know How Fund was a programme set up by the British government that assisted former Soviet bloc nations in the transition to free-market democracies. TACL, Training and Academic Links, was the project arm of the Fund.

Tushinskaya School of Paediatric Nursing was scheduled to open on 1 September 1994, and indeed did open on that date.

Ham & High

Our local newspaper, the *Ham & High,* gave the project a full one-page cover with several photos, and ran an excellent article on "British doctors heal the scars of the past regime. Trust helps children in Moscow."

Paul Waugh, now a national political commentator, wrote, *"It was once known, somewhat forbiddingly, as Moscow City Children's Hospital Number 7. Today, Tushinskaya Children's Hospital has a friendlier name, but it still has many scars from the Communist era.*

In what is supposed to be a children's hospital, parents are kept at arm's length and can only expect to visit once a week. But thanks to Dr Harald Lipman, a Foreign Office Medical Adviser and founder of a charity aimed at helping Tushinskaya offer high-quality, the regime at the hospital is slowly changing."

*

Solzhenitsyn

Aleksandr Solzhenitsyn, novelist, philosopher, historian and outspoken critic of Communism, was arrested in 1945 and initially imprisoned in the Lubyanka prison in Moscow.

When he heard of Germany's surrender, he wrote, *"Above the muzzle of our window, and from all the other cells of the Lubyanka, and from all the windows of the Moscow prisons, we too, former prisoners of war and former front-line soldiers, watched the Moscow heavens, patterned with fireworks and crisscrossed with beams of searchlights. There was no rejoicing in our cells and no hugs and no kisses for us. That victory was not ours."*

Khrushchev released him from exile in 1956, but his Soviet citizenship was removed, and he was deported to West Germany and then travelled to the United States in 1974.

His Soviet citizenship was restored in 1990 and, following his return from the United States in 1994, lived in a dacha in the woods close to the Embassy dacha in Serebryany Bor.

He expressed his disillusionment with post-Soviet Russia in his works and called for the establishment of a strong Presidential republic, balanced by vigorous institutions of local self-government. He also published several short stories, a series of poems and a literary memoir on his years in the West

Chapter 7

Problems in Tushinskaya

Problems in Tushinskaya, Pectopah's death, Russian nurses' arrival, Nelli's resignation, Wellcome Foundation, Surgical team, Evgeni Pasternak, Pharmacy, Hospital infection control, FCC and child development, Tushinskaya problems, Royal Garden Party, Laundry, Hospital management, Painting holiday, First Chechen War, Queen's visit to Moscow, Yeltsin

Problems in Tushinskaya

On the face of it, the project was proceeding well; several departments in the hospital had now opened day clinics, and others were planned. A private clinic, Kalinka, had been opened in one of the hospital buildings, and the profits from this were to be used to help purchase a new car for the hospital.

However, early in the year we heard from several sources that there were serious problems in Tushinskaya, including a breakdown in relationships between Yuri and Nelli.

Potentially even more serious than that problem was that in the Department of Health, Glavk was unhappy with certain procedures in the hospital. Relations between Yuri and Olga Skorobogatova, head of the Paediatric Nursing School, were strained, and there were problems between the administration and the hospital staff – the command structure in the hospital still persisted, and Tushinskaya had a poor relationship with other Moscow hospitals, which were probably jealous of the assistance it received.

Looking at these series of problems dispassionately, the common link appeared to be Yuri Pavlov. He was undoubtedly a good, dedicated, farsighted man, brought up in the command structure system and finding it very difficult to put into effect new ideas, with which we thought he genuinely believed.

It was agreed by the Trustees and committee that Nahid and I should go out to Moscow to try to resolve these numerous problems.

*

Pectopah's death

Unfortunately, the Gods seemed to be conspiring against us. On Saturday 22 January 1994, poor little Pectopah was run over by a car in the street outside our house, whilst we were at the cinema with our brother-in-law Kurt, watching the film version of Kazuo Ishiguro's book *The Remains of the Day*. Amanda, Marc, Nahid and I all said a silent prayer as we buried her in the garden under a cherry blossom tree. She was 18 years old at that time, equivalent to 89 human years, and obviously her reflexes had slowed down and her hearing and sight was impaired, so she had not heard or seen the car that struck her.

We have had no house pets since then, other than occasional goldfish. In memory of our much-loved Siberian Forest cat, a memorial fund was set up in Pectopah's name to purchase educational toys for the children of Tushinskaya Hospital. The FCO Diplomatic Families Spouses Association journal published a short obituary.

*

Russian nurses' arrival

The eight Russian nurses were due to arrive six days later for the two months' training in paediatric nursing in Queen Elizabeth Hospital, and one of Nahid's sisters, Parvaneh, had arranged to stay with us for a few weeks. So, we were unable to depart for Moscow until the last week of February.

On arrival it was snowing in Moscow and the temperature was -8°C. Yuri Pavlov met us with the new hospital car at Sheremetyevo Airport, and we stayed in the hospital flats.

Our first call was on Nelli; she had given notice that she was resigning with effect from 3rd March. She was very welcoming and pleasant, did not agree with the commercial development of part of the hospital, but remained very supportive of the Trust's efforts to help the hospital and would be happy to return there if Yuri were to retire.

She would be taking up an important post in the new government department dealing with medical insurance for children in the "umbrella ministry" which oversees the Ministry of Health. In light of her future professional success, this was the best move she ever made in her career.

When we visited Tushinskaya Hospital, we found that several parts of it had been redecorated in anticipation of the Princess of Wales's postponed visit. Following long and positive talks with Yuri and various heads of departments, followed by lunch in the hospital canteen, we presented our future plans to a meeting of approximately fifty members of the hospital staff.

The following morning, we had a further short talk with Yuri who was very busy involved with a visiting Japanese delegation.

We invited Dr Vladimir Garkusha, Head of the Neonatal department, and Dr Margarita Kalinina, Head of Microbiology laboratory, to visit the UK in April.

In the afternoon we met Olga Skorobogatova and Margarita Kosygina and discussed practical aspects of the relationship between the hospital and the new Paediatric Nursing School.

Speaking with Ivan Leshkevitch, it became obvious that the conservative elements in Glavk were in the ascendancy, and had effectively closed Kalinka, the private clinic, and ordered the proceeds of any income from developments of hospital properties to be paid to Glavk, and not to the hospital.

Many of the accusations made against Yuri Pavlov appeared to be orchestrated by those who were jealous of the attention Tushinskaya received, and were attempts to destabilise the situation. We liked Yuri and in general got on with him well, although we had some reservations, but felt *чёрт знакомый лучше чёрта незнакомого* – *"the devil you know is better than the devil you don't know."*

We recognised that the importance of introducing a management structure was even greater than previously, and we should proceed with this as rapidly as we could, subject to Yuri and Glavk's agreement.

That day we lunched in the German Embassy with my colleague Martin Friedrichs and visited the Republican Children's Hospital with him, where he had an ongoing programme assisting them with supplies of chemotherapy medication for the children. They were using a German protocol for treatment.

*

Wellcome Foundation

The Wellcome Foundation had kindly offered to host a reception for the Russian nurses in their main building, Unicorn House, in Euston Road.

We invited, amongst others, guests from all the many organisations who were involved with the project, some of the other charitable trusts working in the former Soviet Union, the International Relations Department of the Department of Health, representatives from Great Ormond Street Hospital and the Russian Embassy.

Surgical team

Two weeks later I returned to Moscow with a small team of surgeons and an anaesthetist from the John Radcliffe Hospital Oxford: Malcolm Gough, John Stevens, Jennifer Price, and Adrianne and Gordon Hill. We stayed in the hospital flats, and the hospital had arranged for us to have breakfast, and when necessary, other meals in the hospital canteen.

On the Sunday, I had arranged with Olga to show them the main sights, the Kremlin, Red Square and Novodevichy. In the evening we saw a rather poor production of Gilbert and Sullivan's *Iolanthe* in the Bolshoi.

During the next couple of days, they saw and assessed the surgical wards and theatres and ITU, whilst I held rounds of talks with Glavk, Yuri and separately with Nelli.

I also went to a store with Olga and bought a washing machine for installation in one of the flats. Rather surprisingly we found that they had several on offer. I hadn't had time to change my dollars into roubles, and had considerable difficulty in persuading the store to accept foreign currency. By law all purchases had to be made in roubles.

At supper that evening, we had the pleasure of eating with Evgeni and Elena Pasternak. Evgeni, a charming man of about seventy years of age, was Boris Pasternak's son by his first wife, Evgeniya. His grandfather, Leonid, had moved to Oxford before the Second World War, and several generations of the Pasternak family had grown up and lived in Oxford. They were friends of some of the members of the visiting surgical team who had arranged this supper meeting.

*

Three days after my return to London, Nahid, Marc and I were skiing in Chamonix. The day after we arrived back in London, the eight Russian nurses were leaving for Moscow. Ten days later, Sheila Barlow and Linda Dale flew out to Moscow to oversee the second part of the Paediatric teacher training course.

As we discovered later, one of the eight nurses had managed to get pregnant whilst in London, and a very discreet termination had been performed.

Pharmacy

Anne Clohessy, a British Pharmacist, was seconded to Tushinskaya and assisted the Chief Pharmacist in reorganising the pharmacy and establishing procedures for medicinal drugs distribution in the hospital.

*

Hospital infection control

Susan MacQueen and Barbara Kerzman visited to introduce Hospital Infection Control, and Susan Vas Dias and Olga Kurtianyuk advised on Family Centred Care and made an assessment of the Neonatal unit. At the same time, on behalf of the Trust, Margaret Swanwick was teaching child development in Tushinskaya.

*

FCC and child development

Susan Vas Dias was consultant Paediatric Psychotherapist at Queen Elizabeth Hospital, and had prepared a detailed programme for further training in the implementation of Family Centred Care in Tushinskaya. She made regular visits to Moscow over the succeeding three years.

Margaret Swanwick concentrated on child development both emotional and psychological, working with siblings, liaising with nursing and medical staff and coping with bereavement.

*

Tushinskaya problems

Nahid and I again returned to Moscow in May and found several areas where progress was being made.

Nurses were starting to be trained on the wards and these changes we discussed with Sheila Barlow, Linda Dale, Lydmilla and Olga. There was much enthusiasm from the attendants at the English language classes, changes were occurring in the Pharmacy and in the Microbiology department, and in the Neonatal department many positive steps were being taken.

However, in several other important areas there was a considerable diminution in enthusiasm for the change and a certain lack of cooperation. Yuri Pavlov's future seemed to be uncertain, and we were unable to ascertain whether or not he would be continuing as Director of Tushinskaya. During our short visit he'd had a possibly diplomatic illness, and we had no opportunities to speak with him privately.

Nelli's replacement, Dr Lazarev, was a nondescript sort of man who had previously run the now closed Kalinka private clinic, and seemed to be very conservative in his approach to change. On the positive side, however, the Chief Surgeon, Makroosef, who was acting as deputy Director and had previously been very antagonistic to change, now appeared to be supportive of our aims.

Vadim Ivanov, who had been awarded a six-month British Council Fellowship to study in the UK, would shortly be returning to Moscow, but it appeared to be unlikely that he would be offered his previous post as deputy Head of the Infectious Diseases Department. The Trust had put a lot of investment into him, and this would be a considerable loss both to us and the hospital.

On our previous visit we had suggested that liaison committees be set up to cooperate directly with the Trust and to integrate academic and clinical departments in the hospital. Some had nominally been set up, which in theory sounded good, but in practice, they were headed by academicians who in general took a very negative approach to change.

The two Nurse Managers from the hospital, Lydmilla and Olga, were regularly attending the paediatric nursing training course, as were two others of the nurses. Svetlana, the Theatre Sister, had not attended at all, two of the other nurses were completing studies they missed whilst in London and another was trying to attend some other course as well as the Trust's course.

We were having difficulty in obtaining reliable interpreters of an adequate calibre, but hoped that Vadim might be able to help in seeking them on his return.

Galina Romanyuk was very disillusioned with the hospital, and we feared she might well reduce the amount of assistance she was giving to the project.

All in all, we began to wonder if it was worth all the effort we were putting in our end, if in Moscow they were either unable or unwilling to cooperate.

We realised that probably political and economic factors, and certainly infighting within the hospital and Department of Health Moscow, played a significant part in their change of heart.

On our return to Heathrow, we had to drive immediately to the crematorium in Ruislip to attend the funeral of Phillip Angel, a close friend of ours.

The Trust had engaged three Nurse Tutors, Kathryn Jones, Jayne Harris and

Janet Wydell, who would reside in Moscow, teach in the Paediatric Nursing School, and also work on the wards in the hospital. They were all given the opportunity of attending Russian language classes, and in July Katherine and Jayne made a familiarisation visit to Moscow. In November, Jan and Jayne both went to Moscow, and, living in the hospital flats, started teaching in the school and working on the Trauma ward and in the ITU. Kathryn would follow early in the New Year.

*

Buckingham Palace garden party

In July Nahid and I as representatives of the Trust were invited by Princess Diana to attend a garden party at Buckingham Palace.

The invitation, stated, "The Lord Chamberlain is commanded by Her Majesty to invite Doctor and Mrs Harold Lipman to a garden party at Buckingham Palace on Tuesday 12 July 1994 from 4 to 6 p.m.

Morning Dress, Uniform or Lounge Suit."

In light of this advice, I chose my best lounge suit and Nahid wore an elegant dress with a floral design and smart brimmed hat that she had previously worn when we were invited to Ascot.

The Lord Chamberlain is commanded by Her Majesty to invite

Doctor and Mrs. Harold Lipman

to a Garden Party at Buckingham Palace on Tuesday 12th July 1994 from 4 to 6 pm

Morning Dress, Uniform or Lounge Suit

Garden party

The invitation envelope also contained some information: all gates will be open from 3.15 p.m. Chauffeur and owner-driven cars could park in Constitution Hill and the

Mall as directed by the police. Parking is available between 12.30 p.m. and 7.00 p.m. Entry to the Palace – Guests should enter and leave the Palace on foot, leaving and rejoining their cars where the vehicles have been parked.

A label, with a large yellow X on one side, was also enclosed to be affixed to the lower left-hand corner of the windscreen of your car or taxi. The side with written instructions was to face the driver.

We placed the label in the windscreen as instructed and walked up to the Palace gates, where we were waved through on showing our invitations. Surprisingly there did not appear to be a high level of security.

Entering the Palace, we passed through a couple of rooms and then a French window with some steps down to the garden.

The 42-acre garden was originally designed by Capability Brown, and later a large man-made lake was added. It is largely lawned with a number of trees of different species.

For the garden party, several tea tents had been erected where we took tea and sandwiches. Probably a couple of a hundred guests were present. Some we knew from the Foreign Office, whilst some others were members of the Russia Britain Chamber of Commerce.

As a military band played the National Anthem, at 4 p.m. the Queen emerged from the Bow Room and slowly processed through the ranks of assembled guests towards her own private tea tent, greeting those previously selected for the honour, whilst the band continued to play a selection of music.

Over the course of each year, the Queen welcomes over 30,000 guests to garden parties. At each garden party, around 27,000 cups of tea, 20,000 sandwiches and 20,000 slices of cake are consumed.

A memorable occasion.

*

I made another short visit to Moscow which turned out to be a very useful trip. Having had long discussions with Yuri Pavlov, assisted by Kingsmill Bond and further long discussions with Glavk, I also managed to fit in visits to the Paediatric Nursing School and saw Kathryn, Jane and Marina. Sheila Barlow and Linda Dale were due to leave and there was a farewell party for them in the hospital.

Having supped with Sergei and Masha Rezayev, the son-in-law and daughter of Nataly Duddington, I had to return to the hospital flat by metro and then take a bus. Travelling on the bus in the dark, I missed my bus stop and stayed on the bus until it arrived at its terminal after a few minutes. There was nobody around to ask my way, so I set off along the road in what I thought was the right direction. In the dark, all the blocks of flats resembled one another, and half an hour later I finally found the correct block and tumbled into bed.

*

On my return to London, we held a special meeting of the Trustees. I had had a series of meetings with various people whilst in Moscow to try to ascertain the causes of past and existing problems and map out agreed areas for future cooperation. I had also taken the opportunity of speaking with many people, including Russians, with an attempt to try to assess whether there was any significant reversal in Russian political trends which might be affecting the Trust's projects.

I reported on a confidential meeting I had held with Yuri Pavlov. According to his version of the problems which had arisen between him and Nelli, they were because she wished to replace him as Director of the hospital and had organised a campaign against him with the cooperation of her relative in the Moscow government.

The Kollegia investigation established by Glavk had found no evidence of criminal actions on his part, but had revoked some of the hospital's previously granted autonomy and banned involvement in all commercial activities.

During my meeting with Glavk, I had spoken about the Hospital Acquired Infection programme and they were prepared to help with the financing of a project for investigation of the causes of infection in hospitals and ways of controlling it. They wanted our specialists to train their teachers.

We had raised the question of installing a laundry in the hospital and Glavk confirmed they would pay the total cost of installation and equipment.

They agreed that the Trust could send out a British manager to undertake an assessment of hospital management in Tushinskaya. They felt, however, that assessment of estate management should be postponed as there were no funds available for any improvements which might be recommended.

It was agreed that the English language programme could continue, although Yuri had reservations and felt that some of the Russian nurses could not read Russian, let alone learn English.

The Family Centred Care project should continue. Teaching seminars were agreed in principle, but they wished us to prepare a list of proposed subjects.

Discussing the Paediatric Nursing project, Margarita Kosygina was initially very aggressive, demanding and negative, but subsequently changed her approach.

We were in the process of preparing a *Textbook of Paediatric Nursing,* applying the principles which were being taught in the Paediatric Nursing School, and it was agreed that a print run of 25–30,000 copies would be appropriate.

We were also proposing to publish a newsletter in English and Russian which would help to keep the hospital staff and parents informed of the details of the project as they developed.

Both Glavk and the hospital remained very enthusiastic about a future visit by Diana, The Princess of Wales.

At a meeting with Margarita Kosygina, Tatiana Manokhina – deputy Head of Medical School number 24 as Olga Skorobogatova was on leave – Sheila Barlow, Linda Dale, Kathryn Jones and Jayne Harris, with Marina interpreting, the roles of Katherine and Jane were discussed and agreed.

Kingsmill Bond had managed to establish a pool of 12 potential interpreters who would be paid US $75 a week with one month's paid leave annually. He and his secretary, Galina, were extremely helpful in liaising with Tushinskaya and resolving our nurses' day-to-day problems. The monthly cost of Kingsmill's and Galina's services was approximately £500.

Based on all the above arrangements and assuming that, in fact, they were all put into practice, all present at the Trustees meeting agreed that the project should continue.

*

Laundry

All hospital linen was sent to a Moscow-authority-run central laundry which gave a very poor service and whose standards of hygiene were questionable.

We arranged for two specialists in commercial laundry installation, Steve Barrow and Nick Saunders, to visit Tushinskaya, assess requirements, draw up plans for a hospital laundry and give us a costing.

Unfortunately, by the time plans and costings were completed, Moscow City Council had run out of funds and was unable to proceed with development of the laundry.

*

Hospital management

BESO had helped us find a retired Hospital Manager, Leslie Yeoman, who agreed to be seconded to Tushinskaya for three weeks to assess hospital management requirements and draw up and cost a draft scheme to replace the existing command structure.

Yuri Pavlov and all the administrative staff in the hospital were very cooperative, and, surprisingly, quite taken with the idea. Les produced an excellent scheme, but the Russian authorities were in the process of introducing a medical insurance scheme for funding health care, which would fund hospitals on an item-of-service basis rather than bed occupancy, and it put Les's scheme on hold.

Whilst Les was in Moscow, I made yet another visit and we shared one of the hospital flats. By then Kathryn had joined Janet and Jayne in Moscow.

*

Our Embassy, represented by Lady Fall, the Ambassador's wife, formally presented a blood gas analyser to the hospital's Neonatal unit, with full Russian press coverage.

Hugh Carpenter, my successor in the embassy, kindly invited me to supper, and the following day I had useful meetings with Pavlov, Glavk and Olga Skorobogatova. Everything appeared to be running on a pretty even keel.

*

Painting holiday

In 1994, following the early death of our close friend Phillip, we took his widow, Liz, who Nahid had known for many years whilst training as a student nurse, on a painting holiday.

We arranged to have a week's painting holiday in Roujan in France, near the small town of Pézenas in the south of the country. We drove to Dover, boarded the Hovercraft, and 40 minutes later arrived in Calais.

That night we spent in a comfortable hotel, Le Vieux Logis near Fontainebleau, having driven on the autoroute via Senlis. It was always such a pleasure to be in France – good food and wine, a pleasant ambience and the sound of rural spoken French.

My French was moderately good, although far from fluent, and my father used to say I spoke like *une vache espagnole* – a Spanish cow.

The next day Nahid drove us down through Meaux to Vichy.

During the Second World War, following the armistice signed on 22 June 1940, the zone which was not occupied by the Germans set up its capital in Vichy.

The republican system was abolished, and the French State, with Marshall Petain at its helm as Head of State, replaced it.

Next day, after stopping for lunch in Le Puy, we drove along a pretty mountain road and overnighted in a small hotel in the village of Meyrueis, which was full of tourists. During breakfast, the hotel cat, which closely resembled our late Siberian Forest cat, Pectopah, walked over to us purring and rubbed its coat against our legs. We wondered, *Are cats reincarnated?*

Having arranged to collect Liz from Montpelier Airport, we had to press on and arrived there shortly before her plane landed.

Our next stop would be our destination, Le Pigeonnier de Senaux in Roujan, in the region known as Languedoc, famed for its wines, where the painting school was located.

Le Pigeonnier de Senaux is a renovated *maison de compagne* situated amongst vineyards with barely a house in sight. It has three acres of land, bordered by a stream, secluded garden with fruit trees, terrace and swimming pool, where the only real disturbance comes from the sounds of crickets, cicadas and exotic birds.

However, as we quickly discovered, the house had typically poor plumbing. French plumbers, at that time, did not install watertraps in u-bend pipes to prevent the smell of sewage percolating into the house bathrooms and toilets.

The village of Roujan was just 1 km away either along the tree-lined road or by foot skirting the stream and vineyards. Several other picturesque villages were also within reach, and the historic town Pézenas was 10 km away and was bursting at the seams with cafés, galleries, craft shops, *brocantes* and old door knockers.

The painting school resorted with small groups and much emphasis on individual tuition, to encourage each member to develop their painting at his or her own pace, and in his or her's own chosen style.

The emphasis was on freedom of interpretation, thus gaining confidence in our ability to paint.

On the first day of tuition, we attended a colour-mixing class with a group of half a dozen other people. Nahid also attended a photographic class.

We lunched in Pézenas, and ate the evening meal with the other group members. During the night we were woken by thunder and lightning.

Following discussion of our previous day's watercolour paintings, we then visited the nearby monastery and sketched and painted architectural structures. This I always found most enjoyable.

In the afternoon we drove to Béziers, taking Dominique, one of the group, with us. He was a custodian at Hampton Court Palace, and a very interesting young man.

Liz remained in contact with him for several years and when a few years later we all visited Hampton Court he kindly showed us around the Palace and gardens.

There was plenty to sketch and paint including the Cathedral of Saint Nazaire and the Pont Vieux, but there were too many tourists and shops catering for their requirements.

One of our group was a rather plump woman, Joyce, probably in her 40s, who apparently was diabetic, and each evening at supper she would pull up her skirt and give herself her evening injection of insulin. Then her arm would stretch across the table and she would say, *"Does anyone mind if I have the last piece of fruit tart?"* as she put it in her mouth. She was staying in a caravan in the school's garden, presumably because the cost was less than that for a room.

Every evening we would drive to Pézenas to have a pre-prandial cocktail in one of the open-air bars, and after a second night of mosquito bites bought some mosquito netting. If there is a single mosquito within 50 miles of Nahid, unfortunately, it will find its way to her and bite her. Her blood must be very sweet.

The following day was a Monday and when we drove to Pézenas for lunch, after our morning class sketching and painting flowers, we discovered all restaurants closed on Mondays. That evening after supper we all played charades.

Some days we would paint in the studio and on others either in the garden or by the pool, or visit churches or other interesting buildings and streets in nearby villages.

On our final day, after fond farewells to all the group and exchanges of addresses, we drove Liz to Montpelier Airport and then lunched in the grounds of Auberge du Lac near Albi.

We were now driving north slowly along country roads towards the Loire Valley, stopping overnight in comfortable hotels in Le Puy en Velay and then at a lovely farm barn house, La Plumardie Basse in St Alvere, sketching and painting as we went.

Having driven in part on the autoroute, past Périgueux, Angoulême, Limoges and Poitiers, we reached Tours, the gateway to the Loire.

The birthplace of Balzac takes one on a wonderful journey back in time. The old quarter had narrow cobbled *pavé* – streets – half-timbered French houses and the stone facades of the monumental Saint-Galien Cathedral which gave the city a charming medieval air.

After breakfast in our hotel, we drove to the French Renaissance Chenonceau Chateau, built in 1513 and later gifted by Henri II to Diane de Poitiers. In the Green Study is a painting of the Queen of Sheba visiting Solomon, painted by the school of Veronese. The gallery was built by Catherine de Medici. On the first floor is the Room of Five Queens, the two daughters and three daughters–in–law of Catherine de Medici, including Mary Stuart, known as Mary Queen of Scots.

Our next port of call would be Paris to see our friend Françoise Diamant, who I had known since the age of 15 when I made my first visit to France and met her in Le Touquet.

We stayed in a hotel near the Champs-Élysées and parked our car in her garage for a couple of days. As ever she was very welcoming, taking us to several excellent restaurants. Françoise would, on entering a restaurant, before seeking a table, find the kitchen and sniff to see if the food was good.

We visited many other places, including the Musée d'Orsay to view their wonderful collection of Impressionists, and the Racing Club de France in the Bois de Boulogne, which Françoise regularly attended to swim or play tennis.

Returning to Dover by Hovercraft, following a roughish Channel crossing, we arrived home in London in the pouring rain.

Having enjoyed our trip so much, we decided to make painting holidays an annual event, and in subsequent years visited painting schools in various regions of France and Spain.

*

1994 December - First Chechen War

Over the centuries there was a long tradition of armed dissent between the Muslim population of the Caucasus and the Christian population of Tsarist Russia. It is in many ways encapsulated in Tolstoy's short novel *Hadji Murat,* the tale of a Chechen rebel.

Chechnya had declared independence from post-Soviet Russia in 1993, and actively discriminated against non-Chechen members of their population.

Former Soviet Air Force General Dudayev led the governing group, but a significant part of the population opposed him and there were repeated incidents attempting to overthrow his regime.

In late 1994, Yeltsin ordered the warring factions to disarm and surrender, and then ordered the Russian army to restore constitutional order in the semi-autonomous republic.

Following an aerial bombardment of the capital Grozny, Russian troops launched an attack. In Russian the word *Grozny* means menacing or cruel. The Tsar Ivan the Terrible was known as *Ivan Grozny.*

This was the start of the First Chechen War, which was officially reported in the Russian press as *"Armed conflict in the Chechen republic and bordering territories of the Russian Federation."*

*

Queen's visit to Moscow

In 1994, Her Majesty the Queen became the first British Monarch to visit Russia. On her arrival she was wearing a fur coat and pillbox hat. She stayed in the Kremlin as Yeltsin's guest, saw a production of *Giselle* at the Bolshoi, attended an informal lunch at the British Embassy and laid the foundation stone for the new British Embassy.

*

Yeltsin

Yeltsin was increasingly often drunk in public. Visiting Berlin, for the withdrawal of the Russian troops, he grabbed the baton from the hand of the military conductor of the welcoming army band and started wildly conducting them. On another occasion, flying from New York to Moscow, the plane stopped at Shannon Airport, and he was too drunk to disembark to meet the Irish Prime Minister Albert Reynolds.

*

What a difficult year it had been. What would the coming year hold for us and Russia?

Chapter 8

Tushinskaya hospital further developments

Barbra Streisand, Estates management, Our nurses' reflections, Preparing children and parents for theatre, Infection control, Family centred care, Homeopathy

In fact, during the course of 1995 many significant events occurred, and considerable progress was made with the project to enhance the facilities offered by Tushinskaya and thus improve the welfare of the children in the hospital.

*

Nahid was visiting her family in LA, where I would be joining her after making a short visit to Moscow to see how things were going in the hospital and Paediatric Nursing School. Everything seemed to be progressing well and relatively smoothly.

*

Barbra Streisand

Two days later following my return, I flew out to LA and was delighted to see Nahid and many members of her family again.

Whilst there I contacted the Streisand Foundation to see if they might be prepared to assist with funding Tushinskaya Trust.

Barbra Streisand had consulted me with a medical problem shortly before we were leaving for Moscow in 1983, and was very taken by the idea that we were considering living in Russia for some time, as her maternal grandparents had lived in Tsarist Russia. She was at that time in the UK producing, directing and starring in the film *Yentl* based on a short story written in Yiddish by the Polish author Isaac Bashevis Singer.

*

Estates management

Alan Clark spent a week at Tushinskaya assessing the state of repair of the hospital buildings and grounds, with a view to assisting with establishing a programme for maintenance and repair of the buildings.

Our nurses' reflections

I can do no better than quote from those who were directly involved in these tasks.

Jan Wydell, one of our British Nurse Tutors, who worked for the Trust for nine months in Moscow, interviewed two of her Russian nursing colleagues. One of them commented, *"I feel the children receive better care. I know them and everything about their care and treatment. I have good relations with the parents, and because they are 'my' patients I feel more responsible for the care I give."*

The other stated, *"Having one person looking after them is not so frightening for the child. I explain everything so that they are not nervous. The continuity of care makes it much easier and quicker. I feel I can communicate with the parents better. I know what I have to do and feel more responsible. The doctors' and parents' attitude has changed towards me and I feel much more respected. The work is not so monotonous."*

Jayne Harris, who had also been working alongside Russian colleagues during her 12 months in the hospital, expressed her thoughts on working in a different culture.

"We came in November not by spaceship but by plane, bringing new ideas to Tushinskaya Children's Hospital. Russians were as foreign to us as we were alien to them, but the reception was warmer than the weather as I began my work, first on the intensive care unit then on the trauma ward.

It was here that I began to understand the Russian people and the famous Russian 'soul' as I experienced the conditions in which they work and live. This was crucial, because just as a truly Russian system would not work in England, neither can a truly English system fit in in Russia. Much discussion and cooperation was needed in order to modify systems to meet the needs of the people concerned. But, despite barriers, including the language barrier, we are all progressing towards our goals. Strangers with even stranger suggestions, aliens we may have been on arrival, but having learnt to live and work together we are having successes and becoming friends. After all, we came from England, not another planet."

Kathryn Jones spent most of her 10 months at Tushinskaya teaching in the Paediatric Nursing School and reflected on her experiences there.

"Students within the School of Nursing enjoyed teaching sessions with Kathryn Jones and Jan Wydell. Kathryn has been working alongside Russian nurse teachers to help students in the classroom learn using different and unusual methods.

Second-year students have drawn the things that stress them, and described their feelings to each other using comparisons with animals, birds and colours. They have shared ways to relax, and made posters about child development and collages of the health needs of the child. They have enjoyed learning about communications and how to relate to patients and families and of putting newly learnt techniques into practice in ward areas.

Jan has been working with students on the trauma ward to reinforce the learning which has taken place in the classroom. Students have used role play to gain some experience of being a hospital patient, and to learn what it is like to have to stay in bed.

The students from the second year of the paediatric course have been bright and enthusiastic learners, motivated to teach each other and to apply the new knowledge on the wards. Teaching them has been a rewarding experience and continued links with the school should further their development, with the ultimate aim of enhancing the care of sick children within Tushinskaya Hospital.

It is now just over a year since the School of Paediatric Nursing opened its doors to students. Throughout the summer the school remained open to interview new candidates, some of whom have come from the local community where interest in the course remains high."

*

Preparing children and parents for theatre

An important aspect of the project was preparing children and parents for the operating theatre. Naturally, both the child and their parents were scared by the thought of an operation, and from the experience obtained in the UK and other countries it had been found that this increased the postoperative risks of the procedure, and often prolonged the child's stay in hospital.

The theatre staff decorated the preparation room with motifs and a brightly coloured curtain which would help distract the child's thoughts from the operation.

Psychological preparation of both the child and parents would usually take place the day before the operation, and this greatly reduced their anxiety. The nurse responsible for the child established a relationship with both the child and their parents. All aspects of the operation itself, including length of recovery and long-term effects as well as possible complications of surgery, would be explained in simple terms.

The parents and child were advised that the child must not eat or drink for several hours before the planned time of the operation and were given details of the procedure on the day, and the child was given an injection to make them sleepy beforehand.

Postoperative information was also given, and it was explained when the child would be able to start drinking fluids, the possibility of pain and discomfort and the need to inform medical staff if worried, what equipment might be used and its purposes, what the wound would look like, and finally how parents could be involved in the child's care.

*

Infection control

Susan MacQueen made several visits to the hospital on the Trust's behalf to advise on methods of improving current practices of infection control. It had been estimated that hospital-acquired infection could be reduced by approximately 30 per cent if there were an active interested Infection Control Team.

Individuals should not be blamed for the spread of infection, but rather the process by which it occurred should be reviewed so that changes in practice in the hospital could be implemented and monitored. Staff would then feel more secure and were more likely to discuss problems openly, and try to improve practice together.

Susan helped set up an internal Infection Control Team in the hospital consisting of a microbiologist, doctors, surgeons and nurses who would liaise closely together. The team would discuss ways to improve the existing programme and help advise the hospital management on microbiological laboratory services and policies and procedures related to risk of infection, both in patients and staff.

Following her visit to Great Ormond Street Hospital, Margarita Kalinina was improving the laboratory service offered to clinicians at Tushinskaya.

Individuals should not be blamed for the spread of infection, but rather the process by which it occurred should be reviewed so that changes in practice in the hospital could be implemented and monitored. Staff on the Trauma ward were demonstrating the importance of hand washing in reducing Hospital-Acquired Infection, aseptic techniques had been reviewed by the nurses and parents were being taught how to dress their children's surgical wounds.

Overall, the benefits of applying these measures would reduce the hospital stay for the child. Rather than isolating the child, the causative organism would be isolated, and the hospital stay would be a happier one. Very importantly, job satisfaction for the staff would be improved.

The Trauma ward had produced an educational video illustrating how to dress a small child's pin site wounds. Everyone found the film hilarious, as its star, Vera, is shown constantly washing her hands. But as Vera herself said, *"If it gets the message across that good hand washing is the major factor in preventing infection then it is worth it."* The video also stressed the importance of preparing children psychologically for their hospital stay.

The video proved very successful in provoking discussion on these issues and further training videos were planned, as this was the way in which skills could be passed on well into the future.

*

Family centred care

Susan Vas Dias also made regular visits to Tushinskaya Hospital to provide training in emotional child development and communication with, and care of, the sick child and their family.

A Family Centred Care unit had been set up in Tushinskaya, initially concentrating largely on the Trauma ward as the chief trauma surgeon, Victor Shein and his team working with Valentina Rogachkova, the head play specialist, had led the way in transforming the emotional care provided for the children.

They had created a ward in which parents could stay and care for their child in an atmosphere congenial for children. Where once the walls were bare, now they had pictures children could respond to. They also ran a highly successful weekly parents' meeting in which the families could discuss their concerns.

Our paediatric nursing team was working to allow the parents to accompany their children to the operating theatre. Almost every bed in the ward had a child and family member playing happily together.

The FCC's approach to a child's treatment had certainly speeded up the children's recovery. Dr Shein reported that the parents say, *"Tushinskaya is the best hospital in Moscow, because we can be here and take care of our children, which other hospitals won't let you do."*

*

I had developed a troublesome low backache and was admitted to The London Clinic for a few days for investigation, which merely showed some disc prolapse, which resolved with physiotherapy.

Homeopathy

Having recently been offered a locum appointment by GOSH with responsibility for the health care of their staff and the staff of the Royal London Homeopathic Hospital and the National Hospital for Neurology and Neurosurgery, all located in Queen Square in Central London, I was required to attend the hospitals for three half days weekly.

Homeopathy is a system of alternative medicine. It was conceived in 1796 by the German physician Samuel Hahnemann. Its practitioners, called Homeopaths, believe that a substance that causes symptoms of a disease in healthy people can cure similar symptoms in sick people; this doctrine is called *similia similibus curentur,* or "like cures like."

Homeopathic preparations are termed "remedies" and are made using homeopathic dilution. In this process, the selected substance is repeatedly diluted until the final product is chemically indistinguishable from the dilutant. Practitioners claim the preparations, taken by mouth, can treat or cure disease.

Chapter 9

Princess Diana's Moscow visit

Princess Diana's Moscow visit, Chechen rebels, Reception Russian Embassy, Pinewood Corporation, Lord Mayor's Show, Lord Mayor's Banquet

Princess Diana's Moscow visit

Our first grandchild, Rachel, had just been born to Amanda and Hugh when we heard from the Palace that as Prince Charles had recently visited St Petersburg heading a British business delegation, protocol would now permit Princess Diana to visit Moscow in June 1995. The Princess was leading a very busy life and that year apparently would be making ten overseas visits.

It was a complicated business setting her trip up, involving me in numerous visits to the Russian Embassy, the Princess's office in St James's Palace and visits to Tushinskaya. The dates of her visit would be 15 and 16 June.

I recollect a meeting in St James's Palace, three weeks before Diana was due to fly out to Moscow, and they were very concerned about arrangements for visas for herself and those who were accompanying her.

I picked up their phone and rang my contacts in the Russian Embassy, Alexander Prosverkin, the Consul General, and Denis Shulakov, the Ambassador's Private Secretary, and the following day all the visas were delivered to the St James's Palace office.

I am sorry to say that our Embassy in Moscow was not being very helpful and would not let us participate in the scheduling of her visit whilst in Moscow. They must have had other more important matters on hand.

*

Chechen rebels

Perhaps they knew something that we didn't, as tragically on 14 June, Chechen rebels led by Shamil Basayev attacked the southern Russian town of Budyonnovsk, located a hundred kilometres outside the Chechen border, and held a thousand hostages in the maternity hospital.

During attacks by Russian troops in attempts to release the hostages, something in the order of a hundred and fifty hostages died. After four days of fighting, it was agreed that the hostages would be released in exchange for cessation of Russian military actions in Chechnya. Naturally most Russian news coverage concentrated on this terrorist attack, but nevertheless the media gave significant and welcoming cover to Diana's visit.

*

We invited our President, Baroness Caroline Cox, to join us in Moscow for the Princess's visit and suggested her husband, Dr Murray Cox, might wish to accompany her. Murray was the Senior Consultant Psychiatrist in Broadmoor Hospital, and as both of them led such busy lives, seeing relatively little of one another, they were delighted to agree with the proposal.

Broadmoor is a high-security psychiatric hospital in Crowthorne, Berkshire, where many of its patients were sent by the Criminal Justice Service.

Bente Fasmer, our Press Officer and photographer, and a very close friend of ours, Liz, whose husband Philip had recently died, came with us. The four of us flew together on a BA flight from Gatwick, and Caroline and Murray, flying on the same plane as the Princess, arrived later that afternoon.

At Sheremetyevo Airport, Diana, dressed in a beige checked jacket and matching dress, was met by our Ambassador, Sir Brian Fall, who then accompanied her in the Embassy Rolls to the White House, the Russian Parliament building, where on behalf of the Russian government she was formally met and welcomed by the deputy Prime Minister, Yuri Yarov, and the Minister of Social Security, Ludmila Bezlepkina.

The Princess's party consisted of her Private Secretary, Patrick Jephson, her Lady in Waiting, Sarah Campden, her Press Secretary, Geoff Crawford, her dresser and her personal police officer, David Shane.

Following afternoon tea, she and her party were driven to the British Embassy where she would be staying.

Princess Diana was a balletomane who had always dreamt of seeing the world-famous Bolshoi Ballet performing in the Bolshoi theatre. The ballet company, which at that time was in rehearsal, had arranged a special performance of *La Sylphide,* in the version choreographed by Bournonville, for that evening. As the plot was set in Scotland, this was felt to be particularly appropriate for a British Princess. Interestingly, WS Gilbert used the same plot in his opera *Iolanthe.*

Diana, wearing a deceptively simple cream slip dress embroidered with gold beading, was seated in the sumptuous red and gold Presidential box in the Bolshoi.

Caroline was seated next to Andrew Crane, the deputy Head of Mission, and the rest of our party from the Trust were seated in the box immediately located to the left of the Presidential box.

Smiling and looking very happy, Diana stood up and waved to the audience, who applauded loudly. Following the enjoyable performance, Diana mingled and talked with the ballet dancers. The Ambassador had arranged a small reception in the interval at which Caroline represented the Trust.

An excellent evening and the Bolshoi had "done itself proud."

On 16 June, the atmosphere in the hospital was feverish, with everyone excited and a little anxious to be receiving such an important visitor. There were rumours that children were refusing to be discharged because they wanted to meet the Princess.

Princess Diana's visit to Moscow

At 10.30 a.m., the Royal party arrived, and the Princess emerged into the Moscow sunshine to be greeted outside the main building of the hospital by Dr Yuri Pavlov, Baroness Cox, Nahid and myself, as well as crowds of onlookers, staff, parents and children, Russian and British journalists, including Jennie Bond, the BBC royal correspondent, and photographers.

Hello magazine gave a six-page full-colour spread to the Princess's visit. They reported Dr Lipman's words: *"Without the Princess's help we would not have been able to achieve what we have."*

Dr Pavlov made a short welcoming speech. *"We know you not only as a beautiful woman, as an intelligent woman, but also as a mother."* A pretty little Russian girl, presented the Princess, who was wearing an above the knee black sleeveless dress, with a bouquet, and the Princess received a beautiful album of photographs and drawings of scenes in the hospital wards and a traditional red and black lacquered souvenir tea pot.

After visiting Dr Pavlov's office, where he made an overlong speech about the joint projects of the Trust and the hospital, the Princess then moved on to the Trauma ward.

The ward had been completely redecorated with pictures and murals on the walls. Toilets and other facilities had also been improved. In the playroom, Lego, which the Princess had donated to the hospital, was on display. She spent about twenty minutes sitting on the floor chatting with children who had been injured in car and train accidents and their parents, all of whom appeared to enjoy her visit enormously.

One of the hospital employees reported: *"She was a very calm and relaxed woman. She walked calmly around the department, but some of her escort felt faint at the sight of the children's injuries."*

Galina Snopova, a reporter for a Moscow newspaper, recorded a short conversation with the Princess who was being shown an apparatus which was used to observe wound healing. *"Where was it invented?"* she asked. *"In Russia,"* was the reply. *"And where is it being manufactured?"* *"In France,"* was the response. *"Why don't you produce it yourselves here?"* wondered the Princess.

The Princess then visited the Neonatal unit and the School of Paediatric Nursing, where she met Olga Skorobogatova, watched the nurse students practising examinations on dummy babies, talked to several students and their teachers and our British Nurse Tutor Kathryn Jones, and then formally opened the school. After signing two photographs, the Princess departed, still surrounded by a large crowd of onlookers. The whole visit lasted more than two hours.

As she stepped into her car, before it drove off, there was loud applause from the crowd who had gathered outside the nursing school building, and this was followed by noisy and prolonged discussions. Everyone had big smiles on their faces and had obviously enjoyed the opportunity of seeing, and in some cases talking with, a real Princess.

I had kept close by the Princess throughout her visit and discreetly marshalled her. She had asked several very pertinent questions, made relevant and considered comments and she came across as being considerably brighter intellectually than the impression given by her public image.

The Princess was taken on a sightseeing tour around Moscow including the Kremlin. There she visited the magnificent 15th-century Assumption Cathedral and the Armoury, the treasure house of the Kremlin.

Her last duty was to visit Motivation, a British charity which designed and distributed wheelchairs for disabled people.

She had had a very busy schedule, and shortly afterwards was winging her way home again to Britain.

The Princess later conveyed to the Trust how much she had enjoyed the opportunity of seeing at first hand the work of the hospital, and the Trust which she had supported so generously.

Several Moscow newspapers carried reports of Diana's visit. *Medetsinsky Vestnik* – "Medical Bulletin" had a full-page article, with a large photo of Diana and Baroness Cox leaning over a hospital bed speaking with a small boy. The paper commented, *"The Princess was sympathetic, questioning and appreciative of detailed replies."* *Rossinskaya Gazeta* – "Russian Newspaper" – stated, *"Everyone loved her."* The *Moscow Times*, an English-language paper, reported, *"The Princess received high marks from Russians for her charity work and her attention to children,"* And headed its article *"Princess or 'Great Broad', Moscow loves Di."*

A gold-toothed technician at Tushinskaya Hospital had been heard to murmur *Krassnaya baba* – "great broad" – when Diana visited the hospital.

According to *Izvestia* – "News" – *"The Princess of Wales is a whiz at making borshch, can polish a floor with the best of them, and loves nothing more than to iron a shirt to perfection."*

In London, the Russian-language paper, *Londonsky Kyrer* – "London Courier" – on its front page carried a large photo of Diana in the hospital, with a full report of her Moscow visit, and on an inside page, further details of the hospital and Tushinskaya Trust, with several photographs.

The *Daily Mail*, *The Times*, *The Sun*, *Daily Express*, *The Telegraph*, *Daily Mirror*, *The Sunday Times* and *Evening Standard* all carried glowing reports of Diana in

Moscow and many photographs taken in the hospital, including one of her signing autographs for some of the children with *"Diana with love."*

The magazine *Majesty* reported that *"The Princess of Wales's visit to Moscow began in dramatic fashion. She flew into an electric storm which delayed the landing of her aircraft and lightning struck the British Embassy, knocking out communications with London for several hours. Even so, the Princess managed to arrive on time with English punctuality for her first meeting of the engagement, with the Russian deputy Prime Minister."*

*

We lunched with Galina and Sergei Romanyuk and supped with Olga, Sacha, Vadim, Nelli, Dima and Kiril.

Next evening we had supper with my successor's successor in the British Embassy, Dorothy Eggleton, in the restaurant U Piromane across the lake opposite the floodlit Novodevichy convent.

*

The following year when I was visiting Tushinskaya, I went by taxi from my hotel and told the driver that I wished to go to Tushinskaya Hospital in the Heroes of Geroev Street. He smiled and said in Russian, *"Ah, Princess Diana's hospital."*

*

We were all staying in the Ukraine Hotel near the *Kievsky voksal* – "rail terminal" – and across the Moskva river from the White House. That evening we ate supper in the hotel restaurant and Murray told us a most interesting story.

Murray was called one morning to see one of the inmates in Broadmoor Hospital who was a serial murderer and had become very distressed and weepy. Apparently, he had just heard that his aged mother had died. However, it wasn't her death that upset him, but the fact that he had suddenly realised that people could die from natural causes and that during all the years he had been in the hospital he had completely forgotten that.

When we finished the meal, the waiter came and asked that we pay for it in roubles as the cooks in the kitchen had formed an independent cooperative and were not employed by the hotel.

By chance, earlier that day I had refunded Kingsmill his monthly expenses in pounds sterling and he had given me change in roubles. These roubles I used to pay for the meal.

Shortly afterwards, I had an urgent call from the hotel reception asking me to come to discuss the payment with them as they had discovered that the roubles were counterfeit. I'm sure you will agree a very embarrassing situation which we could not account for.

The hotel had called the police, and fortunately amongst our party we had enough roubles, which we had obtained from the official currency exchange office, to cover the cost of the meal.

When we later mentioned this to Kingsmill, he explained that he had been given these roubles as change for a larger note in some shop in which he had made a purchase.

Fortunately, we hadn't ended our visit as "guests" of the Russian government's jails.

Having been delayed by sorting out the currency problem we were in a rush when the car arrived to take us to the airport. One of the porters carried our baggage out to the car as I fumbled in my pocket to find some change to give him as a tip for his services. Turning round, I saw a porter standing on the hotel steps, went over to him and put some loose change into his hand. He looked rather surprised, mumbled "*Spasiba*" and went back into the hotel. As the car drove off, I realised that I had inadvertently given the tip to the wrong porter. In Russian, to give a tip is *davat na chai* – "to give for tea."

*

1995 Reception Russian Embassy

Our reception committee, Liz Angel, Nataly Duddington, Bente Fasmer, Bridget Flavell, who now having left the Foreign Office was helping us as Trust Secretary on a part-time basis, Susan MacQueen, Maggie Postlethwaite and Nahid had been working hard for several months making arrangements for a gala fundraising reception which would be held in the Russian Embassy in July.

The Russian Ambassador, HE Anatoly Adamishin, and his wife Olga had kindly agreed to the Trust holding a reception in the presence of HRH the Princess of Wales in the Russian Embassy. During our posting in Moscow in Soviet times we had met him and his wife when he was deputy Minister of Foreign Affairs in the Soviet Union. He was a seemingly affable man who spoke several foreign languages including English, French and Italian.

On a warm July evening, His Excellency Mr Adamishin and Mme Adamishina welcomed our Patron HRH Princess of Wales to the Embassy of the Russian

Federation. HRH was greeted by three little Russian girls who gave her baskets of white roses and freesias. Floral displays had been donated and arranged by Jessica Mugliston and Maggie Postlethwaite.

Dr Harald Lipman presented our sponsors and the committee to Her Royal Highness in the panelled hall hung with fine Russian paintings, where an exhibition of photographs of Tushinskaya Hospital, taken by Bente Fasmer, was on display.

In a welcoming speech, the Ambassador introduced Baroness Cox, who spoke of the Trust's work and its continuing need for support.

With a little girl, Nadia Fedotova, sitting on her lap, Princess Diana was serenaded by violinist Michael Poel with a piece of music composed for the occasion. Lina Fradkina accompanied him on the piano.

Her Royal Highness then moved through the conservatory and white and gold drawing room chatting with and meeting many of the four hundred or so guests, who including our Moscow Ambassador designate, Andrew Wood.

An auction was held, superbly conducted by Peter Mitchell of John Mitchell and Son. Amongst the many excellent items were a pair of earrings by Cassandra Goad, who also displayed her latest designs in the Embassy conservatory, two framed linocuts by Alexander Ivanov, a silver/gold plate by Stuart Devlin, a framed painting of Kafka by Vavro Oravec, two tickets for the *Last Night of the Proms* and six bottles of Clos d'Estournel 1975.

Raffle tickets were sold by student ballerinas from the London Studio Centre wearing costumes from classical Russian ballets. The winning tickets were later drawn by actors Prunella Scales and Timothy West, who had kindly interrupted a busy schedule to help us.

Raffle prizes included two return tickets to Moscow donated by Russia House, two tickets to the Kirov Ballet and dinner at Simpsons donated by the London Hernia Centre, a beautiful velvet jacket donated by Louise Verity, bottles of champagne from Partridges and Raffles, lunch for two at Shaw's restaurant donated by Atkins restaurant, a five-litre bottle of whisky and a Pink Floyd CD and signed photograph.

Thanks to Jo Ford of Revolver Communications, a new vodka, Smirnoff Black, was enjoyed by all, as was wine given by Cynthia and Andrew Hendry of Cooper's Creek Wine and their wholesalers, Erhmanns.

As the guests left, they were presented with gifts of small bottles of Smirnoff Black and perfume donated by Parfum Givenchy.

The Trust was grateful to His Excellency Mr Adamishin and Madame Admishina for making the Embassy available for the reception. Our thanks went also to Portex Ltd, Lada Cars, The Gosling Foundation, Liz Angel and our many anonymous donors, Russian Connections who provided the excellent food and Tamarind's who supplied the crudities.

Providing the background music were the young Russian musicians, pianist Maria Rostotsky, violinists Yuri Kalnits and Emil Chitakov, viola Devorina Gamalova and cellist Andrei Melik-Parsadanov.

A wider public had been made aware of the strengthening link between our two countries, whilst the funds raised, nearly £14,000, would help in continuing the work of the Tushinskaya Children's Hospital Trust.

*

Nahid and I needed a break, and although we both could swim, we decided to spend a week at a swimming school near Exeter in Devon to improve our technique. It was very helpful and enjoyable. Prior to attending it I had been unable to crawl or swim the butterfly stroke.

On the way back to London we drove eastwards across the country to Brighton. Our brother-in-law, Kurt, had been admitted to a hospital there whilst visiting a relative, and we found that his condition was seriously deteriorating. Several years earlier a Russian doctor, Polyakov, who had developed a system of diagnosing diseased organs, had forecast that he would develop this problem. Sadly, shortly after our visit, Kurt died.

*

Pinewood Corporation

Patrick Jephson, Princess Diana's Private Secretary, had contacted us regarding an offer by an American corporation, Pinewood Corporation, to set up a North American Trust which would fundraise for our charity and would have sole rights to organise any visit by the Princess to the USA.

He asked us to investigate the organisation and let him have our feelings relating to proceeding with this proposal.

With considerable difficulty, we ascertained that in fact Pinewood Corporation was based in Canada, and that Henry Kissinger was one of the board members. I tried unsuccessfully on several occasions to contact Kissinger and discuss their proposals.

Obviously, if this North American Trust had been set up, Tushinskaya Trust would have potentially benefited financially very considerably; however, we felt it would be inappropriate for a non-British organisation to organise and manage the

Princess's American visits. We informed the Palace of our opinion, and they did not proceed with the matter.

Princess Diana had already visited the United States on several occasions, had met Henry Kissinger and established a "mutual admiration society" with him. In fact, she was shortly due to visit New York to receive a humanitarian award, which Henry Kissinger would be presenting to her at a ceremony in the Hilton Hotel.

Apparently, during her acceptance speech at the award ceremony, a member of the audience shouted out, "*Where are your kids, Di?*" She immediately responded, "*In bed*," and this earned her the biggest ovation of the evening. She also revisited the Harlem Children's Hospital where six years earlier she had visited the AIDS unit.

*

Lord Mayor's Show 11 November 1995

The Lord Mayor Elect and Mrs John Chalstrey requested the pleasure of the company of Dr and Mrs H Lipman to watch the outward procession of the Lord Mayor's Show, followed by luncheon in the Mansion House, on Saturday 11 November 1995 at 10.15 a.m.

In a welcome message to the City of London for the 1995 Lord Mayor's Show, John Chalstrey stated, "*The 11th of November in this 50th anniversary year of the end of the Second World War is a day for remembrance. Today the procession will pause and in the silence between 'Last Post and Reveille', sounded by the State Trumpeters of Her Majesty's Household Cavalry, I ask you to remember the men and women who, by their sacrifice all those years ago, made it possible for us to enjoy today.*"

The show progressed through the city streets, along Poultry, Cheapside, St Paul's Churchyard, Ludgate and Fleet Street, from the Guildhall to the Royal Courts of Justice in the Strand, and then returned through the streets, along Victoria Embankment, Queen Victoria Street and Princes Street to the Guildhall. En route on both the outward and return journeys it passed the Lord Mayor's residence, the Mansion House.

During the procession, the Lord Mayor alighted at St Paul's and was blessed by the Dean of St Paul's. He then started the Lord Mayor's Challenge 6 km Road Race, sponsored on this occasion by Eurostar, with teams from London, Paris and Brussels competing for the trophy.

John Chalstrey was a member of Birmingham Tipton Harriers, one of Britain's leading road and cross-country clubs. Now, he had been elected as the 668th Lord Mayor of the City of London.

He was both a good friend of ours and an excellent gastro-enterological surgeon to whom I referred many of my patients. He had introduced "keyhole" abdominal surgery into the UK, in contrast to the "knife, fork and spoon" surgery performed by most surgeons at that time.

John was a very unassuming person who was kindness personified and never raised his voice in anger, and who from an early age had developed a deep interest in the City of London. He became Master of the Society of Apothecaries, and later Master of the Barbers and Surgeons Livery company.

The wonderful gold-decorated carriage carrying the Lord Mayor was at the rear of the procession and followed the 130 floats representing many aspects of City life, including on this occasion a float from the City of London School, which I had attended as a pupil after the end of the Second World War. Their float was in the shape of four huge books representing different aspects of Victorian life.

The Lord Mayor's coach, known as a Berlin and made from richly carved, ornamented, gilded wood, with a red roof, was pulled by six shire horses.

New traffic arrangements were being introduced in the City at that time, and additionally many roads were closed in preparation for the Lord Mayor's Parade, so we took an underground train to the Bank station, just across the road from the Mansion House.

Until the mid-18th century, Lord Mayors used their own houses or Livery Halls for their work as head of the City's governmental, judicial and civic functions. After the Great Fire of 1666, the decision was made to provide a house for Lord Mayors who did not have their own Livery Hall.

A century later, the architect and Clerk of the City's Work, George Dance the Elder, was chosen to design and build the Mansion House. The house was completed in 1758. The first Lord Mayor to take up residence was Sir Crispin Gascoigne.

Imposingly Palladian in style, it is faced by a grand temple portico at the front approached by flights of steps each side. The entertaining rooms were built on the first and second floors. On the first floor is the Salon and the great Egyptian Hall. The second floor has a ballroom and private apartments of the Lord Mayor and family. The third and fourth floors contain meeting rooms and staff rooms. The cellars have storage space and once held prisoners' cells, reflecting the former use of the Mansion House as the Lord Mayor's Court.

Following a short reception served in the Salon, Nahid and I, with many other invited guests, watched the procession from our numbered seats on the balcony of the Mansion House, and then we all enjoyed an excellent lunch served in the Egyptian Hall at elegantly laid tables.

*

Lord Mayor's Banquet

The magnificent Guildhall had been built between 1411 and 1440, and the Great Hall has a maximum capacity for dinners of 700 people. Annually, since 1502, it was the setting for the Lord Mayor's Banquet.

There is a soaring, high-arched ceiling and two huge, Gothic stained-glass windows emblazoned with the names of past Lord Mayors. On the walls are the banners of the 12 oldest City Livery companies.

Prominently displayed are statues of Nelson, Wellington and Churchill. Overseeing all are the two legendary Gods, Gog and Magog.

Tablets set into the wall recall the significant trials for treason of Lady Jane Grey and Archbishop Cranmer, which were held in the Guildhall.

Monthly meetings of the City Common Council take place in the Hall, and there the Liverymen elect the Lord Mayor.

When we arrived at the Guildhall, we immediately felt we were participants on a film set. We crossed the courtyard and entered the building through its classical Gothic arched doorways, and walked along passages lined by soldiers in their traditional colourful embroidered uniforms.

Following a short reception in the Guildhall library, we entered the Great Hall and took our seats at long dining tables adorned with crystal glasses and silver cups.

Here had been entertained heads of States including the Prince Regent, the Russian Tsar Alexander I and the King of Prussia, Frederik III of Hohenzollern.

As on our first attendance at a Lord Mayor's Banquet, two years earlier, there was an excellent menu, starting with dill blinis and smetana, followed by Supreme of Norfolk duck, then a Taittinger Rose sorbet, and afterwards the main course, roast fillets of Scottish beef. The desert was The Lord Mayor's bread and butter pudding with fresh cream custard. From their excellent cellar, each course was accompanied by an appropriate wine.

Following the toasts, music on this occasion was played by the Orchestra of the Honourable Artillery Company, and included the "Radetsky March", "The Merry Widow", "Pirates of Penzance", "Fiddler on the Roof", "The Eton Boating Song", and "The Lord Mayor" written by an anonymous composer.

Nahid and I were seated between two judges and their wives, and we had most interesting conversations with them as well as with the couples seated across the table from us.

The trumpeters of the Household Cavalry in their distinctive Georgian uniforms marched in and played, standing on the balcony between the giant statues of Gog and Magog.

Their coat was crimson velvet with blue velvet collar and cuffs, overlaid with strips of broad gold lace, golden crimson sword belt and dark blue velvet jockey hat with a square peak. The Royal cypher was emblazoned on front and back of the coat.

A single trumpeter introduced the State Address, traditionally given by the Prime Minister, on this occasion John Major.

He spoke about the future of the UK which was at a crossroads, and he felt the State should refrain from trying to do everything performed by the private sector, but must take some responsibility for all apects of our society and economy.

The EU was due for review in 1997, and at that time was considering enlarging in order to include most of the countries in Eastern Europe which had formed part of the Soviet Bloc. There was talk of introducing a single currency in the EU, and the UK would make its decisions on the basis of cool assessment and clear facts.

Chapter 10

Where do we go from here?

Montserrat, Bryan Cartledge, David Ratford, What we have achieved, Looking ahead, Consolidation, Tsewang Pemba, Oslo, Russian Presidential election, Agreement of Cooperation, Mammoth, Downing Street, Mad cow disease, Blair Atholl

Montserrat

In 1995 a dormant volcano on the Caribbean island of Montserrat, known as the "Emerald Isle of the Caribbean", erupted, destroying the capital, Plymouth.

Christopher Columbus had been the first European to set foot on the island. As the island was now a British Overseas Territory, the Medical and Welfare Department of the Foreign Office was involved in the evacuation of two thirds of the population, approximately 2,500 people, to the UK.

One of my Moscow colleagues from the 80s, Tony Longrigg, later became Governor of Montserrat during the period of its reconstruction.

*

Bryan Cartledge

Our Chairman, Sir Bryan Cartledge, had informed the Trust that he wished to reduce his commitments but would remain in his present office until an appropriate successor could be found.

We truly appreciated the enormous efforts Sir Bryan had put into developing the Trust during its first five years. Without his patience, support, wise advice and deep commitment, we would have had no Patron and few achievements.

It would be difficult to find the right person to succeed him, but Bryan approached Sir David Ratford, who we knew well from his time as Minister, deputy Head of Mission, to our Embassy whilst we were posted in Moscow, and who had recently retired from the post of Her Majesty's Ambassador to Norway. We were all delighted when David agreed to take on the post of chairman of the Trust.

What we have achieved and where we go from here

In the Tushinskaya newsletter I wrote a short piece entitled *"What we have achieved and where we go from here."*

The Trust's primary objective had always been to improve the welfare of sick Russian children. We recognised that conceptual changes could only progress slowly. However, already both parents and children were less frightened at the thought of hospital admission, children on the wards were happier and the length of their stay in hospital had been reduced due to more rapid recovery.

We were concentrating on teaching both existing nurses in the hospital and student nurses in the Nursing School how to understand the child's requirements better and how to care holistically for the child.

Paediatric nursing was now recognised as a speciality in Russia, but as the qualifying general nursing exams did not include the approaches in the current curriculum which we were teaching in the new school, student nurses had to be taught in parallel both existing and new methods.

In the Paediatric Nursing School, where previously all the teachers would have been doctors, now the students were taught by nurses as well as doctors. This helped to raise the status of nurses.

*

Looking ahead

We felt that we should now be offering our expertise to other children's hospitals in addition to Tushinskaya, and decided to organise a seminar in Moscow to be held in October 1996, at which representatives from other children's hospitals would be able to learn about our methods.

In the field of nurse education, the Trust, now linked with Southbank University in London, was aiming to advance the training of teaching methodology, and we wished to discuss with the Russian Ministry of Education the paediatric nursing curriculum and qualifying examinations.

In the field of Hospital Acquired Infections, discussions would take place with the Russian sanitary authorities with a view to setting up controlled trials comparing existing Russian and UK methods of control of infection, with the aim of absorbing the best of both these approaches into the monitoring and control systems.

1996

The year 1996 proved to be a year of largely standing still and consolidating the Trust's position in the hospital.

In January, Susan MacQueen and I flew out to Moscow and were advised that, although we were now paying a small rental for use of the hospital flats, they would no longer be available to the Trust. Pavlov told us that they felt that the only benefit the hospital was getting from association with the Trust was the introduction of Family Centred Care, and what they really required were concrete donations, *konkretny*, such as toys for the children!

Unrelated to this, the following month our UK nurses ended their secondment to the hospital and Paediatric Nursing School, but Kathryn had offered to continue making visits to the nursing school on behalf of the Trust.

*

My very close friend, Tsewang Pemba, the first Tibetan to graduate in Medicine in the UK, who I had met on our first day in the University College Hospital Medical School in 1949, had been working in New York, teaching Anatomy for two years, and was returning to Darjeeling.

Tsewang Pemba

He stopped over in the UK for a few days, staying with his brother Norbu, an engineer who lived in Woking, and spent a couple of nights living with us in Hampstead. I arranged a lunch in the Royal Society of Medicine restaurant, where we were joined by Michael Nicholls and Dicky Boyde, contemporaries from our student days.

*

IAPOS Oslo visit

The International Association of Physicians for the Overseas Services, IAPOS, had arranged a meeting to be held in Oslo in May 1996. One of our Norwegian members, Dr Ottar Hals, had arranged the programme and recommended a hotel.

Twenty-four members and partners, including our friend Hannah Saunders from Cape Town who was visiting London, would be travelling together to Oslo by SAS and staying at Holmenkollen Park Hotel, a distinctive building designed in the characteristic Norwegian Dragon Style, which towers over the centre of Oslo and commands a unique view of the city and the fjord with the Holmenkollen ski jump close by. The conference would be held in the hotel.

Hannah had worked in Cape Town with Dr Christiaan Barnard who performed the first human heart transplant in the Groote Schuur Hospital in 1967.

We knew all the members travelling from the UK and would be delighted to see in Oslo our good friends Ing-Marie and Lars Lidstrom from Sweden and several members from the Netherlands.

Ottar and his wife Britt had kindly invited us all to their house for informal drinks on the afternoon of the day we arrived and had sent details of how to find them as it was situated up a tiny unmarked shingle-covered road, and also advised that we travel by taxi for the five-minute journey.

Oslo had been founded in 1040, the Viking period, according to Nordic sagas, by Harald Hadrada, and ultimately became the economic and governmental capital of Norway.

The Kingdoms of Sweden and Norway formed a Union in 1814 with a common Monarch and common foreign policy that lasted until its peaceful dissolution in 1905.

The IAPOS business meeting and four talks had been arranged for members for the following day, and spouses were taken by bus to view the Hadeland Glassverk, a renowned old glass and crystal factory.

In the evening, dinner had been arranged at the Ostmarkseteran restaurant, with its excellent winecellar, set in a park outside Oslo, near a lake, surrounded by beautiful scenery.

The following day, a Saturday, we were taken on a sightseeing tour, which included the National Opera and Ballet House and the Royal Palace, and lunched at DS Louise's restaurant by the harbour.

On Sunday, a bus transported us to Fornebu Airport.

During the drive, everybody was excitedly chattering away and praising the fascinating discussions and excellent arrangements and visits we had experienced during our short trip.

Russian Presidential election

David Ratford and I visited Moscow in July. I flew via Vienna and David from Stockholm. We were staying in the Moskva Hotel, and the windows of our rooms overlooked the Russian Federation Parliament building, the Duma, just across the street.

The second round of the Presidential elections was due to be held during our stay.

In the first round of the election, Gennadi Zyuganov, who presented himself as a kinder gentler Communist who was against the infiltration of Western ideals into Russian society, had been a very close second to Yeltsin, and was confident that he would win.

The results of the second round showed Yeltsin to have won 54 per cent of the votes and Zyuganov 41 per cent, but there was some question about the validity of the result. Yeltsin chose as his Prime Minister someone who was a then little-known associate of the St Petersburg Mayor, Anatoly Sobchak – Vladimir Putin.

During the night, I was woken by the sound of tanks on the cobbled street outside the Duma, and I assumed that the opposition candidate was intending to occupy the building. "*Oh my God*," I said as, half asleep, I scrambled out of bed, stumbled to the window and drew back the curtains. It was pouring with rain and I realised that the noise I had heard was the drumming of the rain on a corrugated iron roof just below my window.

*

Agreement of Cooperation

Next day, somewhat blurry-eyed, a further Agreement of Cooperation was signed between the Department of Health, the hospital, Medical School No 24 and Tushinskaya Trust, with the aims of improving the welfare of sick children in hospital and continuing the teaching of Family Centred Care.

Discussions were initiated regarding the holding of a seminar to be organised by the Trust in Moscow on "The Role of Family Centred Care in the Hospital", under the aegis of the Department of Health Moscow, with the aim of showing other Russian hospitals the principles the Trust teaches and to enhance cooperation between foreign aid organisations working in Moscow.

Susan Vas Dias continued to visit every two to three months to teach Family Centred Care in the hospital and had heard that final-year Russian psychology students had been seconded to the Trauma ward of the hospital as part of their training.

Dr Margarita Kalina was sponsored by Dekomed to attend an international conference on hospital acquired infection control in Dublin in September 1996.

Olga Skorobogatova retired on health grounds from the directorship of Medical School No 24 and the Paediatric Nursing School, and was succeeded by Dr Natalia Alexandrova Lanina, a former teacher of infectious diseases.

Kingsmill Bond, our Moscow representative, had left Moscow but was succeeded at BESO by Russell Bradley.

The Trust now had the services in London of two part-time administrators, Bridget Flavell and Mary Murphy. Mary made a pastoral visit to the hospital in November.

*

Skiing in Mammoth

We visited LA to see Nahid's family that March, and her brother, Parviz, invited us to accompany him on the six-hour drive up to the ski resort of Mammoth, in the Sierra Nevada mountains, lying to the east of Yosemite National Park. They have excellent snow, many well-managed runs with easy access and a "laid-back" vibe.

*

Marc flew in from Savannah, where he was attending a medical conference, as we had all been invited to Liz's daughter Vanessa's open-air wedding ceremony in Saddlerock Ranch in Malibu.

The ranch is set in the rolling hills of the Santa Monica mountains, lined with vineyards, manicured lawns, ancient oaks, rose gardens and horses grazing in the background.

We didn't then know that we would be returning twice to LA later that year.

Nahid's father, my father-in-law, Papa, was unwell and had been admitted to hospital.

We had decided, with Amanda and Hugh's agreement, to take Rachel, then almost eighteen months old, with us.

During the 11-hour flight in a Boeing 767 American Airlines plane, she was extremely good and slept most of the time. However, on arrival at Los Angeles

International Airport, there were long queues at immigration and poor little Rachel became very noisy and hyperactive, running around amongst the passengers, crying and loudly shouting. We remind her of this to this day, but she denies that it could have been her and we must have mistaken her for another small child.

In our hotel she rapidly settled and during the rest of our stay was spoilt by all members of Nahid's large family.

I had to return after a few days to London, with Rachel and Marc, and Nahid decided to stay on in LA.

Twelve days later, Nahid rang and told me Papa's condition was deteriorating, and I flew back to LA. The day after I arrived, Papa died.

The end of an era.

*

Shortly before Christmas, Manda, Hugh and Rachel moved to a house in Stoke Newington.

Marc, as a "Christmas gift", was offered a consultant post in Respiratory Medicine and HIV in the Royal Free Hospital in Hampstead.

What an eventful and sad year it had been.

*

Ambassador Adamishin had invited David Ratford to his Embassy in London, as he wished to discuss some matters with him. David was very surprised to hear the Ambassador state that he had been officially informed that the Trust was spending its money on sending British experts to the hospital, rather than giving it to the hospital.

David politely reminded him that the objective of the Trust was to transfer "know how", not money. The history of the past 70-odd years had left Russian standards way out of line with those in the UK. The Ambassador ended the meeting on the note that it had been most useful to have a frank discussion.

*

Cats

Andrew Lloyd Webber's musical show *Cats* based on T. S. Eliot's *Old Possum's Book of Practical Cats* opened in London in 1981 in the New Theatre and eventually ran for 21 years. The poems detail a tribe of cats as they decide which one would ascend to the Heaviside layer and return to a new life. We had a most enjoyable evening when we eventually saw the show in 1996.

Downing Street reception

Rod Lyne, who had been Head of Chancery in the Moscow Embassy, had been seconded by the FCO to Downing Steet as Private Secretary to Prime Minister John Major, advising on foreign affairs, defence and Northern Ireland.

Nahid and I were invited to his farewell reception in 10 Downing Street, when he was ending this appointment.

On the evening of the reception we had first to negotiate our way into Downing Street past the police at the gate and then were accompanied to the door of number 10.

The house, rather like Dr Who's TARDIS, appears very small from the outside, but inside many rooms lead from one to another. The walls of the staircase to the first floor are adorned with pictures of past prime ministers.

When we were introduced to John Major, the PM, we found him to be a very pleasant and affable person, quite unlike the "grey man" that the media always presented him as.

*

Mad cow disease

An outbreak of BSE, *bovine spongiform encephalopathy*, colloquially known as "mad cow disease", occurred in the UK in 1996. Cattle developed abnormal behaviour and troubles with walking and weight loss, caused by an abnormal protein in their brain known as a prion.

If contaminated meat was eaten by humans, it could cause Creutzfeld-Jakob disease, a progressive degenerative brain disorder.

There is no known treatment, and 4 million cattle were slaughtered and incinerated in the UK. The EU imposed a ban on the export of British beef which lasted for the next 10 years. The ban on importing British beef continued in Russia until 2016.

In the 5th century, Hippocrates had described a similar illness in cattle and sheep.

*

Blair Atholl

For several years, each July we had been salmon fishing in Scotland with Philip and Liz and several other friends. This year we were all visiting Blair Atholl. Sadly, Philip was no longer with us.

Salmon enter rivers from the sea as early as January, the numbers usually building up through spring into Summer and Autumn. Different rivers are known for being primarily "Spring", "Summer" or "Autumn" systems based on the timing of the typical salmon run. The salmon swim upstream against the current and go there in order to breed.

Fly fishing is a method of fishing, typically done whilst standing on a riverbank or in the water wearing hip waders.

Fly fishing poles are long and flexible with a spinning reel or a bait-casting reel. At the end of the line is the artificial fly, from which this method of fishing got its name. A fly is often a flashy and attractive lure that resembles an insect. Fly fishing attracts fish because the fly is weighted and resembles a minnow, which are salmon's natural prey.

The art is in the "casting", and learning it requires precision and patience, otherwise the hook catches in the tree or grass behind you, or worse still in your neighbouring fisher's hair. I remained a novice.

The River Tilt is a mountain river of Perthshire, which runs down from the mountain slopes to join the River Garry at Blair Atholl.

Our party of 14 had rented Forest Lodge for five nights. As our car was giving us some trouble, Nahid and I caught a train from King's Cross for the four-and-a-half-hour journey to Edinburgh and there changed trains for another two-hour journey to a rainy Blair Atholl, where Liz met us and drove us to the lodge. We had arranged to return to London on Saturday with Liz in her car.

The excellent cook, Elisa, pronounced Eleessa, had prepared a very tasty meal for dinner.

After a hearty Scottish breakfast, the next morning Liz, Nahid and I walked along the banks of the Tilt, carving its way down a steep valley, Glen Tilt, where it tumbles delightfully down the Falls of Tarf.

During our stay we visited Blair Castle, home of the Duke of Atholl, who at that time still had his own private army.

On our final day I decided to join the rest of our group who were all ardent fly fishers, but were not catching many salmon. Perhaps a novice could change their fortunes! We wished one another *taight laines* – "tight lines", the Fly Fisherman's Prayer.

The sun was shining, the fish were jumping. We ate our picnic lunch, but there were no catches that day.

Next day, after fond farewells, Liz drove us down to The Tontine, a small friendly hotel and bistro in North Yorkshire, which in 1979 had received Egon Ronay's Restaurant of the Year award.

A tontine is an annuity shared by subscribers to a loan or common fund, the shares increasing as subscribers die until the last survivor enjoys the whole income.

*

We were on holiday in Cornwall with Hugh, Amanda and Rachel when Amanda told us she was expecting her second child. Jacob, our grandson, was born in May 1997.

Chapter 11

Our varied life

UK general election, Harkness Fellowship, Baltimore, Amish, South Africa

UK general election

In May 1997, New Labour, led by Tony Blair, defeated the Conservative Party led by John Major, gaining 146 new seats in a decisive victory.

During the campaign, election-themed beers had been introduced – "Major's Mild", "Tony's Tipple" and "Ashdown's Ale."

*

Harkness Fellowship

Marc had been awarded a Harkness Fellowship and would be living in Baltimore, attached to Johns Hopkins Hospital for the next year, researching managed care.

Managed care is a medical delivery system that attempts to manage the quality and cost of medical services in the United States that individuals receive under their insurance plan. Some managed care plans attempt to improve health quality by emphasising the prevention of disease.

Harkness Fellowships were first offered by the Commonwealth Fund in 1925 and were envisioned as a "reverse Rhodes Scholarship." They are the Commonwealth Fund's flagship International Health Policy and Practice Innovations Programme. They provide a unique leadership development experience for midcareer professionals — policymakers, researchers, clinical leaders, health care executives and journalists — from Australia, Canada, France, Germany, the Netherlands, New Zealand, Norway and the United Kingdom.

During their year in the United States, Harkness Fellows conduct Internationally comparative research on a key health care delivery or policy issue, with mentorship from leading US experts. They gain an in-depth understanding of the US health care system and policy landscape, engage in a series of leadership development activities and build a robust network for cross-national exchange and collaboration. Perhaps most importantly, the Harkness Fellowships give future leaders the space to think and reflect without the pressures of day-to-day job responsibilities.

Later that year, following his return to the UK, Cambridge University awarded Marc an MD.

*

Baltimore

A few months later, en route to Los Angeles, we decided to fly via New York and catch a train to Baltimore to see Marc.

On arrival at JFK Airport in New York, we had an interesting experience whilst travelling by cab to our hotel, the Algonquin.

The road was jammed with traffic, and our cab, travelling in the middle lane, was unable to move. Suddenly, the cab driver opened his door and jumped out. We were stranded in the car, and as the vehicles started to move, they loudly hooted their horns and shouted abuse.

After about 25 minutes, the cab driver returned and apologetically told us that he had realised he had forgotten to carry his cab driver's licence and that was an offence in New York.

Being close to his house, he had felt he could run there and collect it. As he entered the house, he heard a loud noise outside and saw two cars had collided at the nearby road junction. Going over to help them, he recognised one of the car drivers, who was a friend of his in the small village in the Punjab, from which he came. He had taken him to his house, given him some tea and calmed him down.

The Algonquin is located near Times Square, and from many decades was a meeting place for renowned writers, journalists and actors, including Robert Benchley, George Kaufmann, Harpo Marx, Dorothy Parker and Alexander Woolcott, who all met there for a daily lunch.

*

We were contacted by long-standing friends, Buddy and Barbara Solomons, and they took us in their Rolls Royce for lunch to their lovely house in Westchester.

Buddy was a most impressive 6'6" tall stocky man, who some years previously had decided to live in London for several months. Buddy and Barbara rented a small house in a street across Knightsbridge from Harrods, and on arrival discovered that the bed was too small.

He visited the bedroom furniture department in Harrods, saw a super king-size bed and persuaded the staff to immediately deliver it across the road to his house. Buddy, an important figure in New York, was a meat wholesaler. He said to them, *"Are you union members?"* then showed them his American Union card and they agreed to deliver the bed. Six strong men held up the Knightsbridge traffic, crossed the road and carried the enormous bed to Buddy and Barbara's house.

*

"You leave the Pennsylvania Station 'bout a quarter to four
Read a magazine and then you're in Baltimore
Dinner in the diner
Nothing could be finer
Then to have your ham an' eggs in Carolina"

"Chatttanooga Choo Choo", recorded by Glenn Miller in 1941

The next morning, we caught an Amtrak train from Penn Station for the three hours journey to Baltimore. On arrival at Baltimore station, we looked for Marc, our son, and eventually recognised a long-haired, casually clad young man.

After we visited his flat, he drove us in the second-hand car he had purchased on a city tour.

Baltimore, located 40 miles east of Washington DC, had in the 1970s become depopulated, particularly in the area known as Harbour, which contained many abandoned warehouses. Gradually, these had been developed, and by the time of our visit, had been converted into a Science centre, Visionary Art Museum and numerous quirky restaurants.

We spent three days with Marc – it was wonderful being together again and our trip included a fascinating visit to Lancaster, an Amish town in Pennsylvania.

Amish

Amish is a strict Christian Fellowship with Swiss, German and Alsatian Anabaptist origins. People live simply, wear plain clothes, are pacifists and have little modern technology. They value life, manual labour, humility and submission to God's will. Most Amish people speak Pennsylvanian Dutch and refer to non-Amish as "English." The total population at that time was about 150,000.

In 1985 Harrison Ford starred in an Oscar-winning film *Witness* which involved a young Amish boy who witnessed a murder in Philadelphia.

We then flew from Baltimore to LA to spend several days with Nahid's family.

*

South Africa Nov 1997

In the past, we had visited several countries in Africa including Egypt, Sudan, Morocco and Kenya, but had never been to the largest and richest country – South Africa.

South African history

In 1486 the coastline of South Africa had been explored by the Portuguese sailor/explorer Bartholomew Dias en route to the Far East. The southernmost cape was originally called Cape of Storms and was later renamed the Cape of Good Hope.

The Dutch East India Company established a permanent settlement in the Cape in 1652, where passing ships could shelter and be serviced.

Following the French Revolution and the French invasion of the Netherlands in 1794, the Dutch King, William V, fled to England and ordered the colonial Governors to surrender to the British. Britain seized the Cape in 1795 and paid the Dutch £6 million for the colony.

Following abolition of slavery by the Brits in 1836, many inhabitants of Dutch origin trekked northwards from Cape Colony and established their own separate states.

In 1860 the first Anglo-Boer war with the Dutch, known as Boers, occurred with the Boers being victorious, and in 1899 the second Anglo-Boer broke out. Eventually, after three years, the Boers were defeated, and the Union of South Africa was formed.

*

The three of us, Nahid, our friend Liz and I met at Heathrow Airport on a Saturday early in November and caught the Virgin Airbus 11-hour overnight flight to Johannesburg, arriving the following morning. We were staying at the Holiday Inn Garden Court Hotel.

It was overcast with a few drops of rain, but the temperature was 25°C.

We toured Joburg by car, visiting, amongst other places, the large shantytown where many of the African population lived in very poor and inadequate conditions.

Dinner that evening was in the Carnivore restaurant – South Africans eat a lot of meat. We were met at the door by a *Dawa*, medicine man, who offered us a welcome cocktail. There was an extensive buffet, with a huge open fire, where joints of meat were skewered on large Masai swords and grilled. The waiters carried the swords to our table and carved the meat directly onto our cast-iron plate.

Next morning, we left Joburg, drove north through spectacular mountain passes, forests and waterfalls to Mpumalanga, a nature reserve. The territory was endless bushveld shimmering in the haze above hot plains with antelopes, buffalo, elephants, rhino and leopards. That night we dined in and stayed overnight in Hotel Malaga.

Poor Nahid had a nightmare and a bad night.

We all had to leave early next morning for a full day tour of Eastern Transvaal including Pilgrims Rest, a replica pioneer village, with stunning views from the natural wonder, God's Window, of Bligh River Canyon. In the late afternoon we checked in at the Kruger Skukuza Rest camp, on the bank of the Sabie River, in the famous Kruger National Park, where we spent two nights.

The park is home to an enormous variety of animals, and we were fortunate to see leopards, impala, baboons, bushbuck and vervet monkeys. The following day we saw elephants and giraffes and rhino. That night the skies opened and the rain poured down. We were due to leave for Swaziland that day.

The Kingdom of Swaziland is a tiny, 26,000 sq kilometers in size, landlocked country in Southern Africa, bordered by Mozambique to its northeast and South Africa to its north, west, south and southeast.

Its present boundaries were drawn up in 1881 in the midst of the Scramble for Africa. After the Second Boer War, the Kingdom, under the name of Swaziland, was a British protectorate from 1903 until it regained its independence in 1968.

*

Driving along the road, we could see the Lebombo mountains towering in the background. We continued along the scenic route, passing several small African villages and fruit farms until we reached the capital Mbabane.

On arrival at Lugogo Hotel, following our long and tiring drive, we were met with a welcoming cold drink with ice cubes.

This I shortly discovered was a big mistake. One should never drink tap water in Swaziland, or in many other African locations, as the giardia parasite resides in it, causing a very unpleasant bowel infection when soil, food or water has been contaminated with faeces from infected people or animals. Eventually when the condition was diagnosed it resolved following a long course of the drug Metronidazole.

The Swazis are renowned craftsmen and local markets are full of exquisite basketware, colourful fabrics, carvings and mother of pearl *objets d'art*.

Our next port of call would be the city of Durban, lying six hours' drive south along the costal road, passing through Zululand, flanked by the Indian Ocean. We lunched in a tribal *boma*.

As we arrived at our hotel, the Holiday Inn Crowne Plaza, we saw a man walking along the pavement being bundled into a police car. Crime was a serious and common problem.

Tired, we sat by the pool, then walked along the promenade and had a rather poor supper in a nearby restaurant.

Next morning entailed an early start, missing breakfast, as we had to fly by South African Airlines to Joburg to catch a flight to Port Elizabeth and then follow the Garden route to Cape Town.

After a city tour and lunch, Liz unfortunately was feeling unwell, but we all had to push on driving along the coastline and through the stunning Tsisikamma Forest, where we saw the impressive yellow wood Big Tree. Eventually we reached the Wilderness Reserve and our hotel, the Garden Court.

Another heavy rainstorm during the night, and another early start the following morning, then the sun came out of hiding, and we could admire the beautiful sea and luxuriant forests, arriving late in the day at Knysna, lying beside the Knysna Lagoon and two sandstone cliffs. The town is renowned for its huge oysters, swilled down with local beer, but frankly none of us felt up to trying them.

Following a dreadful night, we embarked on a safari, starting with a fascinating visit to an ostrich farm and then to the limestone Cango caves. At the farm some intrepid visitors were riding the ostriches, but we decided not to join them.

Then taking the Outeniqua pass we returned to the coastal road and drove to Mossel Bay en route to Cape Town. It was here in 1488 where Bartholomew Dias, the Portuguese explorer, first set foot on Africa, naming the bay "Bay of St Blaise."

We passed through many fruit orchards, with very tasty apples and soft fruits such as plums and apricots.

Cape Town, overlooked by Table Mountain, is one of the most beautiful cities in the world, with interesting shops and craft markets and many good restaurants.

We set out from the De Waal Holiday Inn where we were staying to explore the city, and took a bus to the waterfront with its many shops and open-air restaurants, busy with visitors. By then feeling much better, we supped in one of them and afterwards caught a shuttle bus back to our hotel.

The next day was overcast with some falling light rain, but we took a coach along the Atlantic Ocean coastal road with its magnificent white and sandy beaches and quaint seaside villages of Hout Bay and Noordhoek. Crossing Chapman's Peak, we took several photographs of the breathtaking scenery as we passed the wildlife reserve, the Cape of Good Hope, home to 1,222 species of indigenous plants and small mammals including antelope, zebra and ostriches. Then travelling on to Cape Point, the most southwesterly tip of Africa where two oceans, the cold waters of the Atlantic and the warm waters of the Indian Ocean, meet.

After lunch at the Black Marlin fish restaurant, we stopped at the Penguin Colony, Boulder's Beach to view the African Penguin in its natural habitat. Passing Simon's Town, with its naval atmosphere and quaint shops, we drove back to Cape Town.

Cape region wines are renowned internationally, so on a rainy day with periods of sunshine we set out on a tour of the winelands.

We visited KWV, *Ko-operative Wijnbouwers Vereniging,* for a wine-tasting and at Fairview tasted their wines with a selection of their cheeses, bread and olive oil. Then we travelled on to Stellenbosch and Franschoek, where in 1668 Protestant French Huguenots, who had fled persecution in Catholic France, had settled and introduced the first vineyards.

Following an excellent lunch in Boschendal, we returned to Cape Town. Stellenbosch Village Museum is located in a typical Dutch-style house, built in the early 1700s, which was owned by Hendrick Betterman, the last magistrate, *landdrost,* to be appointed by the Dutch East India Company.

That evening, our friend Hannah invited us to dinner in her flat, where we met the US Consul General and the Italian Ambassador.

On our last day in South Africa, we took the cable car up Table Mountain, 3,500 feet above sea level, and after lunch caught a SunAir flight to Joburg for a four-hour stopover before a Virgin Airbus flew us back to the UK.

Chapter 12

Princess Diana's death

On Saturday 30 August 1997, Nahid and I returned from a reunion of "old Moscow hands," organised by Alistair and D Fyfe, the Military Attaché during our time in Moscow, which was held in their country house near Ilchester, where we reminisced with many of our colleagues.

At 7 a.m. on Sunday 31 August, our radio alarm woke us with the news that Diana had been seriously injured in a car crash in Paris. Whilst later, lunching in Liz's garden in Harrow, we heard the tragic news that Diana had not survived her injuries and had died.

Henri Paul, who was apparently intoxicated, was driving Princess Diana, Dodi Fayed and her bodyguard, Trevor Rees-Jones, at high speed to avoid paparazzi when he entered the Pont de l'Alma underpass. Both Diana and Dodi were killed and her bodyguard was seriously injured.

There was an enormous outpouring of grief worldwide. A book of condolences was opened in St James's Palace, and people queued the length of the Mall to sign it. More than 1 million floral bouquets were placed outside Kensington Palace, where the Princess had resided.

The *Evening Standard* reported, *"It was as if the nation had no home to go to. Thousands of mourners spent the night holding a candle-lit vigil outside Kensington Palace. Others remained outside Buckingham Palace itself. Outside the Princess's home they stood silently in front of the gates, gazing at flames and petals blowing in the wind."*

A journalist wrote of *"a fairy-tale failing to end happily – twice. First when she divorced and now that she has died."*

Kofi Annan, UN Secretary-General said, *"Princess Diana's death has robbed the world of a consistent and committed voice for the improvement of the lives of suffering children worldwide."*

Boris Yeltsin praised Diana's charity work and stated, *"All know of Princess Diana's big contribution to charitable work and not only in Great Britain."*

"Who will be comforting William now?" asked *The Telegraph*.

*

Diana's funeral was held in Westminster Abbey on 6 September.

Nahid and I had been invited to represent the Trust in the Abbey and we took with us Nataly and Sasha Duddington.

Princess Diana's funeral

*

The gun carriage carrying the coffin, draped in the Royal standard, drawn by three pairs of horses, was escorted by eight members of the Welsh Guards and an escort of mounted police from Kensington Palace to Westminster Abbey. More than 2.5 billion people viewed the cortege on TV screens worldwide.

The Duke of Edinburgh, Prince of Wales, Princes William and Harry and Charles Spencer, Diana's brother, walked behind the coffin.

Several members of the Trust marched in the funeral procession behind the Royal family, alongside 500 representatives from Diana's many charities.

*

We were each sent small brown cards with black decked edging inscribed.

- Westminster Abbey
- Funeral of Diana, Princess of Wales
- Saturday 6th September 1997 at 11 am
- Signed by the Dean of Westminster Abbey and the Lord Chamberlain

- Entrance Poets Corner Door (opposite the House of Lords) from 9.30 am
- No admittance to the Abbey after 10.15 am
- Dress: Non-Ceremonial Day Dress or Lounge Suit
- We would be seated in the South Transept.
- The use of private cameras, videos or sound recording equipment was not permitted in the Abbey.
- On the reverse side of the card was a map of the Abbey marking the entrance.
- If coming by car the approach to the Abbey was by way of Victoria Street to set down at the Great West Door.
- A red label with a large black X should be displayed inside the windscreen of the car and was for "setting down" only. No parking facilities were available.
- On arrival, by taxi, we were each handed a large booklet containing details of the order of the service.
- From 10.10 a.m. during the Procession of the cortege from Kensington Palace, the Tenor Bell was toiled every minute.
- The service was sung by the Choir of Westminster Abbey, conducted by Martin Neary, Organist and Master of the Choristers.
- The organ was played by Martin Baker, Sub-Organist of Westminster Abbey.
- Music before the service, played by Stephen Le Prevost, Assistant Organist, Westminster Abbey, included " Grave and Adagio Organ Sonata, no.2", "Prelude on the hymn tune 'Eventide'", "choral prelude: *Ich ruf' zu dir, Herr Jesu Christ,* Fantasia in C minor, Largo", "Ninth symphony, 'Nimrod' variation No 9."
- All stood as the Procession of Visiting Clergy moved to their places in the Sacrarium.
- The members of the Spencer Family were received at the Great West Door by the Dean and Chapter of Westminster, and all stood as they were conducted to their places in the North Lantern.
- Members of the Royal family were received at the Great West Door by the Dean and Chapter, and all stood as they were conducted to their places in the South Lantern.

- Her Majesty the Queen, Her Majesty Queen Elizabeth the Queen Mother and His Royal Highness Prince Philip, Duke of Edinburgh were received at the Great West Door by the Dean and Chapter, and all stood as Their Majesties and His Royal Highness were conducted to their places in the South Lantern.

- The Collegiate Body of St Peter in Westminster moved into place in the Nove.

- All remained standing as the cortege entered the Great West Door.

- All sang the National Anthem.

- The cortege, preceded by the Collegiate Body, moved to the Quire and Sacrarium, during which the choir sang "The Sentences."

- All remained standing and the Very Reverend Dr Wesley Carr, Dean of Westminster, said The Bidding: *"We are gathered here in Westminster Abbey to give thanks for the life of Diana, Princess of Wales; to commend her soul to almighty God, and to seek his comfort for all who mourn."*

- All remained standing for the hymn "I Vow To Thee, My Country."

- All sat. Lady Sarah McCorquodale, Diana's sister, read: "Turn Again to Life". *"If I should die and leave you here a while."*

- All remained seated. The BBC Singers, together with Lynne Dawson, Soprano, sang "Verdi's Requiem."

- All remained seated. Lady Jane Fellows, Diana's elder sister, who was married to the Queen's Private Secretary, read *"Time is too slow for those who wait, too swift for those who fear."*

- All stood to sing "*The King of love my Shepherd is.*"

- All sat. The Right Honourable Tony Blair, MP, Prime Minister, read: 1 Corinthians 13: "*Though I speak with the tongues of men and of angels, and have not love, I become as sounding brass, or a tinkling cymbal.*"

- All remained seated. Elton John sang "Candle in the Wind."

- *"Goodbye England's rose: may you ever grow in our hearts. You were the grace that placed itself where lives were torn apart. You called out to our country, and you whispered to those in pain. Now you belong to heaven, and the stars spell out your name. And it seems to me you lived your life like a candle in the wind: never fading with the sunset when the sun set in. And your footsteps will always fall here, along England's greenest hills; your candle's burned out long before your legend ever will."*

- All remained seated for the tribute by Charles Spencer, 9th Earl Spencer, Diana's younger brother. His eulogy criticised the press and indirectly the Royal family.

- *"We are all united not only in our desire to pay our respects to Diana but rather in our need to do so. For such was her extraordinary appeal that the tens of millions of people taking part in this service all over the world via television and radio who never actually met her feel that they too lost someone close to them in the early hours of Sunday morning. It is a more remarkable tribute to Diana than I can ever hope to offer her today."*

- There was spontaneous applause from the congregation in the Abbey.

- All stood to sing *"Make me a channel of your peace: where there is hatred let me bring your love, where there is injury, your pardon, Lord, and where there's doubt, true faith in you."*

- All sat. The Most Reverend and Right Honourable Dr George Carey, Lord Archbishop of Canterbury, Primate of All England and Metropolitan led the prayers for Diana, Princess of Wales, for her family, for the Royal family, for all who mourn, for the Princess's life and work, for ourselves.

- All remained seated. The Choristers sang *"I would be true, for there are those that trust me."*

- The Archbishop continued with "The Lord's Prayer", and then said "The Blessing."

- All stood to sing *"Guide Me, O Thou Great Redeemer."*

- Standing before the catafalque the Dean said the commendation: *"Let us commend our sister Diana to the mercy of God, our Maker and Redeemer."*

- All remained standing as the cortege left the church, during which the Choir sang *"Alleluia. May flights of angels sing the to thy rest."*

- At the west end of the church the cortege halted for the minute's silence, observed by the nation.

- The half-muffled bells of the Abbey were rung.

- All remained standing as the processions moved to the west end of the church.

- Music after the service consisted of Bach's "Prelude in C Minor" and Saint-Saens's "Maestoso", from Symphonie no 3.
- Members of the congregation were requested to stay in their places until invited by the stewards to move.

Two thousand people attended the ceremony in the Abbey, amongst them Hillary Clinton, Jacques Chirac, Pavarotti, George Michael, Nelson Mandela, Margaret Thatcher, Henry Kissinger, Queen Noor of Jordan, Tom Cruise, Suzanne Mubarak, the King of Spain, Edward Heath and many, many other well-known figures.

A memorable occasion which we have many times described in detail to friends, acquaintances and our grandchildren.

On the day of the funeral, *The Guardian* carried a special 16-page section dedicated to Diana, which stated *"Today Diana is laid to rest and will enter our legends."*

In a remarkable break with tradition, the Queen paid tribute to the Princess of Wales in an unprecedented television and radio address to the nation from the balcony of Buckingham Palace. *"Diana was an exceptional and gifted human being. In good times and bad, she never lost her capacity to smile and laugh, nor to inspire others with her warmth and kindness."*

Her friend Rosa Monckton remembered the girlfriend she had lost, and recalled a visit they had made together to Greece. *"In a small village called Kiparissi, we went together to a Greek Orthodox church. We lit candles for our children, and as we left the church Diana turned to me and said: 'Oh Rosa, I do so love my boys.'"*

Diana's coffin was conveyed in a hearse to Althorp, the Spencer family home where she grew up, and she was buried on a small island known as the Oval, in the centre of an ornamental lake in the grounds. It is reported that a rosary given to her by Mother Teresa was placed in her hands. The Bishop of Peterborough had consecrated the ground where she was laid to rest.

A local villager who had lived in the village for several years said, *"It was her home and they must have many happy memories of her there with the family."*

The Sunday Times, in a 48-page special issue devoted to Diana, led its front page with a full-page photograph of Prince William, Prince Harry and Prince Charles, their faces filled with emotion, watching as the body of Princess Diana was driven from Westminster Abbey after the service.

In 1988 we were invited to visit Althorp, where Diana had grown up as a child, and pay our respects at her grave on the island – The Oval.

On 6 June 2021, Diana's 60th birthday, Andrew Marr wrote in *The Sunday Times*, "*Had Diana survived to see her seventh decade, what would her life, and the lives of her sons, have looked like in the Britain she changed for ever?*

What has changed in the balance of power? 'Metropolitan' values, despite Brexit, despite the waning of Labour, seem increasingly dominant. The empathetic, open, informal, democratic side of Diana's legacy is more potent – and perhaps more dangerous for the monarchy itself – than the establishment side. Some see the division being played out in the different characters of her sons."

Chapter 13

A change of tack

Southeast Asia haze, Russian inflation, Diana Memorial Fund, Diana, Princess of Wales Tushinskaya Memorial Scholarships, Scholarship criteria, IELTS, Scholarship benefits, Scholarship applications, Stockholm, Paediatric nurse teacher training, Paediatric Nursing School, Uncle Aby

Southeast Asia haze

A "slash and burn" policy, particularly in Indonesia, in order to create land for agricultural use by cutting down forests, caused, over the years, repeated episodes of fire-related air pollution which was conveyed by winds to Malaysia and Singapore. Business activities and air travel were seriously disrupted, and people living in affected areas had to wear face masks and protect their eyes. Those who suffered from asthma in many cases had to be admitted to hospital.

With our medical responsibility for diplomats and British nationals in the affected countries, the Medical and Welfare Department of the FCO played a significant part in advising, and when appropriate, evacuating affected Brits.

Eventually, when the delayed monsoon started, the fires were extinguished.

*

1998 Russian inflation

Inflation in Russia had risen to over 10 per cent, and in an attempt to combat this new rouble notes were issued. One new rouble was equivalent to 1,000 old roubles. In September 1998 the rouble was devalued and Internationally its value fell by two thirds. Many Russians lost much of their savings.

These economic problems and the widespread corruption would lead to Yeltsin's resignation at the end of the next year. Yeltsin had chosen as his successor Vladimir Putin, who then became the acting President.

Princess Diana Memorial Fund

In September 1997, the Diana, Princess of Wales Memorial Fund was set up largely at the instigation of Anthony Julius of Mishcon de Reya, Diana's divorce lawyer, and her elder sister Lady Sarah McCorquodale. The Fund's objectives were to continue Diana's humanitarian work in the UK and overseas. Funds of over £100 million had been received from private donations by members of the public, investments and sales of "Candle in the Wind". Andrew Purkis was appointed chief executive.

The six organisations which Diana had been supporting at the time of her death would share £8 million, and £5 million would be made available to the other hundred charities which she had supported, including Tushinskaya Trust.

Diana, Princess of Wales Tushinskaya Memorial Scholarships

The Trust felt that, in view of Diana's known interest in the welfare of children and her desire specifically to assist Russian children, a fitting memorial would be the establishment of an annual Scholarship for young Russian paediatricians and paediatric nurses to study in the UK to assist in improving and broadening their opportunities for training.

In conjunction with Great Ormond Street Hospital for Children and South Bank University, an application was submitted by the Trust to the Diana Memorial Fund, and they granted the sum of £60,000 to cover the first three years' Scholarships.

A joint British/Russian Selection Board was established. The Russian members were Professor Larisa Stepanova Baleva, Principal Paediatrician of the Ministry of Health of the Russian Federation, Professor Natalia Anatolvna Geppe representing the Union of Russian Paediatricians, Dr Oleg Povarnin, Director of Surgical Planning Tushinskaya Children's Hospital and Dr Ivan Alexandrovitch Leshkevitch, deputy Head Department of Health Moscow.

The British members were Dr Michael Nicholls who would be Chairman of the Selection Board, Dr Robert Dinwiddie, Director of Postgraduate Medical Education GOSH and Mark Whiting, Senior Lecturer in Community Children's Nursing South Bank University. In 1999, Mark was succeeded by Louise Soanes, Host Defence Directorate Great Ormond Street Hospital, representing South Bank University.

Scholarship criteria

Doctors applying for Scholarships needed to be no older than 35 years, and following graduation have had a minimum of two years' training in their paediatric speciality. Nurses must have had at least two years' work experience in paediatrics following graduation.

All applicants required a good understanding of spoken English and would need to achieve a minimum mark of 5.5 in the Academic IELTS examination.

IELTS

The International English Language Testing System, IELTS, assessed four elements of language – listening, reading, writing and speaking – and at that time it was run by the British Council.

Scholarship benefits

The scholarships offered generous benefits and paid the IELTS and visa fees, return air fare Moscow to London, accommodation in London, local transport in London, twelve weeks' tuition as Clinical Observer in Great Ormond Street Children's Hospital, and subsistence for twelve weeks.

Scholarship applications

A detailed application form had to be completed in English, and include details of the benefits they hoped to receive from the Scholarship and how they hoped to apply the knowledge gained on their return home.

Each applicant was requested to sign statements that said that, if offered a Scholarship, they agreed to remain at the post in the UK for the full term of the Scholarship, namely twelve weeks, would return to their present post in Russia on completion of the Scholarship, and submit a detailed report by the end of the Scholarship, and then annual reports for three years.

The Russian Head of their department was requested to confirm that they recommended them as a competent candidate to apply for a Diana, Princess of Wales Tushinskaya Memorial Scholarship, and certify that they would be re-employed in their present, or more senior, position on their return to Russia after completion of the Scholarship.

*

Stockholm

In May 1998 Dr Ing-Marie Lidstrom invited IAPOS members to Stockholm for a three-day visit.

Stockholm is the capital and largest city of Sweden with a population of almost 1 million. The city stretches across fourteen islands where Lake Mälaren flows into the Baltic Sea. Outside the city to the east, and along the coast, is the island chain of the Stockholm Archipelago.

The area has been settled since the Stone Age in the 6th millennium BC, and was founded as a city in 1252. For several hundred years it was the capital of Finland as well, which then was a part of Sweden.

Stockholm is the cultural, media, political and economic centre of Sweden. The city is home to some of Europe's top ranking universities, such as the Stockholm School of Economics, Karolinska Institute, KTH Royal Institute of Technology and Stockholm University and is the seat of the Swedish government. It hosts the annual Nobel Prize ceremonies and banquet.

Stockholm Palace is the official residence and principal workplace of the Swedish monarch, and Drottningholm Palace serves as the Royal family's private residence.

*

The Nobel Prizes are five separate prizes in the fields of Physics, Chemistry, Physiology or Medicine, Literature and Peace that are awarded to those who, during the preceding year, have conferred the greatest benefits to mankind.

Alfred Nobel was a Swedish chemist, engineer and industrialist most famously known for the invention of dynamite. He died in 1896, and in his will he bequeathed all of his "remaining realisable assets" to be used to establish the prizes which became known as "Nobel Prizes." The first Nobel Prizes were awarded in 1901, and they are widely regarded as the most prestigious awards available in their respective fields.

The prize ceremonies take place annually and each recipient, known as a "Laurate", receives a gold medal, a diploma and a monetary award.

*

Forty-seven members of IAPOS met at Heathrow Airport to catch the BA flight to Stockholm where Ing-Marie and her husband Lars were waiting for us with a coach to transport us to the Grand Hotel Saltsjobaden, situated in the middle of a beautiful archipelago overlooking the sea with its own grand marina.

After an excellent breakfast next morning, in the hotel conference room, we had a full day of lectures, with a very varied programme: a lecture about Carl von Linne, the botanist and Professor of Medicine; the traditional lifestyle, health and diseases of the Lapplander population; electromagnetic fields, and before the IAPOS business meeting, psychophysiological aspects of expatriation.

Members' partners were taken on a city sightseeing tour, with a visit to the Town Hall, a guided tour through the Old Town and lunch in one of Stockholm's oldest restaurants. Dinner that night was in the Queen Silvia Pavilion at Ulriksdals Wardshus situated in the Royal Park of Ulriksdal.

On Saturday we visited Skansen, the world's first open-air museum in the Djurgarden, and the Museum of Modern Art.

On our final, hot and sunny day, we walked by the sea then took a bus to the airport, accompanied by Ing-Marie.

An excellent and most enjoyable short trip.

*

Paediatric nurse teacher training

David, Susan and June Hutt, consultant for Childrens' Nursing, Practice and Education, with Inessa Ray as interpreter, visited Moscow in January at the invitation of Dina Zelinskaya. We heard from Olga Dmitrieva that Dina's fax inviting us to Moscow had been sent following Nelli Naigovzina's intervention. It was pleasing to know that our friends from Tushinskaya remained loyal to us.

They had several meetings with Dina Zelinskaya, Chief Nurse Manager at Childrens' Republican Hospital, and Emilia Ispolatovskaya, lecturer at Academy of Postgraduate Education in Minzdrav, and were told that a postgraduate diploma in paediatric nursing was planned. Emilia, who was friendly and sympathetic and had a basic grounding in hesitant spoken English, was a close friend of Dina since medical school days, and she would be organising this.

The diploma would give specialised training in the care of children to nurses who already had general nursing qualifications, and would consist of several modules each lasting for five weeks. Despite considerable probing it was not possible to reach a clear understanding of the syllabus, who would be teaching it and whether it consisted exclusively of classroom work or if it also included practical aspects. They requested that the Trust provide assistance with training the teachers who would instruct these courses.

With the objective of encouraging Minzdrav to recognise the value and resources of a multidisciplinary approach, which they regarded as novel and different from their customary working methods, our team suggested that a Joint Working Group be set up comprising members with experience of nursing, medicine, management and education.

Later in the year, June Hutt and Lesley Robertson, principal lecturer in Child Health Thames Valley University, went out to Moscow to help organise the Joint Working Group for the development of the curriculum for Childrens' Nursing, and arrange a course to be held in Moscow for training teachers of paediatric nurses.

They also visited the Paediatric Cardiological Research Centre, but Acamedician Veltishev was absent following an eye operation, and they were received by Maria Shkolnikova, who was very grateful to receive the articles from *Paediatric Nursing* which they had brought with them, which would be included in their Institute's own bimonthly journal.

At the Paediatric Oncological Research Centre they got a rather cool welcome from Dr Mentkevitch when they suggested that the centre might wish to associate itself with programmes aimed at the improvement of nursing and the holistic care of sick children. He criticised the prevailing low standards in the nursing profession due, amongst other things, to low pay and low public esteem.

Inessa spoke with Dr Lanina on the phone and established that the Paediatric Nursing School was still running and that they would welcome continuing contact with us.

*

We followed up the two earlier visits later that year when David, Harald, Michael, June, Leslie and Inessa spent five days in Moscow, staying at the Moskva Hotel, even though it still had Soviet-style bedrooms with hard beds.

Inessa and I spent all morning ringing around to arrange appointments to see various people, with varying degrees of success. We managed to fix a very useful meeting with Dina Zelinskaya in Minzdrav and had supper with Olga and Sasha Dmitrieva.

It was pouring with rain the following day, and our appointment with Glavk was cancelled; however, we visited BESO's office and discussed with Gregory Horobin the possibility of him acting as the Trust's representative.

June and Leslie went to see Emilia Ispolatovskaya and received a rather cool welcome, whilst we visited Vadim in the American Medical Centre where he now worked. We had a useful meeting with Leshkevitch in Glavk, and in the evening we all had supper with the Romanyuks.

The next day we went to see Tushinskaya Hospital and the Paediatric Nursing School, and then went back to Minzdrav to meet Dina, Larisa Baleva and Natalia Geppe – everyone got on well. We invited Emilia Ispolatovskaya and her team to supper with us in the hotel.

We were departing the following day and David, Michael and I visited our Embassy to put them in the picture, whilst the others saw some of the sights and visited GUM.

A difficult but successful trip.

*

Paediatric Nursing School

In 1998, a further 48 student children's nurses graduated from the Paediatric Nursing School and a similar number in 1999. By then there were 235 students in the nursing school, spread over four years.

The curriculum included a two-year course on the philosophy of nursing, involving many aspects of Family Centred Care and holistic childcare. Much of the students' training took place on the hospital wards.

Both Tushinskaya Hospital and the nursing school were visited by Trust representatives who had found the majority of the concepts and changes the Trust had introduced were still being applied.

*

Uncle Aby

As was our custom in July, we went on our annual salmon fishing trip to Scotland with Liz and a group of friends. That year we stayed in a rundown castle to the northeast of Fort William.

Walking across a somewhat desolate heath, surprisingly we saw a telephone box in the middle of nowhere. Knowing we would be driving back through Glasgow, I decided to ring my Uncle Aby Caplan, my mother's youngest brother, who lived there.

He picked up the phone and I said, "*Uncle Aby, this is your nephew, Harald.*" His immediate comment was, "*Och, it's 34 years since I last saw you.*" I later realised that he was referring to 1964 when he came to my mother's funeral in London. As you can appreciate, we are a very close family!

Chapter 14

Balkans and eastern Europe

International Space Station, Good Friday Agreement, Former Yugoslavia, Balkan states, Belgrade, Tirana, Sarajevo, The House by the Dvina, Kafka's Dick

International Space Station

In 1998, 16 nations agreed to develop and man an International Space Station which permanently orbits the Earth. The crew of six or seven were transported to and from the station in Russian Soyuz capsules which were launched from Baikonur Cosmodrome in southern Kazakhstan. The crew's main activities related to research projects in biology, human biology, physics, astronomy and meteorology amongst others, and their average stay is for six months.

Long-term residents in space have been shown to develop medical problems, largely due to weightlessness, such as muscle atrophy, thinning of bones and disturbances of balance. A proportion of the crew members suffered stress and developed impaired immune systems.

*

Good Friday Agreement

The Good Friday Agreement was signed on Friday 10 April 1998 and ended most of the violence of the "Troubles" in Northern Ireland that had prevailed until that time.

The Agreement was between most of Northern Ireland's political parties, and the British and Irish governments. Northern Ireland was granted a devolved system of government, based on "power sharing."

The Democratic Unionist Party (DUP) was the only major political group in Northern Ireland to oppose the Good Friday Agreement.

Many people made major contributions, including Tony Blair and Bertie Ahern, the leaders of the UK and the Republic of Ireland at the time. The talks were chaired by United States special envoy George Mitchell.

*

Former Yugoslavia

The Foreign Office had asked me to make a ten-day visit to the former Yugoslavia and Albania. I would be visiting Belgrade, Tirana and Sarajevo. One of the problems would be that, although they were geographically fairly close to one another, it was not possible, for political reasons, to fly directly from one city to another.

*

Balkan states

Prior to the First World War, the Balkan states of Serbia, Croatia, Bosnia-Herzegovina and Slovenia had been part of the Austro-Hungarian Empire, and at an earlier stage in history part of the Ottoman Empire.

After the war ended, the states joined together to form Yugoslavia, the Land of the Southern Slavs.

In 1941, German, Italian and Hungarian troops occupied the country. There were two rival partisan resistance groups, the larger more powerful one the Communist group led by Josip Broz, known as Tito, and a smaller royalist group, the Chetniks.

Fitzroy Maclean, a British diplomat, was chosen by Churchill to act as liaison officer in central Yugoslavia working with Tito's group of partisans, and he played a very significant role in the final defeat of the German army in the Balkans. He had been posted to Moscow during the time of Stalin's purges in the 1930s. In the late 1980s when he was paying a visit to Moscow, I met him walking down the grand staircase in the British Embassy and we had a short talk. Some people believe that he was the model for Ian Fleming's 007.

Following the end of World War II in 1945, the Federal People's Republic of Yugoslavia was formed, led by Tito. It was initially a satellite of the USSR, but three years later Yugoslavia, whilst remaining a Communist state, split with the Soviet Union.

In 1961, Tito, in collaboration with Nehru of India, Sukarno of Indonesia, Nasser of Egypt and Nkrumah of Ghana, all neutral states in the Cold War, formed the Non-Alignment Movement.

Following Tito's death in 1980, long bottled-up ethnic tensions began to reappear. The republics within Yugoslavia declared independence, and a bloody war broke out which lasted for 10 years. Many atrocities were committed by all parties involved. Eventually in 2001 a peace agreement was brokered by NATO.

Belgrade

I flew the two-and-a-half-hour flight to Belgrade, and on arrival there was snow on the ground. A car took me to the Hyatt Hotel and in the evening I was invited to a buffet supper by David Landsmann the Ambo, where I met an American friend of the Moreys and a local Dermatologist, and an ENT specialist.

Next day, I saw a dozen patients in our Embassy and visited the US Embassy.

Dr Levi, the Director had invited me to visit the Gradska Orthopaedic and Trauma Hospital, but a visit to the Urgenti Centre, the A&E clinic, was cancelled. In the evening at the British Embassy Club, I joined a quiz team and surprisingly we were the winners.

Serbian is a highly inflected language and is digraphic; that is, it can be written either in the Latin or Cyrillic script. In practice, most people use the Cyrillic script.

The history of Belgrade, the White City, situated on the confluence of the Danube and Sava rivers, dates back 7,000 years. For 300 years it was held by the Turks. It became the capital of Yugoslavia in 1918 and remained so until the final dissolution of Yugoslavia in 2006.

*

Tirana

My next port of call was Tirana, capital of Albania, but there were no direct flights from Belgrade. So, this entailed a JAT Yugoslavia Airline two-hour flight to Zurich, queueing for immigration, collecting my baggage and politely pushing my way to the front of the queue for the Crossair flight in an Avro RJ 85 plane to Tirana.

Albania, with an Adriatic and Ionian Sea coastline, became a Communist state following the Second World War. Enver Hoxha was their leader until the revolution in 1991. After Stalin's death, the relationship with the USSR deteriorated and it developed closer ties with Communist China. However, the country remained very isolated for 40 years.

In post-Communist times it tried to develop a capitalist economy, but many rogues took advantage of this, and with the connivance of the government developed "Ponzi" pyramid schemes, which following their collapse in the mid-1990s, left much of the population in poverty.

Albanian is an Indo-European language, but it is not closely related to any other European languages. It is, however, rather disconcerting that when Albanians say no – *Jo* – they nod their heads and when they say yes – *Po* – they shake their heads. This of course is the opposite of the way that people gesticulate by head movement in the majority of countries.

Nene Tereza – Mother Teresa – Airport was chaotic. There were armed guards lining the roofs of the buildings and the majority of the men on the ground were wearing black bomber jackets with the suspicious bulge of a pistol under their armpits.

The Albanian Mafia was very active and there was a large demand in Albania for Mercedes and BMW cars. Individuals who wished to acquire a car would give details of the specific model and colour they required. A few days later, it would be delivered to their doorstep having been acquired who knows how or from where, and driven across the border.

On one memorable occasion, whilst I was in Tirana, an Albanian government Minister who was due to attend a high-level meeting in a nearby country was stopped at the border control and the stolen official car in which he was being driven was confiscated.

On arrival at the airport, passengers' luggage was piled up on the floor in a small room, and we had to sort out our own bags. Eventually, after a small boy had tried to run off with my bag, I found the Embassy car and driver who took me to Europe Park Hotel, which surprisingly was reasonably comfortable.

There were only a few patients to be seen, but I was advised that it was unsafe to walk about in the street, and all Embassy staff were forbidden to go out unaccompanied. The previous weekend, three members of the Embassy staff had gone out to the countryside in a car for a picnic and had been held up by armed robbers. When they tried to drive away, the robbers started shooting, and one member of our Embassy had been wounded in her arm.

The next day, the sun was shining and the sky was blue. I visited several clinics run by foreign nationals, and with our Ambassador visited the Ministry of Health. After lunch at the residency, he drove me to the airport and later that day I was safely ensconced in the Hotel Europe in Zurich, writing my reports.

*

Sarajevo

After a good breakfast, I took a bus to the airport and Crossair flew me in one and a half hours comfortably to Sarajevo. Driving through the streets, there was much evidence of war damage to the buildings. The Grand Hotel was located in a rather isolated part of town, but it was comfortable enough.

In the past, Sarajevo, the capital of Bosnia-Herzegovina, had been known as the "Jerusalem of the Balkans", with a mosque, Catholic church, Orthodox church and synagogue all sited in the same neighbourhood.

Gavrilo Princip, a Bosnian activist, assassinated Archduke Ferdinand of Austria in 1914 in Sarajevo, and this act in many ways sparked the Great War.

In 1992, the Serbs, with the stated intention of safeguarding Serbs living in Bosnia-Herzegovina, had declared a new state, *Republika Srpska,* which included large parts of north and east Bosnia-Herzegovina.

For four years, following the Bosnian declaration of independence, Sarajevo was under continuous siege by Serbian troops, with constant bombardment and sniping from the surrounding hills. Over 11,000 civilians lost their lives.

There was a road tunnel very close to the hotel and I decided to walk through it to see where it led to. I came out of the tunnel into the daylight some way up a hill, and looking down into the valley, could see a large cemetery. Many people and open-backed lorries were gathering there. When I inquired what was happening, I was informed that during the siege many who had been killed were buried in mass graves, and now they were being disinterred and individually reburied.

In the city there were many white Jeeps and vehicles with the letters SFOR emblazoned on their sides. The Stabilisation Force in Bosnia-Herzegovina was a NATO-led peacekeeping force, whose objective was to contribute to a secure environment. At that time there were a total of 26 foreign agencies and 33 Embassies or Consulates in the city.

During my stay in Sarajevo, I saw several patients, visited a dental clinic, an IVF clinic, the state hospital, the general military hospital and a gynaecologist.

Walking through the city, I viewed the 16th-century Al Pasha Mosque, Isa Bey's Hamam, the Catholic cathedral and the Bazaar.

I caused a minor problem in the hotel when I blew the fuses in my bathroom. I had decided to boil some water to make a cup of coffee with a small electric coil that I had brought with me. I plugged it into the shaver socket, and all the lights went out. There was no reading for me that night.

*

The House by the Dvina

I had brought with me a copy of Eugenie Fraser's fascinating story *The House by the Dvina*, in which she relates the story of her upbringing by a Russian father and Scottish mother living in northern Russia near Archangel. In the time of Tsar

Alexander II, known as the Emancipator of the Serfs, her great grandfather had fallen in love with and eventually married a serf girl.

*

Following a "wash up" with Ambassador Gordon Hands, a discussion about health problems and morale in the Embassy, but mentioning no one by name, I left for the airport. The Austrian Airways plane was delayed, and by the time I arrived in Vienna I had missed my connection.

Eventually, managing to find a BA flight to Heathrow, on arrival there I passed through immigration and waited and waited at the carousel for my baggage, but it didn't turn up. Someone in Vienna had forgotten to load it onto the plane. Some days later my missing suitcase arrived in London.

*

Kafka's Dick

We always enjoyed Alan Bennett's plays, and having met him in Moscow in 1988, when he was visiting Moscow with five other authors to meet members of the Soviet Writers Union, we could not miss seeing his play *Kafka's Dick*, when, on New Year's Eve, it was on stage in the Piccadilly Theatre. It tells the story of Franz Kafka and Max Brod, long after their deaths, returning to visit a Yorkshire couple.

As Kafka lay in his death bed, he had instructed his friend Brod to destroy all his works. Fortunately, Brod had not observed this wish.

Chapter 15

Scholarships and visits

Patrons Memorial Scholarship, Baleva Geppe Povarnin visit, Scholarship Selection Board, Warsaw and Bratislava, Pickpocket, Teachers' training course 2008 and Textbook, Teacher training manual, Warsaw Bratislava Prague Budapest

We were still awaiting consent from the Palace to name the scholarships "Diana, Princess of Wales Memorial Scholarships."

*

Baleva Geppe Povarnin visit

Having invited Larisa Baleva, Natalia Geppe and Oleg Povarnin to visit London as our guests, we arranged a reception for them to meet representatives from the Trust, Great Ormond Street Hospital and the Institute of Child Health, the Diana Memorial Fund, the Department of Health, the Know How Fund, the British Council and the Russian Ambassador Yuri Fokin and his wife, amongst others.

We organised a comprehensive programme for them in Great Ormond Street Hospital, the Royal Free Hospital and the Whittington Hospital, and had discussions on a wide range of subjects relating to training of British doctors and training of children's nurses in the UK.

*

Scholarship Selection Board

The first Scholarship Selection Board met in Moscow in June. By then it had been agreed that the Scholarships could be named "The Diana, Princess of Wales Tushinskaya Memorial Scholarships."

Dr Michael Nicholls as Chairman, Dr Robert Dinwiddie representing Great Ormond Street Hospital, Louise Soanes representing Southbank University, Dr Olga Crawford assisting with interpretation, Elena Broumarova who was invited as an observer on behalf of the British Council, Professor Larisa Baleva representing the

Russian Ministry of Health, and Harald and Nahid Lipman, attending as observers, were all present.

There had been 25 applicants, of whom 10 were shortlisted by our Russian colleagues, nine doctors and one nurse, and they, with varying degrees of fear and trembling, attended the Selection Board. It was not the Russian custom for a Board to make selections, so this was a first-time, rather daunting, experience for all of them.

On this occasion, only one of the applicants satisfied all the criteria of the Selection Board, including proficiency in English language, and he was awarded the first annual Memorial Scholarship, to be attached as a Clinical Observer to the Institute of Child Health in London for a three-month course of study commencing in February 2000.

During the next 18 years we would award a total of 56 scholarships.

Don't worry, I won't bore you with full details of each Scholar, but will instead regale you with selected highlights.

Dr Sergei Vladimirovich Vaganov, aged 26, was a Paediatric Physician in the Department of Children's Anaesthesiology and Intensive care in Samara Regional Kalinin Hospital. He was married to a Neurologist.

*

Warsaw and Bratislava

I was due to visit our Embassies in Warsaw and Bratislava,, and Nahid accompanied me on the first leg of the trip as our friends from Moscow days, Peter and Judy Harris, were now posted in Warsaw.

We flew in a British Midland Boeing 737 to Warsaw and then took a taxi to Hotel Mercure. Our first visit was to our Embassy, where I met the Management Officer and Joanna Litynska, our locally engaged nurse.

The Harrises had arranged to take us to the premier of a Polish film, *Fire and Sword*, the story of a Cossack uprising in the 17th century. It was the most lavish and expensive Polish film ever made.

At the reception following the film, we were introduced to the Director Jerzy Hoffman and the Polish Foreign Secretary.

The following day, whilst I was engaged with my professional activities, Judy looked after Nahid and took her around the city. In the evening, we supped with Peter and Judy and met again their three lovely sons, who were now much more grown up than when we had last seen them.

The following day, having seen a few patients, Nahid and I walked to the Royal Castle and Old Town and then caught a bus to take us back to the hotel.

The bus was very crowded, and as it rumbled over the cobbled street, the passengers who were standing would bang against one another. I noticed that the tall man next to me, who was carrying a plastic bag over his arm, and who had gently bumped against me on a couple of occasions when the bus swayed, spent his time playing with his mobile phone.

The bus stopped, the doors opened and many of the passengers got out. Just as the doors were closing, the tall man jumped out off the bus. I was a little surprised, and instinctively put my hand inside my zipped anorak and felt for my wallet. Realising that the tall man must have taken it, I managed to open the bus door before the bus started and saw him further up the pavement walking rapidly away.

On returning to the hotel, we informed the reception and our Embassy, and they called the police. We were due to depart Warsaw early next morning, and were very impressed when shortly after it was reported, a Polish police officer arrived in the hotel and took a statement. Apparently pickpocketing and handbag-snatching was very prevalent in Warsaw at that time. The police would inform the Embassy if there were any developments.

Nahid caught a British Midland flight to London, and I took an Austrian Airlines flight to Vienna. I was met on arrival at the airport by an Embassy car sent from Bratislava and driven the one-hour journey across the border to the comfortable Hotel Danube in Bratislava.

*

Bratislava, straddllng the banks of the Danube, is the capital of Slovakia, previously one of the states of federalised Czechoslovakia. In 1993, an entirely peaceful divorce, known as the "Velvet Divorce", had split Czechoslovakia into the Czech Republic and Slovakia. The division occurred following longstanding political and nationalistic disagreements. President Vaclav Havel, who favoured the continuation of Czechoslovakia, had resigned.

Over the centuries, the city has been influenced by inhabitants of many nationalities including Austrians, Bulgarians, Czechs, German, Hungarians and Slovaks.

For 200 years it was the coronation site of the Kingdom of Hungary.

Particularly in the Old Town, these varied influences are reflected in the architecture, of historical buildings – the Baroque palaces, the Gothic Cathedral of St Martin, the Francescan Church, and Bratislava Castle, rebuilt in 1950 in the Theresian style, following destruction in a fire.

The bridge over the Danube commemorates the Slovak uprising.

During my visit, I was consulted by several members of the Embassy staff, visited the Diplomatic Clinic where I met an extremely good local GP, Dr Koller, visited a Gynaecological clinic and drove across the Austrian border to see a patient who had been transferred to an Austrian medical centre near the border.

That evening, I listened to an excellent recital by a Klezmer band in the City Gallery. Klezmer is based on traditional Ashkenazi Jewish music often blended with jazz. It is a very expressive music reminiscent of the human voice.

Following a visit to the Diagnostic Oncological Centre which was well-equipped, I was driven to Vienna Airport from where BA flew me comfortably back to Heathrow.

*

Teachers' training course and Textbook

The Trust funded, and our representatives in Moscow, Gregory Horobin and Elena Popova of BESO, assisted with organising the first teachers' training courses in paediatric nursing in conjunction with the Russian Academy of Postgraduate Education.

A prime objective was to underpin the development of the first nurse teachers of children's nursing course in Russia as well as the principles of holistic childcare.

Dina Zelinskaya and Emilia Ispolatovskaya had recently visited London as our guests to review the teacher training course.

Twelve Russian doctors and nurses, from widely scattered regions of the Russian Federation, attended a two-week course held in Moscow, at the Republican Children's Hospital. Lesley Robertson, June Hutt, Emilia Ispolatovskaya, Dina Zelinskaya and Marina Nikovskaya all participated, with Inessa Ray interpreting.

A further training seminar was held in Kaluga, in May 2000. On that occasion, 14 nurse managers from the Kaluga region attended the two-week course.

Kaluga, 150 km southwest of Moscow, is the birthplace of the founding father of modern rocketry and astronautics, Konstantin Tsiolkovsky.

The following year, the third teacher training seminar was held in Vladimir, the ancient capital of Rus. There were 28 participants on this occasion, and all were nurses from the region.

The final seminar in 2002 was held specifically for the nursing staff of the Central

Republican Hospital Moscow. They had the opportunity to explore alternative teaching and learning skills, become change agents, and teach experienced nurses how to teach, thus further developing appropriate nursing services for children.

*

In 2008, the Trust in conjunction with Dina Zelinskaya and Emilia Ispolatovskaya published in Russian a Teaching Manual of Paediatric Nursing.

*

Warsaw, Bratislava, Prague, Budapest

I was due to visit Warsaw and Bratislava again and then travel on to Prague and Budapest.

Arriving at the Hotel Mercure in Warsaw, I found rather surprisingly that no room had been booked for me. The rest of my stay there was uneventful and included visits to several hospitals and clinics as well as medical consultations with several members of the Embassy staff.

*

My visit to Bratislava was also pretty routine and fortunately there were no serious medical problems to deal with.

*

From the Bratislava airport on a CSA flight, it was only 45 minutes to Prague. Having now the rank of Counsellor in the Foreign Office, equivalent to a Major General, I was entitled to fly Club class, and I stayed at the Corinthia Hotel, standing atop one of Prague's hills with breathtaking, panoramic views of the beautiful city.

This would be my first return to the city since the fall of the Communist regime. That evening, I saw a good production of *Carmen* in the neoclassic State Opera House.

Whilst in Prague on this occasion, I visited the Motel Paediatric Hospital, a dental clinic, the Na Frantiska Hospital and saw a member of the Embassy staff who was in the Na Homoice Hospital.

Several members of the Embassy staff consulted me, and I felt that staff morale was low.

The following morning after discussions with the deputy Head of Mission, a car took me to the airport. The CSA flight had been cancelled, and, after a six-hour wait, I eventually caught a flight to Budapest, where a car met me and took me to the comfortable Hyatt Hotel.

*

Budapest

I had last visited Budapest 16 years previously when we flew down from Moscow and met up with our brother-in-law, Kurt.

Walking to the Embassy, which was fairly close by the hotel, I found it now a very different city.

Budapest, said to be one of the most beautiful cities in the world, was the co-capital with Vienna of the Austro-Hungarian Empire. In the 16th and 17th centuries, it had been under Ottoman rule. There were many famous inhabitants including Franz Liszt, Houdini and Zsa Zsa Gabor.

The extremely difficult and complex Hungarian language belongs to the group of Finno-Ugric languages, which also includes the Finnish language. Interestingly, I once had a Finnish secretary who had a Hungarian husband. Their young son was one of the few people in the world who could speak both Finnish and Hungarian, which he had learnt from his two sets of grandparents. The wheel had come full circle.

There were several patients to be seen, and I had a meeting with the Ambassador. I took the opportunity of lunching at Kempinski, as ever an excellent meal, and then visited Korhaz Hospital where I met several staff doctors including an Iranian dentist.

The next day the nurse from the US Embassy came to visit me and we went together to see the Falk clinic where city ambulances were based.

A bus to the airport, and BA brought me safely back to Heathrow where I was met by Nahid and her sister Parvin who was visiting us.

I wouldn't be visiting Budapest again for another six years and then under very different circumstances, when Nahid had arranged to take a group of the Diplomatic Neighbours, with the assistance and guidance of ZsuZsa, the wife of Bela Szombati, the Hungarian Ambassador to the UK.

Chapter 16

Tushinskaya Hospital

Los Angeles burglary, Tushinskaya Hospital, Lithuania, Diplomatic Neighbours, Millennium, Sergei Vaganov, Reception Russian Embassy, Second Scholarship Selection Board, Moscow reunion, Russian Service BBC, People's Peers

Los Angeles burglary

We were visiting LA to attend a family wedding and Nahid had brought some of her jewellery with her to wear at the event.

On the way to Chez Sahim, Nahid's parents' house, driving a car we had picked up at the airport, we decided to stop at a small restaurant for a coffee. I parked in their carpark and opened the car boot, known in US English as the "trunk", to take out my wallet and some dollars.

On returning to the car, after finishing our coffees, we realised that someone had broken into it and stolen, amongst other items, the bag containing Nahid's jewellery. Naturally, she was very upset.

We drove to a police station and reported the theft. Obviously, the thief must have been watching the carpark and seen me open the boot. Sadly, no one was caught and Nahid had lost some of her best jewellery.

A salutary tale – showing how careful one must be.

*

Tushinskaya Hospital

Yuri Mikhailovitch Pavlov had retired on medical grounds, and his deputy, Dr Sergei Lazarev, who strongly opposed the changes we were introducing in the hospital, acted as Director until a successor could be found. It was he who, in 1997, when the UK Department for International Development was evaluating the Health Small Partnerships Scheme, had been very critical of our project to assist the hospital to modernise and given DFID a very false impression of the actual benefits which the hospital had received.

Eventually a successor was found, Dr Vassily Philipovitch Smirnoff, who turned out to be a rather difficult person to relate to.

However, during a recent visit to the hospital, our representative reported that it was very pleasing to see that on Trauma ward, Dr Victor Shein and his staff were still applying the principles of holistic childcare taught by the Trust's nurses. A Clinical Psychologist was now attached to the ward with responsibility for children, parents and staff.

Children's parents were counselled before admission and before operations. Effectively, open visiting hours for parents were now applied in most wards of the hospital, and mothers could assist with some aspects of their nursing care and could stay in the hospital with their children.

The principles taught by the Trust relating to Infection Control, modified in accordance with the statutory requirements of the Russian Sanitary Institution, were being applied. Several of the Russian nurses who had attended the GOSH nurse training course six years previously were still teaching in the Paediatric Nursing School.

*

We also had had news of the Trust's nurses. Sheila Barlow had retired, Kathryn Jones was a lecturer at the Royal College of Nursing, Jayne Harris was a ward manager in the Chelsea and Westminster Hospital and Jan Wydell, who had married, was working in the Gulf.

*

Lithuania

We didn't have an opportunity to visit Lithuania or Latvia during our Moscow postings in the 80s.

However, in 1999 and 2001, we made trips to Lithuania.

*

Diplomatic Neighbours

Nahid, on our final return from Moscow in early 1991, was responsible for a London branch of Diplomatic Neighbours, an organisation set up by the Foreign Office to help spouses of foreign diplomats who were posted in the UK obtain some understanding of and adapt to the British way of life.

She thus met and entertained many wives, and often the husbands, of foreign diplomats who were at that time posted in London. Amongst them, she became very friendly with Laima Paleckiene, the wife of the Lithuanian Ambassador.

Laima offered to arrange and accompany a group of members of Diplomatic Neighbours and their spouses on what turned out to be a very successful, fascinating and enjoyable cultural trip to Lithuania.

*

Lithuania, which was once the largest European medieval empire, stretching from the Baltic to the Black Sea, has a dramatic and varied history. Vilnius, being for centuries the capital of a multinational state, has accumulated features of many cultures. Looking at the ancient buildings, one could enjoy the influence of various schools of architecture – apart from Lithuanian – Italian, Jewish, Austrian, Polish, German and Russian.

Andrew Mueller, a British journalist, is convinced that *"Vilnius is Europe's most deeply and bafflingly buried treasure,"* and stated that *"the elegant capital should by now be firmly established as the new Prague."*

*

Twenty-five guests would be accompanying Liama, Nahid and me on this visit, including representatives from the Norwegian Embassy, the Foreign Office, House of Commons, the Malaysian High Commission, International Social Services, the art critic of the *Evening Standard*, the editor of *Travel Weekly*, a representative of the British-Lithuanian Society and several of our personal friends.

The cost of the four-night package including airfare, hotel, museum tickets, transportation and interpreters was merely £346.

On 3 June, we all met in the late afternoon at the Lithuanian Airlines desk in Terminal Three Heathrow, which is near the Canada Airlines desk, and checked in on flight TE 453. On arrival at Vilnius Airport three hours later, we were transferred to Hotel Centrum, which is situated just 10 minutes' walk from the Old Town.

A tour exploring Vilnius by night was followed by dinner at a restaurant in the Old Town.

Next morning, after a good night's sleep and an excellent Scandinavian breakfast, we walked through the narrow and crooked streets of the Old Town, visiting Vilnius Cathedral and its crypt where Lithuanian dukes and Royal family members were buried. We then paid a visit to St Peter and St Paul's church, the masterpiece of 17th-century Lithuanian baroque.

Lunch was in the Iron Wolf restaurant, which combined the Soviet era's food and a wide collection of that period's memorabilia. Nahid and I felt very much "at home."

After lunch, on the Vilnius city tour we popped into the amber, ceramics and antique shops, and then visited the Vilnius artists' village, where we took afternoon tea.

In the evening we enjoyed a traditional Lithuanian dinner in Rita's Tavern with folk music and dances.

Saturday, the next day, we were driven by coach to Trakai, a distance of 28km, the former capital of the grand Duchy of Lithuania with a 15th-century castle amidst the lakes.

A picnic lunch in a country house near Trakai was followed by a boat trip on the lake, and later a tour of the KGB museum, guided by a former inmate. This was followed by visits to Lithuanian State Jewish Museum, with an introduction to the Jewish culture in Vilnius which used to be an intellectual centre for Jews across Europe for many centuries, until the tragedy of the Holocaust in the 20th century.

In the evening, we attended a concert in the Vilnius University churchyard in memory of Yehudi Menuhin. The programme included Schubert's "Symphony No 4" and Rossini's "Stabat Mater", performed by the Sinfonia Varsovia Orchestra and Kaunas State Choir, with a German soprano, Teresa Seidl, a Portuguese mezzo, Liliana Bizneche-Eisinger, a Lithuanian tenor, Algirdas Janutas, and Benno Schollum, an Austrian bass.

Sunday would be our final full day in Lithuania and we departed by coach for Kaunas, Lithuania's second largest city, where we walked in the Old Town, visited the Art Gallery of Ciurlionis, the outstanding Lithuanian painter and composer, and then viewed the private collection at the Devils Museum.

Breaking for lunch, which had been arranged in Ona Ribakoviene's bakery, we observed how the unique Lithuanian wedding cakes, known as *Sakotis*, were prepared.

That evening there was a ballet performance at the Lithuanian Opera and Ballet Theatre of Herold's *La Fille mal gardée*.

Next morning, after time to wander around the city and do some shopping, we had a light lunch and departed for London on the Lithuanian Airlines flight TE 452.

All in all, a most fascinating and enjoyable trip.

*

It happened that Prince Edward, Earl of Wessex, the Queen's youngest son, was due to marry Sophie Rhys-Jones shortly after we returned to London. Nahid was requested by the Lithuanian Embassy to liaise with the Palace, as they wished to present the couple with a traditional Lithuanian wedding cake. The cake is made by slowly dripping egg-rich batter onto a hot rotating spit and can be several feet high. The cone-shaped cake is then decorated with flowers.

*

A couple of years later, with Laima's help, I organised a medically orientated trip to Lithuania for Liverymen of The Worshipful Society of Apothecaries of London and their spouses with visits to several hospitals and institutes.

*

Millennium

As the end of 1999 and the coming of the year 2000, the millennium, approached, there was International concern related to the storage of calendar data, which became known as the "millennium bug." Software programs represent four-digit years, but only show the final two digits, and thus there was widespread concern they would be unable to distinguish between 1900 and 2000. When midnight arrived on 31 December 1999, they would "think" next year 2000 would be 1900. As so many aspects of modern life depend on software, this would cause absolute chaos.

Fortunately, no serious problems occurred. In fact, the century ends on the last day of the final year in the century, not the first, and the millennium ended on 31 December 2000.

*

2000 Sergei Vaganov

On 29 February 2000, Nahid and I were standing in the crowded arrivals hall in Terminal One Heathrow expectantly awaiting the arrival of Sergei, our first Scholar. After about 30 minutes or so we saw a tired, slightly anxious-looking Sergei carrying a rather small suitcase and two plastic bags. We hailed him and saw a smile spread over his face.

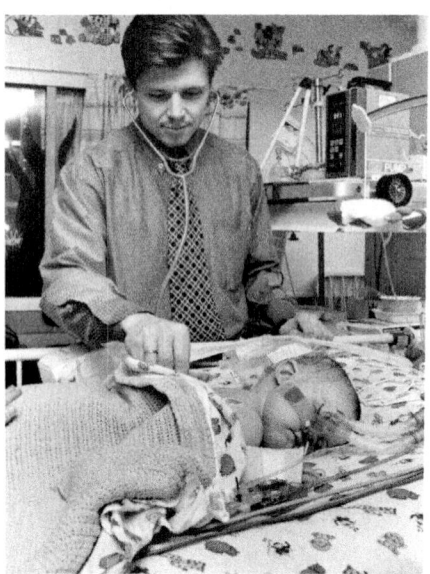

Sergei Vaganov

During the journey in the car back to our house, he was talking excitedly and frequently exclaiming about the houses, cars and people he could see through the car's window. On arrival at our house, he appeared to be impressed but became somewhat subdued.

Nahid had prepared lunch for him, and afterwards I took him up to Hampstead underground station to purchase a travel pass and to a local mobile phone store to obtain a SIM card for his mobile phone.

We had prepared a welcome pack for him containing a telephone list, an underground and bus map, maps of Hampstead and the area around Great Ormond Street Hospital and a small London guidebook. Sergei, and each subsequent Scholar, would receive a similar pack and four weeks' subsistence in £ notes of various denominations. Subsequent scholars' packs would include copies of earlier Scholars' reports and lists of acronyms used in the hospital.

He would be staying with an English family in their house in Holloway, with the hope that they would speak to him and help him practise his English. Later that afternoon we drove him to their house and on the way showed him the closest underground station.

Susan MacQueen had arranged to meet him the following morning, Sunday, take him to GOSH, show him around and then take him out to lunch. On Monday morning he would need to find his own way by Tube train to GOSH where Susan would meet him and take him to the Institute of Child Health for registration.

Sergei was attached as a Clinical Observer to the Department of Anaesthetics and to the paediatric Intensive Care Unit under the watchful eye of distinguished Professor David Hatch. He was able to obtain new insights into the management of severe head injury, use of computers in Intensive Care, local analgesia and epidural pain management.

He told us that he found the biggest initial problem to be understanding the numerous acronyms and abbreviations used in the hospital.

During the tenure of the Scholarship, he attended the Association of Paediatric Anaesthetists' Conference in Birmingham and the annual Conference of the Royal College of Paediatrics and Child Health held that year in York, making many contacts with medical colleagues both in the UK and overseas which would be of inestimable value to his future career. He also visited the Portex factory in Hythe to see the production of respirators and equipment used in his department.

Being farsighted, whilst in the UK he sat and passed the Professional Linguistics Assessment Boards test, PLAB, an essential examination should he wish to apply for temporary registration with the General Medical Council at some future date.

At the end of his Scholarship, he presented a report which highlighted the benefits he had obtained from the Scholarship and the opportunity to inform British doctors about the health care system in Russia.

He also produced a briefing sheet, "Tips for Scholars", which would be very valuable for future Scholars who would be asked to add their own contributions.

Whilst Sergei was in London, Nahid and I arranged to show him many of the sights, entertained him with meals either in our house or in restaurants and introduced him to many English people.

Following his return to Samara, he gave several talks to his professional colleagues about his experiences in the UK.

During the next two years he sent us annual reports regarding his professional and personal life.

*

Reception Russian Embassy

We had discussed with the Russian Ambassador, His Excellency Yuri Fokine, who was shortly to return to Russia, the possibility of holding a reception in his Embassy to celebrate the arrival of our first Diana Memorial Scholar. He kindly agreed to host it jointly with Baroness Cox, and then had to hurry back in a rush to Moscow on the day of the reception.

The Ambassador in his welcoming speech laid aside his manuscript and spoke spontaneously *ot dusha*, "from his spirit", giving a generous endorsement of the Trust and all the work they were doing to support Russian doctors and Russian children.

In her speech, Caroline Cox welcomed Sergei. She spoke of the collaboration between Russian and British colleagues which had led to many exciting initiatives and encouraged mutual learning to enable Western paediatric care practices which might be applicable to the Russian context to be taken back to Russia and developed in ways appropriate to Russian culture and Russian health care systems.

She also thanked our hosts in the Embassy for the delightful reception and this little taste of Russian hospitality. The word "hospitality" reminded her of a definition jokingly once suggested by Archbishop Coggan. *"Hospitality is the art of making someone feel at home when you wish they were at home."*

There was an excellent recital by the Bekova Sisters, Eleonora piano, Elvira violin and Alfia cello, who were born in Kazakhstan and studied at the Moscow Conservatory. They performed Beethoven's "Piano Trio in D major", Rachmaninov's "Elegy", Prokofiev's "March from The Love of Three Oranges" and Stravinsky's

"Russian Dance from Petrushka." A raffle was then drawn by Baroness Cox, with prizes of a "weekend for two in Moscow", donated by Russia House and two seats for *Madame Butterfly* at the Royal Albert Hall, donated by Bente Fasmer.

*

Second Scholarship Selection Board

In May 2000 the joint British-Russian Selection Board awarded three Scholarships. Dr Elena Samoshkina, a fluent English speaker working as a Paediatric Endocrinologist in Saransk, 400 miles southwest of Moscow in the region known as Mordovia; Dr Anastasya Ossipova, married to a dentist with a three-year-old daughter Anna, who worked in Tushinskaya Children's Hospital as a Paediatric Urologist; and Dr Galina Treskina, married to a Sociologist and who was working as a Paediatric Neurologist in Archangel in the far north of Russia on the White Sea.

*

Moscow reunion

Amongst our many friends, from the days we all spent together in the 80s in Moscow, the Military Attachés were the most diligent in maintaining contacts. John and Sam Cheshire had organised a reunion in their lovely house in the village of Batcombe, near Shepton Mallet.

The sun was shining as we sat in their garden chatting away with the thirty or so colleagues, many of whom we had not seen for the last ten years. Egil and his wife Dagmy Torgerson from Norway, with whom we exchanged Christmas cards each year, had joined us. On the way back after visiting Wells Cathedral, we had arranged to meet Tony and Agni Morey, who lived in Sherborne, at a small country inn.

*

Russian Service BBC

Georgina Wilson, with an Alexander Onassis bursary from the Russian service of the BBC, spent six weeks in Moscow informally interviewing staff members in Tushinskaya Hospital.

People's Peers

In 1997, the so-called New Labour Party led by Tony Blair, after 18 years of Conservative government, won the general election by a majority of 179 parliamentary seats. In their manifesto they had included a policy of reforming the unelected House of Lords: *Modernising Parliament: Reforming the House of Lords*.

Three years later, they asked the public to self-nominate or nominate others to be appointed to the House of Lords, to be known as "People's Peers." Those elected would be independent non-party peers: "cross benchers."

A total of 3,164 nominations were received, amongst which was one from Dr Harald Lipman, largely based on his experience in medical practice, political affairs related to work with the Foreign Office and his charitable work. His referees were Baroness Cox, who kindly arranged for him to sit in in the House of Lords for several hours during a debate, Sir David Ratford, Dr Carol Dow, Chief Medical Officer FCO and Dr Michael Nicholls.

At 2.30 p.m. on Tuesday, 10 October 2000, when, as a guest, I sat in the House of Lords, the Notices and Orders of the day, amongst others, related to the Griffiths report reviewing the research framework in the North Staffordshire National Health Service Trust, whether HMG was satisfied that teachers have sufficient powers to deal with disruptive children in the classroom, how many Welsh miners' claims for chest and lung diseases compensation were outstanding and how many secondary schools had changed to the comprehensive system.

Twenty per cent of the nominees to be People's Peers were female, 15 per cent were from ethnic minorities, 15 per cent were disabled and 61 per cent were aged 60 or under. Forty-five per cent lived in Greater London or southeast England.

The Appointments Commission, whose members were Baroness Dean, Chairwoman of the Housing Corporation, Lord Dholakia, Chairman National Association for Care and Rehabilitation of Offenders, Dame Deirdre Hine, President Royal Society of Medicine, Lord Hurd of Westwell, Political Honours Scrutiny Committee, Felicity Huston, Chairwoman Northern Ireland Consumer Committee for Electricity, Angela Sarkis, CEO Church Urban Fund, and the Chairman Lord Stevenson, Chairman of Pearson and Halifax, had formulated criteria for all nominees.

Any UK, Commonwealth or Irish National aged over 21 years could be nominated and must undertake to contribute to the work of the House of Lords.

The Commission was looking for those with an outstanding record of personal success and achievement, independence and integrity and commitment to the highest standards of public life.

Assessment of the nominations would be in five stages, initially based on the supporting documents supplied and checks to ensure that they complied with the Commission's criteria. Then, following a more detailed assessment, a "long list" of nominees for consideration would be agreed. From further assessment of that list, a shortlist of potential recommendations would be made and references taken up. Nominees from the shortlist would be interviewed to discuss the works of the House of Lords and how they might contribute to it.

Eventually, the Prime Minister invited the Commission to put forward 15 people for appointment to the Peerage. *The Times* newspaper, in its edition of 27 April 2001, commented that, "*The great and good dominate the list of People's Peers.*"

These included Victor Adebowale, CEO Centre Point, Richard Best, Director Joseph Rowntree Foundation, Amir Bhatia, co-founder Ethnic Minority Foundation, Sir John Browne, CEO BP Amoco, Professor Michael Chan, Ethnic Health Liverpool University, Sir Paul Condon, Commissioner Metropolitan Police, Professor Ilora Finley, Vice-dean School of Medicine University of Wales, Professor Susan Greenfield, Director Royal Institution of Great Britain, Sir David Hanney, UK Ambassador UN New York, Valerie Howarth, CEO Childline, Lady Howe, Chairwoman Broadcasting Standards Commission, Sir Robert May, President Royal Society, Sir Claus Moser, Chairman Royal Opera House, Sir Herman Ouseley, Chairman Commission for Racial Equality, and Sir Stewart Sutherland, founder of Ofsted.

Peter Riddell stated, "*The cynicism and shallowness of government's thinking on the future of the House of Lords has now been fully exposed.*"

*

The House of Lords is the second chamber of the United Kingdom Parliament. In the 11th century, councils known as the Parliament in the Witans were consulted by Saxon Kings, and by the 13th century attendance included representatives of counties, cities and boroughs. A century later, two distinct houses emerged. One known as the Commons, composed of shire and borough representatives, and the other, the Upper House, consisted of religious leaders, Lords Spiritual and Magnates and Lords Temporal.

Lords Temporal, almost entirely hereditary and male, became known as 'Peers'; that is, equal amongst themselves, but with five ranks – Duke, Marquis, Earl, Viscount and Baron. The Lords Spiritual consisted of Bishops, Abbots and Priors.

In 1968, the then Labour government introduced a Parliamentary Bill which would have created a two-tier House of Lords, in which some of the members could speak and vote and others could speak but not vote, but the bill was held up and abandoned.

In 1999, the rights of most hereditary Peers, numbering in total 742, to sit and vote in the House were removed, but 92 hereditary Peers were permitted to remain.

The function of the House of Lords is to process and revise legislation, to act as a check on the government, provide a forum of independent expertise and to act as a final Court of Appeal.

Chapter 17

Scholars

Skiing St Moritz, Scholars' accommodation, Foot-and-mouth disease, Bella, Mentoring scholars, GOSH reception, World Trade Centre, Selection Board, Fundraiser, White powder

Skiing St Moritz

That year when Nahid and I were skiing in St Moritz, visibility was poor, snow soft and she had a bad fall, bruising her face and chest. The "blood wagon" was called and she was taken down the mountain to a clinic for an X-ray. The rest of the week she was very uncomfortable and sadly couldn't ski again.

*

Scholars

Anastasya, who preferred to be known as Nasya, and Elena arrived in February and settled in well with their host families. In April, Galina arrived and the three of them had a one-month overlap.

Unfortunately, Nasya was knocked down by a cyclist and the Royal Free Hospital telephoned us to tell us that she was in their Casualty department. Fortunately, her injuries weren't serious. So, during the last week of her Scholarship, she was able to attend the European Society of Paediatric Urologists' meeting in Denmark.

During Elena's stay she made a presentation in GOSH about the medical education system, postgraduate training and work routine of Paediatric Endocrinologists in Mordovia.

Galina was very impressed by the role of nurses in the treatment of the children in their care and their attitude towards the children and their parents. She and Elena had the opportunity of attending the Spring meeting of the Royal College of Paediatrics and Child Health in York and made some very useful professional contacts.

*

Foot-and-mouth disease

Foot-and-mouth disease is a specific virus-caused, highly infectious disease, which affects cloven-hoofed animals such as cattle, pigs, sheep and goats. Fortunately, it is very very rarely transmitted to humans.

As there is no effective treatment, the affected animals, and animals which were likely to acquire the infection from them, have to be killed. On this occasion, although there were only 2,000 cases in the UK, 6 million cows and sheep were killed and their bodies buried in quicklime. The total cost to the Exchequer was £8 billion.

In order to limit the spread of the infection, the Cheltenham Festival was cancelled and the general election due to take place at that time was postponed by one month.

*

Bella

In our personal lives, one of the most important events of the year was the birth of Amanda's third child, Isabella, later known to all as Bella. She was very beautiful; she'd inherited her mother's appearance and could have been a Persian Princess. Who would have thought, at that time, that 19 years later she would be co-authoring and editing her grandfather's memoirs, *Memories of Moscow*.

*

Mentoring scholars

As well as giving our Scholars the opportunity of increasing their medical knowledge, and thus ultimately assisting the care of the Russian children who would be their responsibility, we also wished to introduce them to some of the ways of British life and keep a close eye on them whilst in the UK to try to prevent or reduce any problems during their stay and ensure that they enjoyed their Scholarships to the full.

They knew that they could contact us at any time, and we would speak with them at least once a week by phone or contact by email, as well as arranging for them to come to us for a meal either in our house or in a local restaurant. Some of them would prepare a national dish in our kitchen for all of us to enjoy.

Most Scholars made their own arrangements to visit Oxford and Cambridge,

Windsor, Edinburgh and in some instances other cities or regions of the British Isles. Usually, they would arrange to go to at least one musical, and most preferred *The Lion King*. Some arranged to use a gym, and some attended English language classes.

We would take them on visits to Hampton Court, the Wallace collection, the Victoria and Albert Museum, the Royal Academy and other places of interest. Many of them commented that their eyes had been opened to a completely different, previously unknown way of life.

*

GOSH reception

We organised a reception, hosted by Baroness Cox, in the boardroom of Great Ormond Street Hospital to introduce our Scholars and thank the hospital's staff and some of our donors. The Russian Ambassador HE Grigori Karasin and several members of their Embassy staff attended. As is the Russian custom, we never knew who would actually attend until they either came, or didn't come.

*

World Trade Centre

On Tuesday, 11 September 2001, now universally known as 9/11, al-Qaeda, an ultra-orthodox Wahabi Islamist terrorist group, hijacked four American Airlines passenger airliners and crashed two of them into the Twin Towers of the World Trade Centre in New York. Almost three thousand people were killed and approximately six thousand injured.

A third plane was crashed into the Pentagon building, and the fourth crashed into a field in Pennsylvania when a group of passengers attempted to resist the hijackers. This attack has been described as *"the deadliest terrorist attack in human history."* The repercussions of which continue to this day.

US president George Bush declared a "war on terror", and in October 2001 US and UK troops invaded Afghanistan to try to destroy Al Qaeda. In 2011 their leader, Osama bin Laden was eventually found, shot and killed.

*

Selection Board

In May, the Selection Board chaired by Dr Michael Nichollls and accompanied by Dr Olga Crawford travelled out to Moscow again and awarded two Scholarships for the coming year. Dr Anya Turkova, who was a qualified translator of English medical literature and worked as a consultant in Infectious Diseases in Archangel Children's Hospital wrote in her report prior to leaving London, "*My stay in London has enriched me intellectually, culturally and spiritually*."

Whilst he was in the UK, we arranged for Dr Stanislav Nikolsky, a Paediatric Cardiologist from Kazan who was a weightlifter and keen fitness exponent, to visit the British Olympic Medical Centre in Northwick Hospital in Harrow where he discussed creating a screening programme to measure the adverse effects of strenuous physical exercise on the cardiovascular systems in 10 to 18-year-old athletes.

*

At that time, the British board members' visas required a letter of invitation from the Russian Institute of Paediatrics and Children's Surgery, and as this was causing some delays in obtaining them it was proposed that a formal Partnership Agreement should be signed between the Institute and the Trust. Knowing how ponderous, bureaucratic and prolonged legal agreements in Russia would be, we decided in future to travel on visitors' visas. This turned out to be a very satisfactory and much simpler procedure, merely requiring a letter of confirmation of room booking from the hotel, which was obtained by our travel agents, The Russia House.

All British board members were advised to be immunised against poliomyelitis, diphtheria and hepatitis A and to bring with them clean US $ notes issued after 1991, as creased or torn notes would not be accepted by the money exchange bureaus, *obmen valuty*. The exchange rate then was 30 roubles to the US dollar, 50 roubles to the pound.

*

Fundraiser

The Trust engaged a part-time fundraiser, Mark Pargeter, who acted in that capacity for Keston Institute. His stated aim was not "fundraising", but "friend raising."

The Keston Institute, founded by the Reverend Canon Dr Michael Bourdeaux, specialised in the study of all religions in Communist and former Communist countries.

*

White powder

Following the attack on the Twin Towers, letters and parcels containing a "white powder", were sent from unkown sources. In a few instances this apparently was anthrax, but in most cases it contained no harmful ingredients and had been sent as a stupid hoax.

There were numerous episodes in the United States and in the UK of individuals from all walks of life receiving such letters.

Nevertheless, the UK authorities correctly alerted the general population to the potential risk and circulated advice on how suspicious letters should be dealt with.

I was sitting in my office in the Old Admiralty Building one afternoon when the telephone rang. At the other end of the line there was a very anxious voice speaking from an office in a different part of the building, saying that they had just received a suspect letter and requesting advice as to how to deal with it.

I immediately told them not to handle or open it, to thoroughly wash their hands and I would alert the security services who would come over to their room and deal with it in a secure manner. In fact, it turned out not to be anthrax, but a hoax.

Chapter 18

Balkan visits

Bratislava, Scholarships, David Ratford, House of Lords, Belgrade / Tirana / Sarajevo / Pristina / Skopje / Zagreb, My Fair Lady, Scholars' arrival, St Helena

Bratislava

The first week of December, I visited Bratislava again. I had been due to visit Prague as well, but for operational reasons that had been postponed.

It was snowing in Bratislava, and in the main square they held their annual Christmas bazaar, with stalls selling wooden toys, local food, mulled wine and Slovak glass, with traditional music playing in the background. A truly joyous event.

I was consulted by several patients, visited a children's hospital and several clinics and was invited in the evening to the Opera to see Verdi's *Luisa Miller* based on Schiller's *Kabale und Liebe*, "Intrigue and Love", sung by some excellent voices.

All in all, a most enjoyable way to start Christmas. I had really grown quite fond of Bratislava.

*

Scholarships

During the next 16 years, the Trust granted a further 49 Scholarships to young Paediatricians from Russia and Kazakhstan.

Scholars came from many parts of the Russian Federation and Kazakhstan including Archangel, Samara, Moscow, Kazan, Saransk, Ufa, Ekaterinburg, Xabarovsk, Nizhny Novgorod, Vladikavkaz, Ulan Ude, Kemerovo, St Petersburg, Almaty, Ust-Kamenogorosk and Astana.

They had interests in and practised in a great variety of medical disciplines – Paediatric Intensive Care, Endocrinology, Urology, Infectious Diseases, Cardiology, Neurology, Onco-haematology, Nephrology, Gastro-enterology, General Surgery, Radiology, Endoscopy, ENT, Neonatology and Cardiac Surgery.

*

Dr Larissa Prikhodina, a Nephrologist from Moscow, married with an eleven-year old son, stayed in Rosie Oxley's small house on the edge of Hampstead Heath. Rosie annually arranged concerts in St Stephens, a former church building in Hampstead.

Larissa had compiled lists of the approximately eighty acronyms used generally in the hospital, and a separate list which was specific to the Urology department. From then on copies of these lists were included in each Scholar's welcome pack. On her return to Russia, she was very successful in her career, and later was awarded a Professorial Chair.

*

The Trust's Russian partners had been Professor Larisa Baleva, until she retired, then the Institute of Paediatrics and Childrens' Surgery, Moscow, and by this time Professor Ismail Osmanov, Director Tushinskaya Childrens' Hospital, Moscow.

The British partners consisted of representatives from the Trust and from Great Ormond Street Hospital, London. When Bob Dinwiddie retired, he was succeeded by Dr Quen Mok, Head of the Paediatric and Neonatal Intensive Care Unit GOSH, the largest Paediatric Intensive Care Unit in the UK.

*

David Ratford

David Ratford, after 15 years as Chairman of the Trust, regretfully stood down in 2011. His tenure had seen the establishment of the Diana, Princess of Wales Tushinskaya Memorial Scholarships and the commencement of the Raisa Gorbachev Foundation Scholarships. His wise judgement, tact, eloquence, knowledge of Russia, the language and the people, and epistolary skills would be sorely missed. He graciously agreed to be an honorary Vice President of the Trust.

Quen Mok and Susan MacQueen had become Trustees of the Trust, in addition to Michael Nicholls and myself. Nahid remained Honorary Secretary.

It was agreed that the Trust should not search for a successor as Chairman until the future of the Trust was clearer, and meanwhile Harald Lipman was invited to act as Chairman. In fact, he remains in that position today.

*

House of Lords lunch

Baroness Cox invited the scholars, Nahid and I, Sir Cyril Chantler, a Paediatric Urologist who was the Chairman of GOSH, and Dr Bob Dinwiddie to an excellent, enjoyable lunch in the House of Lords.

*

Belgrade/Tirana

In January I flew Alitalia to Belgrade. On arrival at the Hyatt Hotel I found that no room had been booked for me.

The following morning, after a visit to the Embassy to see some patients, I was taken to view the Care Centre for Serbia, National Blood Transfusion Centre and the Zeptar Dental Clinic.

Next day, I saw some more patients in the Embassy, visited the Orthopaedic hospital and another couple of clinics. Following a "wash-up" with the Ambassador Charles Crawford, I was very kindly invited to a supper party in the residency.

On checking out of the hotel next morning, I discovered that the hotel had not received notice from the Embassy confirming their responsibility for settling the account. A phone call to the Embassy resolved the problem.

A JAT Boeing flew me to Zurich where I collected my baggage, passed some time in the Swissair lounge, and then boarded an Avro 87 for the two-hour flight to Tirana in Albania. Since my previous visit, Tirana Airport had improved considerably. On this occasion no one grabbed my suitcase and ran off with it.

An Embassy car took me to the Hotel Rogner and then to the Embassy where I was supping with the Ambassador David Landsman and his wife Catherine.

After seeing some patients in the Embassy the following day, I visited the Military hospital, where after a 45-minute wait there was still no sign of the Director. Most unusual for military personnel to be so inefficient. Then to the ABC clinic, where I met the American Regional Psychiatrist who was visiting it. My final port of call was the Mother Teresa Hospital, which was very rundown.

Visits the next day included the Maternity and Gynaecological hospital, the Marie Stopes clinic, and most interestingly, the enormous "waste dump" in the city suburbs – a quite incredible sight.

My return flight involved an Albanian Airways Tupolev 134 to Rome, where there was a long delay collecting baggage and passing security, and finally a BA Airbus back to Heathrow.

*

Ski Club of Great Britain

A week after my return, Nahid and I flew off, with the Ski Club of Great Britain, SKGB, to Zell am See in Austria. It was our first experience of skiing with a group of people.

The snow was good, the hotel comfortable and our companions pleasant. One of them, an elderly lady who still skied very elegantly, regaled us with tales of taking a train up the mountain, as in those days there were no ski lifts, skiing down unmarked pistes, turning with the now old-fashioned telemark technique and then tying fur skins to their skis and trudging on foot up the lower slopes.

*

Telemark

Telemark skiing is a technique that combines both alpine and Nordic skiing elements. Telemark skiers are often known as "free-heelers."

The boots used are clicked into toe bindings that leave the heels free. The free heel gives it the appearance of cross-country skiing, but it also has a look of alpine skiing in the downhill phase, even though the style used is completely different.

As opposed to alpine skiers, telemark skiers will bend their knees every time they have to turn. The heel is attached to the front of the binding by a hinged cable.

*

Sarajevo/ Pristina/Skopje/Zagreb

A month later, I was due to visit Sarajevo, Pristina, Skopje and Zagreb. This would entail several journeys by air as there were no direct flights between some of the cities.

The first leg was relatively simple. An Austrian Airlines Airbus from Heathrow to Vienna, and following 30 minutes' wait, an Austrian Airline's flight to Sarajevo. There I was met by an Embassy car and driver and taken to the comfortable Holiday Inn.

I visited Kosovo Hospital, the VIP clinic and an Obstetric unit before I saw several patients from the Embassy. Next day, I visited the Epidemiological

Institute, with its very well-equipped laboratory, and had supper in the residency with HMA, Ian Cliff, where I met two local Paediatricians.

The following day, the fun started. I had an early flight, so left the hotel before breakfast and checked my baggage at the airport with Croatian Air through to Vienna. We stopped in Zagreb where there was a 40-minute transit wait, and then I took another Croatian Air flight in a different plane to Vienna.

On arrival in Vienna there was no sign on the carousel of my baggage, and on inquiry I discovered that it had not been loaded on at Sarajevo. Meanwhile, I had missed the flight to Pristina. Many of you I am sure have experienced similar troublesome situations. I can assure it doesn't get any easier to resolve, even if you have had to deal with similar events in the past.

I checked in to the airport hotel, rebooked the flight to Pristina for the following day and phoned the Embassy in Pristina to inform them that I had been delayed. Eventually, my baggage was delivered to the hotel.

The next morning, I caught an Austrian Airlines Airbus to Pristina, approximately a two-hour flight. As we were landing at the airport, there were very strong crosswinds, and after a couple of attempts, the landing was aborted and the plane returned to Vienna.

I decided to cancel my visit to Pristina and booked a flight for the following morning to Skopje in Macedonia. That evening, I attended a piano recital in the Konzerthaus, in Vienna, with the Russian pianist Mikhail Pletnev giving a masterly performance of Beethoven and Tchaikovsky pieces.

Next day, Austrian Air flew me down to Skopje where I was met and taken to the residency where I would be staying. Lo and behold, the Ambassador and his wife were George and Yelena Edgar, who I had last met in Moscow in 1983. They now had two small daughters, Anna and Katerina.

It was the weekend and they took me to the City Museum, some of the local shops and then to an excellent supper in a fish restaurant.

Skopje, the capital of Macedonia, situated on the banks of the Vardra river, was part of the Ottoman Empire and then of the Kingdom of Serbia, and subsequently formed part of the Yugoslavian republic. It became independent in 1991. A major earthquake had destroyed large parts of the city in 1963, but many of the buildings had been reconstructed.

The languages spoken there are Macedonian – a south Slavic language – and Albanian, an Indo-European language.

The religion practised is now largely Christian Orthodox, and I visited the St Panteleimon Monastery, with its beautiful frescoes.

Everybody in the small Embassy seemed remarkably healthy. I visited the Trauma and Paediatric units in the State hospital, the City Surgical hospital, the City Maternity hospital and the Military hospital. Later, I gave a short talk to the Embassy staff about HIV.

*

A very early departure for the Croatian Airlines flight to Zagreb, where I just managed to avert my luggage being sent on to London. On arrival in Zagreb, an Embassy car took me to the Sheraton Hotel, having en route visited a mother and newborn baby, one of the Embassy staff, in the Petrova Maternity hospital.

There were no major medical problems that required my attention.

Two of the Embassy staff took me to visit the Children's hospital and the University Saluta hospital. In the evening, I accompanied them to a fish restaurant in Ban Jelacic Square, the lovely main square with its fountain, surrounded by houses with antique facades.

After breakfast, I checked out of the hotel and was driven to the Embassy to meet the Ambassador, Nicolas Jarrold, and the Management Officer. A Croatian Airlines Airbus flew me back to London and, somewhat surprisingly, on arrival on the carousel there was my suitcase.

*

My Fair Lady

Trevor Nunn's excellent production of *My Fair Lady*, the musical based on Shaw's *Pygmalion*, was presented in The Theatre Royal, Drury Lane, with Alex Jennings in the role of Professor Higgins and Joanna Riding playing Eliza. A most enjoyable evening.

*

Scholars' arrival

It had been our custom to meet Scholars on arrival at Heathrow Airport, but when Irina Belousova, a Urologist from Moscow, was due to arrive, Nahid and I had prior commitments and so arranged for a car and driver to meet her.

We advised her to pass through immigration and customs, and when she entered the main hall where passengers are met, to look for a man holding a board with her name on it. All went smoothly, and the driver brought her to our house.

After supper, we took her to Sana Short's house in Hampstead, where she would be staying. In light of this very successful procedure, as driving out and back to Heathrow was very time consuming, we decided that all future scholars would be met by a car and driver.

In her final report she wrote in both English and Russian, *"I am grateful to all members of Tushinskaya Trust who organised this unique scholarship for all their advice and help."*

*

St Helena

Back in my office the telephone rang, and I was advised that the Governor of St Helena wished to speak with me.

St Helena, a British Overseas Territory, was a small windswept volcanic rocky island set in the South Atlantic 2,000 km, 1,200 miles, west of the southwest African coast, with a total population of about 3,000 people. It had no airfield and depended both for access and supplies of all necessities, including food and medication, on the safe arrival from Cape Town of the passenger cargo ship RMS *St Helena*, which visited three times a year. It was a five-day journey.

In 1815, Napoleon, following the French defeat at the Battle of Waterloo, had initially been exiled to the island of Elba, from which he had escaped. On his recapture, he had been exiled by the British to St Helena, where he died six years later at the age of 51, from a possible cancer of the stomach.

The Governor, when he spoke to me, sounded very tired and anxious, and he was speaking with a tremulous voice. He felt very isolated and lonely, was sleeping badly and was having vivid frightening dreams.

I managed to establish a rapport with him, counselled him and suggested some practical measures he could take to help allay his fears. I arranged to speak with him again by phone after a couple of days, and continued to counsel him over the course of the next two to three weeks.

Meanwhile, I arranged that a doctor from Cape Town would travel out on the next scheduled visit by RSM *St Helena*, to accompany him back to South Africa.

Fortunately, the Governor managed to cope reasonably well until he arrived safely in Cape Town.

Chapter 19

Politics and war

Khodorokovsky, Politovskaya, Litvinenko, Nemtsov, Belgrade, Pristina, Tirana, Kosovo, Curate's egg, Moscow theatre hostages, Linguistics, SARS

Khodorokovsky, Politovskaya

All was not well in Russia, and activists from several fields of life were being suppressed.

In 2003 Mikhail Khodorokovsky, an oligarch who owned Yukos oilfields, was arrested and charged with fraud and money laundering. He was at that time imprisoned and finally pardoned in 2013.

A Russian journalist and human rights activist, Anna Politovskaya, was assassinated in 2006.

*

Litvinenko

Aleksandr Litvinenko was an FSB officer who had disagreed with some of the Russian government policies and defected to the UK in 2000.

Inessa Ray, who acted as our interpreter, at that time assisting Vanessa Redgrave, was introduced to him, and he became one of her English language students.

In 2006 he was admitted to a London hospital, seriously ill, and eventually was found to have been poisoned with radioactive polonium-210, which apparently had been administered by FSB operatives. This unprovoked attack, on British soil, on an individual granted asylum, led to a significant worsening in British–Russian relationships.

*

Nemtsov

Boris Nemtsov, a physicist and liberal politician who had previously been the governor of Nizhny Novgorod, was assassinated in a Moscow street in 2015.

*

Belgrade, Pristina, Tirana

I was due to make my last visit to the former Yugoslavia, and fully intended to reach Pristina, the capital of Kosovo, on this trip. To ensure that I actually got there on this occasion, I would travel overland from Belgrade.

An uneventful flight to Belgrade, via Vienna, with Austrian Airlines and I found myself back in the Hyatt Hotel. My routine there was not dissimilar to that on previous visits.

Several consultations, visits to hospitals and clinics and the Public Health Institute, whilst members of the Embassy staff looked after my social programme.

*

Kosovo

Kosovo was part of the Ottoman Empire from the 15th century until the First World War. A pyrrhic victory in the Battle of Kosovo at the end of the 14th century, when the onward advance of the Ottoman Empire was stopped, still lived in Serbian memory.

Kosovo had a large Albanian population, and in the 1990s formed the Kosovo Liberation Army, which in an attempt to gain independence rebelled against the Serbs. NATO, without UN approval, intervened, and commenced an aerial bombardment of Serbia, during which the Chinese Embassy in Belgrade was damaged.

Russia, an ally of the Slavic Serbs, sent troops to Kosovo, and occupied the Pristina airport. Eventually Russian and Finnish negotiators successfully cobbled together an agreement, and the Serbs withdrew. In the year 2000 the Serbian president, Slobodan Milosevic, resigned. In 2008 Kosovo declared its independence, which was recognised by the United States and the EU, but not by the UN Security Council.

*

Pristina

Sadly in 1947 the slogan of the Communist Yugoslav regime was "destroy the old, build the new", and now few Ottoman buildings survive in the city of Pristina.

*

An early start, and a three-and-a-half-hour drive in an Embassy car on a rather bumpy road on a hot, misty morning, and eventually I arrived at the border with Kosovo. The border posts were all sandbagged, and the border guards carried machine guns.

I was met in Pristina, the capital of Kosovo, by a British Army officer who took me to lunch and then on a visit to the University Hospital, a rundown building which was undergoing reconstruction. The hospital Director showed me their ambitious 10-year development plan.

Having visited the Embassy, I was taken to the Hotel Baci, where I would be staying, and my luggage on arrival was locked in a room. Eventually, with some difficulty, I managed to retrieve it.

I spent next morning with Lieutenant-Colonel Jeremy Owen of BRITFOR, who showed me their barracks, a primary health centre and took me to lunch in the barracks. Traffic was very heavy on the roads and many of the vehicles bore NATO logos.

A visit by Jeep had been arranged for me to the vast Camp Bondsteel, the US headquarters, situated 30 km outside Pristina. I was shown round the quite remarkable modern, excellently equipped hospital and many of the facilities such as the PX store, which resembled a large supermarket. Close by, parked on the airfield, one could see the latest models of military aircraft.

Before departing for the airport for my flight to Tirana I was taken to view the 14th-century Serbian Orthodox Gracanica Monastery.

The small airport was a madhouse. There were no obvious check-in desks, crowds of people milling around, and from time to time there were announcements over the loudspeakers which were impossible to comprehend. After sitting there for three hours, I eventually discovered that the flight had already departed.

I took a taxi back to Baci Hotel and checked in for the night. After several complicated telephone calls to our Embassies in Pristina and Tirana, to the Foreign Office in London and to Nahid, I had supper in the hotel.

I arranged to catch an Albanian Airlines flight to Tirana the following morning, and rather surprisingly I had quite a reasonable night's sleep. The embassy driver stayed with me at the airport until the half-hour flight was called, and on arrival at Tirana I was met and taken to the Hotel Rogner.

I saw some patients and was then driven in a tropical downpour to the rundown Military hospital, and then to the Greek Orthodox clinic which was run by an American Medical Missionary, Doctor Charles Lindeman. Later I visited the Mother Teresa Hospital, which was good in parts like the proverbial curate's egg, but was very short of medication.

*

Curate's egg

The term "good in parts" derives from a cartoon published in the humorous British magazine Punch on 9 November 1895. Drawn by George du Maurier and titled "True Humility", it pictures a timid-looking curate eating breakfast in his Bishop's house. The Bishop says: *"I'm afraid you've got a bad egg, Mr Jones."* The curate, desperate not to offend his eminent host and ultimate employer, replies: *"Oh no, my Lord, I assure you that parts of it are excellent!"*

*

The following day was Nahid's birthday, and when I arrived at Heathrow, I found that no taxi was waiting for me, so, at considerable expense, I took a taxi from the taxi rank. When I arrived home, I found that poor Nahid had driven all the way to the airport, missed me, and then driven back home through the traffic. Fortunately, during my stopover from Tirana in Vienna, I had bought her a birthday present.

*

A few days after my return, we flew down to Brantome in the Dordogne with our friend Liz, stayed in a château and had a most enjoyable and relaxing week painting.

*

Moscow theatre hostages

Approximately fifty Chechen rebels attacked the Moscow Dubrovka theatre during a performance of the musical *Nord Ost* and took several hundred hostages. They demanded that Russia withdraw its troops from Chechnya.

Following the killing of two hostages, Russian special forces introduced a narcotic gas into the theatre auditorium and then entered the theatre via the roof and underground sewers. Most of the Chechen guerrillas and 120 hostages in the audience were killed in the attack.

*

Linguistics

I had several other interests, quite apart from medicine and acting as an honorary "benevolent lepidopterist."

Language had always fascinated me. Now, as I was reducing some of my medical commitments, I decided to study Linguistics.

There are five main parts of linguistics: the study of sounds – phonology – the study of parts of words, like "un-" and "-ing" – morphology – the study of word order and how sentences are made – syntax – the study of the meaning of words – semantics – and the study of the unspoken meaning of speech that is separate from the literal meaning of what is said – pragmatics; for example, if you were to say "*I'm cold*" when what you actually want is someone to turn off the fan.

I contacted my alma mater, UCL, and met with Professor Neil Smith, head of the Department of Phonetics and Linguistics. They offered an intensive one-year conversion course for an MA in Linguistics which was suitable both for those with some prior knowledge of the subject and for appropriately motivated beginners. On a part-time basis it could be pursued over two Academic years. I opted for the part-time course, as I was still working part-time with the Foreign Office.

It was pleasing to discover that the department was located in a house in Gordon Square, backing on to the grounds of UCL. The first nursery school I had attended, Gordon Hall School, over sixty-five years previously, had been based in the next-door house. The wheel had truly come full circle.

I found the course quite hard going, as I had not studied intensively for many years. I was again sitting in the lecture theatre with twenty or so knowledgeable students, most of whom had a BA in linguistics and were about fifty years younger than I was, though I found they were very considerate and great fun. It was pleasing to see how wrong one's stereotyped view of 21st-century students was.

*

SARS

An outbreak of Severe Acute Respiratory Syndrome, SARS, caused by a previously unrecognised coronavirus, and probably spread from bats to civet cats and then to human beings, had been diagnosed in China. This caused severe flu-like symptoms, and by human-to-human transmission spread to 26 other countries, largely due to the absence of adequate infection control precautions such as frequent hand washing.

Eventually, 8,000 people worldwide were infected, and approximately 10 per cent of these died. All people arriving by air from affected regions were screened and isolated, and fortunately after about eight months the threatened pandemic ceased.

There were four cases of SARS in the UK, and the sufferers all survived. In Russia only one case was reported.

Some Russian, and later Chinese, scientists speculated that the virus was probably man-made in the United States to be used as a biological weapon. No evidence has ever been found to corroborate this theory.

The risks of further similar pandemics in the future remained high as has been evidenced by the recent outbreak of Covid-19.

Chapter 20

A dreadful year

Marrakech, Midnight's Children, Iraq war, Amanda, Abramovich, Skiing Ortisei, Dalai Lama, Scholars' reunion, Yasnaya Polyana, Selection Board Cosmos, Stent, Master & Margarita, Olga visit, History Boys

Marrakech

We had for many years wished to visit the Magreb, the name the Arab countries Algeria, Tunisia, Morocco and Libya in northwest Africa are known by. *Magreb* in Arabic means "the West."

The Mediterranean coast became known as the "Barbary coast", named after the indigenous inhabitants of Morocco, the Berbers, known as Moors.

In January 2003 we made a short visit to Morocco, flying to Casablanca, the capital, shades of Humphrey Bogart and Ingrid Bergman in the 1942 memorable romantic drama film, *Casablanca,* and then by car to the old capital, Marrakech.

It had colourful souks – markets selling spices, leather goods, fruit and vegetables, carpets, jewellery and many other items – and quiet courtyards and the snaking alleyways of the historic Medina, surrounded by ramparts.

We saw wonderful Moorish mosques, palaces and gardens and small palaces, known as *riads*, made from rammed earth.

One evening we ate supper in the restaurant in Hotel Mamounia, a renowned hotel. Winston Churchill on several occasions wintered there, painting his watercolours; Chaplin, Mastroianni, Coppola, Roosevelt and de Gaulle, amongst many other famous guests, had also stayed there.

Travelling in a four-wheeled drive, with a couple of New Zealand young women and a guide, we visited a Berber village with ochre-coloured soil in the Ourika Valley in the lower foothills of the Atlas mountains.

*

Midnight's Children

The RSC's production of Salman Rushdie's novel depicting the story of two children born on the date of the Indian subcontinent's division into India and Pakistan was showing in the Barbican Theatre.

Midnight's Children, the play, starts with video footage of Nehru's historic speech, delivered in 1947, projected on a screen that serves as the backdrop of the stage.

"Long years ago we made a tryst with destiny, and now the time comes when we shall redeem our pledge, not wholly or in full measure, but very substantially. At the stroke of midnight hour, when the world sleeps, India will awake to life and freedom."

On stage, there were two beds, two women in labour, two children born at the stroke of midnight: Saleem and Shiva, the most gifted of Midnight's Children.

In the foreground, Saleem Sinai, squatting on the floor, starts to tell us his story as plump, muscular Padma sits next to him and listens. The neon lights of Braganza pickle factory are suspended over the stage.

A most impressive version of the story.

*

Iraq war

Internationally, 2003 was a bad year for the world.

Unsubstantiated claims had been made that Iraq possessed weapons of mass destruction (WMD) and the US and UK drafted a UN resolution that Saddam Hussein comply with disarmament obligations.

In the UN Security Council, France and Russia vetoed the resolution.

The Iraq War was a protracted armed conflict, lasting from 2003 to 2011, that began with the invasion of Iraq by the United States-led coalition which quite rapidly overthrew the Iraqi government of Saddam Hussein.

The war began on 20 March 2003, when the US, joined by the UK, Australia and Poland, launched a "shock-and-awe" bombing campaign. Iraqi forces were quickly overwhelmed as coalition forces swept through the country. The invasion led to the collapse of the Ba'athist government. Five weeks later, the American President George Bush announced, "mission completed."

The rationale for the invasion was based on claims that Iraq had weapons of mass destruction and posed a threat to the United States and its allies. No stockpiles of WMDs or an active WMD programme were ever found in Iraq. Kofi Annan, then the UN Secretary-General, called the invasion illegal under international law, as it violated the UN Charter.

A DREADFUL YEAR

*

Amanda

For us personally, 2003 was a dreadful year. We were visiting LA, and on returning to our hotel, following a performance by comedian Jackie Mason, Amanda rang. She informed us that she had discovered a lump in her breast, probably a cancer. The date, Wednesday 11 June, is engraved on our hearts.

This was the start of her sadly unsuccessful, courageous eight-year struggle to control and defeat it.

*

Roman Abramovich

Roman Abramovich, the owner of Chelsea Football Club, was for eight years the Governor of the autonomous *Okrug*, "district", Chukotka. It is situated in the far east region of Siberia along the Bering Strait with a population of 50,000, and its income is derived from reindeer herding. The Governor poured money into it. He built schools, hospitals, roads and houses, and developed gold and coal mine industries.

He also arranged with the Russian Institute of Paediatrics and Child Surgery that medical teams be sent out three or four times a year from Moscow.

One of our Scholars, Alexei Krapivkin, a Neurologist by training, was a member of one of these teams. Six weeks into his Scholarship he received an urgent command from Moscow to return immediately as he was required to visit Chukotka. Neither he nor the Trust had any choice, so he departed and missed the benefits of half of the scholarship.

*

Skiing Ortisei

In early April we all, including Amanda, who celebrated her birthday there, skied together in Ortisei in the Dolomites and had a most enjoyable time. Hugh had been unable to join us as his mother was ill, and sadly she died whilst we were away.

*

Dalai Lama

I met His Holiness the Dalai Lama on two occasions whilst he was visiting London.

The Dalai Lama

In 2004, in the presence of Prince Charles, the Dalai Lama was due to speak at the L M Singhui-Temonos Interfaith Lecture to be held in the Central Hall Westminster.

Shortly before the event, I was informed that His Holiness was unwell. He consulted me and the problem was treated appropriately.

The next occasion when I was fortunate to meet him again was in 2013 in St Paul's Cathedral, where he was presented with the Templeton Prize. During his speech he warned against feeling helpless and hopeless.

In front of the High Altar, eight Tibetan Buddhist monks, in their maroon shirt and skirt robes, were chanting Tibetan Buddhist mantras.

Heinrich Harrer in his 1952 memoirs *Seven Years in Tibet* related his experiences in Tibet from 1944 to 1951, when he became one of the young 14th Dalai Lama's tutors.

*

The first Dalai Lama, spiritual leader of Tibetan Buddhists, lived in the 14th century AD. The present incumbent is Tenzin Gyatso, the 14th, and possibly the last. Following China's annexation of Tibet, he escaped over the mountains to India and now lives in Dharamsala.

Following the death of a Dalai Lama, his soul transmigrates to another young child's body and often, after he has been located, is only recognised several years later, when he has satisfied numerous criteria.

Scholars' reunion

The Trust had decided to hold reunions for past Scholars every four years to coincide with the Selection Board meeting in Moscow to select new Scholars for the following year.

At Heathrow we met with David, Michael, Bob, Louise, Susan and John, Sandra, Inessa and, as usual, Olga arrived late. BA flew us to Domodedovo Airport in Moscow, where we stayed in Hotel Budapest close to the Bolshoi.

We had arranged to see Tchaikovsky's ballet *Sleeping Beauty*, which was a patchy performance, but good on the whole.

Larisa Baleva had arranged for us to visit the Institute of Paediatrics and Children's Surgery where we had useful discussions with the Director, Professor Alexander Tsaregorodtsev and his deputy, Ismail Osmanov who, following Larisa's retirement a few years later, would succeed her as our Russian partners.

In the evening, following the Selection Board where we had chosen two Scholars, our Ambassador Sir Roderic and Lady Mandy Lyne had invited us all to a sumptuous reception in the residency. They were wonderful welcoming hosts, mixing freely with the fifty or so guests.

*

Yasnaya Polyana

We had last visited Yasnaya Polyana, Tolstoy's estate, in 1990, with our friends Michael and Pam, when they were visiting us in Moscow.

Some fifteen years later, in 2004, we revisited Yasnaya Polyana for the first reunion of our Diana Memorial Scholars.

Our Russian partner, Professor Larisa Baleva, a Paediatric Endocrinologist, had arranged with a friend of hers for us to take all the past Scholars and members of the Tushinskaya Trust Committee to stay overnight in a sanatorium which her friend ran in the estate grounds. Young children suffering from thyroid problems caused by their mothers' exposure to radioactive dust released during the Chernobyl disaster in 1986 were lodged there.

We had arranged a coach to bring us all from Moscow. After lunch, we held a meeting of the Scholars where they told us about their activities, professional and social, since returning to Russia after their three-month Scholarships as Clinical Observers in Great Ormond Street Hospital.

In the evening, we had a dinner that Larisa's friend had arranged in a local restaurant where several of the sanatorium staff joined us, and everyone ate and drank too much and sang and danced the night away.

We slept soundly and were woken early by the knocking on our bedroom doors by the young children who wished to greet us with their few words of English. *"Good morning. What is your name?"* A truly lovely and unforgettable experience.

Next on our agenda was a visit to Tolstoy's mansion and the armoury in Tula. We discovered, by chance, that the coach company had forgotten to register our booking to return to Moscow, and this required a few phone calls before we managed to sort the problem out.

In later chapters, you will be able to read in greater detail the full story of Tushinskaya Trust.

*

Selection Board Cosmos

An interesting event happened whilst I was staying in the Cosmos Hotel.

Following Larisa Baleva's retirement, the date for the Scholarship Selection Board had been moved to October to coincide with the National Paediatric Congress which was held annually in Moscow.

Although for us climatically it wasn't the best time of year to go there, it was very helpful for the Scholarship applicants as they could coincide attendance at both the Congress and the Selection Board. Thus, they didn't have to request special permission to attend the Board and would be remunerated for their travel and accommodation expenses in Moscow.

I went down to breakfast, and on my return to my room I couldn't find my mobile phone. I called the hotel security and three burly men tapped on the door and I invited them in.

When I explained that my phone was missing, they suggested that perhaps I had dropped it somewhere. One of them went over to the wardrobe, and I could hear him say "Here it is", or the Russian equivalent, *Vot*, as he emerged with the phone in his hand. He said he had found it in the pocket of my jacket. I knew that it hadn't been there, as earlier I had thoroughly searched everywhere myself.

Times obviously hadn't changed; someone had taken the phone from my room whilst I was having breakfast, presumably in order to copy the names and contact numbers of the people in my address book.

All our past Scholars were attending the Congress and we had the pleasure of seeing them again and the opportunity of catching up on all their news.

Irina Belousova, a Urologist from Moscow, had written in her final Scholarship report, which she had presented in both English and Russian, "*I am grateful to all members of Tushinskaya Trust, who organised this unique scholarship, for all their advice and help.*"

*

That year marked the 75th anniversary of the founding of the Paediatric Institute, and David, in his most eloquent Russian, gave a short speech congratulating them and explaining the purpose of our Scholarships. When he was first invited to speak, we had understood that this would be at the opening plenary session; however, the powers that be decided that only Russians associated with the Institute could participate in the opening session, and David was invited to speak at the closing session. As commonly happens at conferences, by the last day most people have drifted away and, sadly, he delivered his elegant speech to only a handful of people.

*

Stent

I had developed some chest discomfort, initially thought to be due to acid reflux, but it was subsequently diagnosed as related to my heart and I had a stent inserted into one of the blood vessels supplying blood to the heart muscle. This has stood me in good stead for the last 20 years.

*

Master & Margarita

In September we drove down to Chichester to see Edward Kemp's innovative adaptation of Bulgakov's *Master & Margarita*, portraying the master as a flawed seeker after truth. We had last seen a very different version of the play in Moscow in 1989.

*

Olga visit

Olga Dmitrieva came to visit and stay with us in London for a couple of weeks shortly after we had moved back to our Hampstead house; Marc then moved into our flat in Hampstead.

She told us that sadly she no longer worked with the Embassy, as a staff member had revealed that she was employed by the Russian authorities, implying that she was engaged in spying upon us. This of course was not a new revelation, as everybody knew that all the Russian staff employed in the Embassy had dual functions, one of which was to obtain information when possible and report back across the river to the Kremlin.

*

History Boys

On New Year's Eve we saw Nicolas Hytner's production of Alan Bennett's *History Boys* staged in the National Theatre. The play takes place in a northern grammar school in the Thatcherite 80s and presents the arguments between beleaguered humanism and pragmatic functionalism, presented in Bennett's typically humorous style.

Chapter 21

ICHARM

London bombing, Abortive 1905 revolution, Stethoscope, Heart disease in Russia, Moscow Selection Board, Ken Lovett, Amanda, Hugh and children, Hermitage Foundation, St Dorothy's hostel, The Government Inspector, UCHMS 50th reunion, Atheneum, FCO

London bombing

On 7 July 2005, four suicide bombers, adherents of al-Qaeda, with rucksacks full of explosives, attacked central London, killing 52 people and injuring hundreds more. It was the worst single terrorist atrocity on British soil. Three bombs exploded on the underground at Aldgate, Edgware Road and Russell Square. A fourth bomb partially destroyed a London bus outside BMA house in Tavistock Square.

*

Abortive 1905 revolution

The year 1905 was a momentous year for Tsarist Russia and my mother's family. Russia had been soundly defeated in the Russo-Japanese war, Tsar Nicolas II had been forced to create the Duma, the Russian Parliament, and grant the introduction of a Russian constitution.

Due to failed state-level leadership and policy, inflation, poverty, hunger, the rise of reformist and revolutionary groups and the Bloody Sunday massacre of demonstrators, workers and peasants revolted and the punitive Imperial Russian Army executed and deported many thousands of people.

My mother's family lived in the town of Orel, 230 miles southwest of Moscow, situated in the Pale. Her father was a master stonemason who, although Jewish, specialised in restoring Orthodox churches and must have been a relatively well-off man.

Those of you who have seen the musical show or film *Fiddler on the Roof*, based on a story *Tevye and his Daughters*, written by Sholem Aleichem, will have some idea of life in the Pale of Settlement of Imperial Russia in or around 1905.

The Pale of Jewish Settlement was created in the late 18th century, encompassed parts of modern-day Lithuania, Poland, Moldova, Ukraine and Belarus, and stretched from the Baltic to the Black Sea. It is estimated that 4 million Jewish people lived there.

They suffered increasing state persecution, *pogroms*, which worsened in severity after the abortive 1905 revolution, and many including my mother's family decided to emigrate.

With considerable difficulty, and, doubtless, after expenditure of a considerable sum of money, in 1907 they managed to obtain a Russian passport which would permit them to travel abroad, although not in their own family name.

They probably travelled by train to the port of Odessa on the Black Sea coast and there embarked with many other emigrants on a steamship which would take them to America.

En route, the ship stopped in the port of Glasgow to restock and refuel, and all the emigrants, doubtless tired and confused, thinking they had arrived in America, disembarked.

Speaking no English, they were directed to immigration where the officials, being unable to understand their names or family relationships, arbitrarily named them. For example, in one case the Scottish official on hearing a name he could not understand was reported to have said *"that's a faine name"*, and his document was completed in the name of Faine. My mother's family for reasons unknown to me were called Caplan, although their Russian passport showed the family name as Stool.

My mother, then aged five, grew up in Glasgow, attended school there and subsequently entered St Mungo's College to study Medicine.

My father was born in London, but his father, who had lived in a small village, Chinares, in Lithuania, close to the Polish border, had emigrated from Lithuania in the late 19th century. My paternal grandfather apparently had been an inn keeper and much of the alcohol he sold, or so I was told, had been smuggled over the border.

When the family emigrated to the east end of London, he developed a new skill and became a skilled journeyman tailor.

My father, Isaac, was very bright, studied Medicine in Kings College London and graduated from the Westminster Hospital at the age of 21 in the early 1920s.

He first met my mother when she came to London, and he tutored her in Anatomy prior to her sitting her qualifying medical examinations.

My father told me a story about when he was a medical student in Westminster

Hospital, which was then located across Parliament Square from the Houses of Parliament and is now the site of the Supreme Court.

Sir Adolphe Abrahams, a renowned Cardiologist, who wore a frock coat, was conducting a teaching ward round. His brother was Harold Abrahams, the Olympic runner who you may have seen in the film '*Chariots of Fire*.'

Stopping at the foot of a patient's bed, he asked one of the students to examine the patient's chest and listen to his heart. The student took out a stethoscope, applied it to the patient's chest and after some minutes was asked to detail his findings. He talked about hearing the heart sounds and a heart murmur and gave a detailed report.

Sir Adolphe took a silk handkerchief out of his lapel pocket, placed it on the patient's chest, and then placed his left ear on the handkerchief, which was still the custom amongst some of the older generation of Consultants. He stood up, looked at the medical student and said " *Young Sir you gave a detailed account of what you heard through a stethoscope. When I examined the patient, I could hear nothing except the sound of the London traffic outside.*" A Salutary tale.

*

Stethoscope

René Laennec invented the stethoscope in 1816. He rolled up a sheet of paper into a tube and placed one end on the patient's chest. The rolled-up piece of paper was soon replaced by a hollow wooden tube. Laennec named his invention the 'stethoscope.'

In the 1890s, the hollow wooden tube was replaced by two rubber tubes and now by plastic tubes. The binaural stethoscope is much like stethoscopes that are used today. In these days a stethoscope hung around the neck is now one of the most popular images of the medical profession.

A foetal stethoscope, placed on a pregnant women's abdomen to hear the foetal heart sounds, is shaped like a monoaural ear trumpet, resembling Laennec's original design.

David Littmann, an American Cardiologist whose parents were born in Ukraine, then part of the Russian Empire, developed an acoustically improved stethoscope in the 1960s.

*

Moscow old hands reunion

Nahid and I decided to arrange a reunion of Moscow "old hands" in our house in 2005, to commemorate the events which had occurred 100 years previously.

We sent about one hundred invitations to our colleagues whom we had been with in Moscow in the 1980s, and their spouses, and eventually forty or so came to the event. There was much reminiscing and updating and a good time was had by all.

*

Heart disease in Russia

I had been giving much thought to how, in addition to our work with Tushinskaya Trust, we might assist with Russian health care.

Dr Richard Wyse was introduced to me. His background initially was working in GOSH as a paediatric Cardiologist, and then he took an MBA and moved into the pharmaceutical services. He was particularly interested in health economics, patient outcomes and disease management programmes. Now, he is Global Director of Research and Development of the Cure Parkinson's Trust.

Following numerous discussions, we decided to set up a not-for-profit organisation to assist Russian health care with reducing heart disease and stroke in the Russian Federation.

In the next chapter you will be able to read about this in greater detail.

*

Moscow Selection Board

When visiting Moscow the Selection Board now stayed at the Pekin Hotel, which, although a Soviet-style hotel, was well located for many of the places we wished to visit, within walking distance or easy travel by the metro from Mayakovskya metro station.

Bob Dinwiddie was due to retire and both he and Dr Quen Mok, who had kindly agreed to replace him as the GOSH representative on the Selection Board, accompanied us to Moscow.

Moscow was changing rapidly with many new buildings and increasing numbers of private cars jamming the streets. Many International shops and stores had opened branches there and there were many new restaurants serving excellent food, numerous banks and international hotels. The shops were full of mainly imported goods.

However, inflation was high, pensions were low and one could still see poor people in the streets offering one or two items for sale. For those who had money to spend, there were plenty of places to spend it in including bars, nightclubs and casinos.

Whilst in Moscow I took the opportunity of discussing the proposed ICHARM health care project, which we were considering, with Nelli Naigovzina, who by then was effectively responsible for health care in President Putin's "kitchen cabinet." I also discussed it with some of the members of our Embassy in the economic section and DFID, Department for International Development, as well as the then embassy medical adviser, Dr Ian MacDonald . All were enthusiastic about it but could foresee numerous problems.

We managed to fit in an interesting production of Tchaikovsky's opera *Eugene Onegin* at the "new" Bolshoi. The actual original Bolshoi theatre was *na remont,* under repair, and would remain closed for almost three years.

*

Ken Lovett

The following week, we heard the sad news that our close friend, and treasurer of the Trust, Ken Lovett, had died. We had first met Ken and Susi Lovett in Moscow where he was the Defence Attaché at the Embassy. Later in the year a very touching memorial service was held for Ken in Keble College Oxford, where, after leaving the Airforce, he had been the Bursar.

*

Amanda, Hugh and children

During our Moscow visit, Amanda, Hugh and their three young children, Rachel, Jacob and Isabella, had been touring California in a Winnebago campervan whilst the kitchen and bathroom in their house were being replaced.

On their return to London, they stayed with us in Hampstead for six weeks which was great for us, but poor Hugh had to drive them halfway across London to school each morning, and then repeat the journey later in the day when he collected them.

*

Hermitage Foundation

The Hermitage Foundation represents The State Hermitage Museum in the UK, facilitating cultural exchange and fundraising to support a range of Hermitage projects, exhibitions in the UK and St Petersburg and study visits to the UK for Hermitage research staff.

From 2000 to 2007, paintings owned by the Hermitage in St Petersburg were exhibited in the Hermitage rooms in Somerset House in London.

An exhibition entitled "Beyond the Palace Walls", Islamic Art, loaned by the Hermitage, was due to open in Edinburgh in collaboration with the National Museums Scotland, and Geraldine Norman, Director of the Hermitage Foundation, invited us to attend the opening.

There were many representatives from Russia including the Director of the Hermitage, Professor Mikhail Piotrovsky, and a large reception was held, followed by dinner.

During the visit to the exhibition, Nahid pointed out to the Professor that many of the exhibits on show were in fact Persian in origin and in some cases pre-Islamic.

*

St Dorothy's hostel

For several years, we had continued to accommodate our Scholars with families. Now we were experiencing some difficulties in finding family homes where our scholars could stay.

Ultimately, we came to the conclusion, as some of the Scholars experienced homesickness and were missing their families and in some cases children, that it would be better to have them living together, even if that might mean they spoke more Russian when they were together. and tried several students' hostels, but they only accepted long-stay residents. Eventually we were introduced to St Dorothy's Hostel in Hampstead where the Mother Superior, Sister Pauline, a very lovable person, was very welcoming. This turned out to be so successful that we continued to use it for our future female scholars.

Charles de Gaulle, later to become French President, lived in Frognal House, now occupied by St Dorothy's Convent, whilst exiled in London from 1942 to 1944, during which time he led the Free French Forces against Nazi Germany in World War II.

St Dorothy's Residence offered accommodation to single young ladies between the ages of 18 and 35, of any creed or nationality, who were coming to study in London. They found it to be a welcoming, safe and friendly place to live in as they faced the strange challenges of foreign city life whilst involved in their studies.

Sister Pauline introduced us to Netherhall House run by Opus Dei, also located quite close to our Hampstead home, where our male scholars could stay.

Netherhall House is open to students of all faiths and backgrounds and has a large range of facilities. It has its own library, computer and laptop rooms, newspaper reading room, its own outdoor sports pitch, used mainly for 5-a-side football and basketball, music practice rooms, a coffee lounge, an auditorium and a TV lounge.

*

The Government Inspector

The Guardian's literary editor wrote, "*Chichester Theatre's production of The Government Inspector, translated by Alistair Beaton, goes back to the source and faithfully captures Gogol's strange mix of realism and grotesquerie.*"

Alistair McGowan played Khlestakov, the minor pen-pusher mistaken by gullible provincials for a St Petersburg bigwig, looking like an attenuated dandy, and had good moments, such as when he stretched out his long legs and vaingloriously announced: "*I'm also known for my balls.*"

Martin Duncan's production succeeded in capturing the play's nightmarish theatricality. The show began with an ominous flash of lightning; it was filled with echoing sound effects and set on what might have been a footlight lit Russian provincial stage.

My longstanding friend from my medical school days, Michael Nicholls, lived in Birdham, not far from Chichester, and the day following the performance we met for lunch at a restaurant called Crouchers, quite close to his house. He was a great support on the board of Tushinskaya Trust, and would play a major role in organising the 50th reunion of students from UCHMS, University College Hospital Medical School.

*

UCHMS 50th reunion

I had qualified as a doctor from the University College Hospital Medical School in 1955, and decided, following discussion with several of my contemporaries, to organise a 50th year reunion in 2005.

Four previous excellent reunions had been held – the first in 1976 and the most recent in 1991 – but all the organisers had decided that, for various reasons, they did not wish to undertake the work entailed in arranging further meetings.

I obtained from UCL a list of all UCL graduates from 1954 until 1957 and contacted 134 by email or land mail to assess the likelihood of them attending a reunion to be held at UCL in October 2005. Six of my contemporaries, Michael

Nicholls, Ray Radford, Peter Lachmann, Alison Smithers, Hugh Platt and Tony Jacobs, agreed to sit on the organising committee with me.

Ray Radford kindly offered to trawl the medical register for the hundred or so missing addresses. The events department in UCL were very helpful and agreed to organise a reception and dinner and undertake the catering.

Each committee member was responsible for different aspects of the reunion organisation.

The programme would include a tour of the new University College Hospital, which had recently opened nearby, and a visit to the old Cruciform building, which we all had attended as students in the 1950s.

Eventually, 89 contemporaries, including some spouses, coming from many parts of the world, attended the meeting, of whom 70 stayed for the reunion dinner.

Our guest speaker was Dame Professor Margaret Turner-Warwick, a renowned consultant in Chest medicine at UCL and the Royal Brompton Hospital. She had been elected the first female President of the Royal College of Physicians, and by chance, in 2005 had recently published her autobiography.

We also invited Dr Arthur Hollman, a Cardiologist at UCL who had taught all of us as students in the 1950s. He had pioneered the use of the heart-lung machine, as well as being a medical historian and plantsman. In 1959 he had been invited to visit Moscow with a small surgical team, following the purchase by the Soviet Union of one of these machines. The team performed operations on four Russian children, each with a different variety of congenital heart diseases.

We had arranged for eight speakers to present talks – Sir Peter Lachmann, "Unplanned and Unexpected 12 years in Carlton House Terrace", Peter Gillam, "Ethics, Etiquette and Integrity", Lord Nic Rea, "Doctor in the House", Alice Godfrey, "My visit to a Witch Doctor", Professor Peter Curzen, "From a Profession to a Vocation", Pauline Munro, "Neurology in Russia Where? What? Why? How?", Ann Johnson, "Looking Backwards at Breast Cancer", and John Baker, "Medical Experiences in Nigeria."

Following a buffet lunch in the south cloisters of the College, we all gathered on the portico steps for a group photograph.

Each attendant had been allocated to a group for tours of the Cruciform building and then the new University College Hospital. Following the tours, a reception was held in the south cloisters, where all could mingle and talk of old times.

We had arranged to dine in the old refectory, where we enjoyed smoked salmon and quail eggs, fillet of blue Rossini, Mousse au Cassis and finally coffee with mints.

Vegetarians were offered alternative vegetarian dishes, and we all drank too much Sancerre La Graveliere 2004 and Fleurie domaine de la Madone 2004.

Then Peter Lachmann introduced our guest speaker, Dame Margaret. Following her excellent speech, toasts were made to Her Majesty the Queen and to absent friends. Nahid presented her with a bouquet of flowers, and I gave thanks to Dame Margaret, proposed a toast to invited guests and thanked all the Committee and all UCL staff who had assisted us and those who arranged and accompanied us on the hospital tours.

I ended my thank you speech with one of Ronnie Barker's favourite jokes, which seemed appropriate for a medical gathering:

"An elderly man goes to his doctor and tells him that he no longer gets any pleasure from sex. The doctor looks at him and asks, *'How old are you and your wife?'* *'I'm 81 and my wife is 79,'* he replies. *'When did you first notice the problem?'* the doctor asks. *'Ah,'* he replies, *'twice last night and once this morning.'*"

*

During the next 12 years I organised a further four reunions. The last one was held in 2017 and we had hoped to have a final reunion in 2020 to mark the 65th anniversary of our graduation. However, due to the Covid pandemic, that reunion never took place.

The 2010 reunion and the two subsequent reunions were held in Christ's College Cambridge, thanks to the assistance and influence of Peter Lachmann. These in many ways were even more ambitious than the 50th anniversary, as they entailed two overnight stays in the college rooms.

Breakfast was in the Upper Hall, lunch in the Old Combination Room, tea in the Junior Common Room, the early evening reception in the Fellow's garden and the formal dinner in the Hall. This was followed by an organ and College Choir recital in Christ's College Chapel.

Powerpoint talks by several participants and a guest speaker took place in the lecture room of the Yusuf Hamed Theatre.

During the afternoon there were optional visits to Kettle's Yard, the Fitzwilliam Museum, New Hall Art Collection and various other venues.

The New Hall visit was particularly interesting and evocative for Nahid and myself as Amanda had read English in New Hall in the late 1970s and early 1980s.

*

To mark the 55th anniversary of our graduation prior to the 2010 reunion, I had requested all our colleagues to submit short biographies. Thirty responded, and these we then collated and distributed to all.

Christ's College Cambridge, then known as God's House, was established in in 1437.

Lady Margaret Beaufort Court refounded the college in 1505 and it became the leading Puritan College in Cambridge. In 1625 John Milton was admitted to the College and the Fellow's garden still boasts Milton's mulberry tree.

Charles Darwin was a Christ's man in 1828, and 30 years later published *On the Origin of Species*.

*

Numbers of active participants were dwindling due to natural attrition, aka "old age."

Michael Nicholls suggested that in 2017 we have a small dinner in the Athenaeum Club, where he had been a member for many years. He arranged the lunch with the club, but, unfortunately, due to ill-health, he was unable to personally join us on the day.

Three speakers gave short talks after lunch and then we walked the short distance to the Foreign Office, where I had arranged a guided tour.

*

Atheneum

The Athenaeum Club was founded in 1824 by John Wilson Crocker and designed by Decimus Burton at the then enormous sum of £2,000. The frieze around the outside was a copy of the Elgin marbles.

"*I am John Wilson Crocker, I do as I please, instead of an Ice House, I give you a 'frieze'.*"

The club was founded as a meeting place for men and women who enjoy the life of the mind.

The wide interests of members are reflected in the literary riches contained in the library.

The smaller dining room where we lunched is known as the Picture Room and is hung with portrait sketches.

FCO

The Foreign & Commonwealth Office located in King Charles Street was designed and built by George Gilbert Scott and completed in 1875. He wished to impress foreign visitors, and this is exemplified in the lavish design of the Grand Staircase.

The main three-storey-high area is a combination of chrome-red and gold marble and is surmounted by a vast dome decorated by female figures representing countries that had diplomatic relations with Great Britain.

The murals on the first floor depict the origin, education, development and expansion and triumph of the British Empire.

The Secretary of State's office looks out over St James's Park, and from this room in 1914 the then Foreign Secretary, Sir Edward Grey observed, "*The lamps are going out all over Europe.*"

The Locarno Suite consists of three rooms, the largest of which looks out to the Main Quadrangle. The Conference Room has a gilded ceiling supported by metal beams covered with majolica decorations.

Part of the building is known as the India Office, containing the Durbar Court, with three storeys of columns and piers supporting arches. The name dates to the coronation celebrations of King Edward VII. The third storey is adorned with portraits of great figures in Anglo-Indian history.

The Oval Room has the notable feature of a pair of entrance doors, which are said to have been installed so that two visiting Indian princes of equal rank could be received simultaneously.

Chapter 22

ICHARM pilot project

The Bahamas, ICHARM, London visit, Leonardo da Vinci, Heart disease & stroke, State of the Nation, Platonov, ICHARM pilot project, REMRF seminar, A salutary thought, Zhenya, Blair/Brown, Scholarship Selection Board, Moscow World Bank meeting, BEARR seminar, Project funding, Peter Hambro, Prague 2007

The Bahamas

"Oh, island in the sun
Willed to me by my father's hand
All my days I will sing in praise
Of your forest, waters
Your shining sand"

The Caribbean singer Harry Belafonte wrote and recorded "Island in the Sun" in 1957.

During the extremely cold winter of 1962/63, I came across an advertisement offering for sale four plots of land, totalling one acre, located in the centre of Great Exuma Island in The Bahamas. This sounded very tempting as the price was cheap, £1,230, which would be paid over ten years, interest free. My mother Rachel, my sister Annette and I decided to jointly purchase it, with a view to building a bungalow there for vacation use.

Each year we had to pay the Bahamian government a small tax for undeveloped land, as we had never got around to proceeding with the building of a bungalow, nor even viewed the land.

Forty-three years later, Nahid and I decided to visit The Bahamas en route to Los Angeles, flying comfortably in a Virgin Airlines Boeing 747 for nine hours to Nassau, the capital of The Bahamas.

Situated in the Atlantic to the east of Florida, The Bahamas consists of an archipelago of over seven hundred coral-based islands. Most of the population is centred on New Providence Island, where Nassau is located, and Grand Bahama

Island. The 760-mile-long chain of islands, cays and reefs stretches southwards to about sixty miles from northeast Cuba. Sandy beaches, fishing and boating attract many tourists, particularly from the US mainland.

In the 1960s the Duke, the late King Edward VIII, and the Duchess of Windsor, following his renunciation of the British throne, was appointed the Governor of The Bahamas.

A hotel minibus took us from the rather badly designed Nassau International Airport to the comfortable and well-located British Colonial Beach Resort Hotel, with its private artificial white sand beach. The hotel had been used as a backdrop for the James Bond film *Never Say Never Again*. We took a short walk to nearby Bay Street, the main street in the city, had an early supper and a rather disturbed night.

The following day, a trip in a semi-submarine boat, from which we could view through the windows the fish and coral, took us to the nearby Paradise Island, lying just 200 yards north of Nassau.

We lunched in the Atlantis Paradise Hotel Resort and Casino and then viewed the island's beautiful foliage with brilliant red hibiscus and a grove of casuarina trees forming a tropical arcade.

On arrival at the ferry terminal to return to Nassau, a Junkanoo band dressed in ornate and bizarre costumes was playing on the quay, reggae and calypsos, on goombay drums, cowbells and "rake'n' scrape" saws.

Our main reason for staying in Nassau was to view the land and resolve the Great Exuma land property tax situation, so whilst Nahid was at the hairdresser, I visited the Public Treasury and Valuation Department and sorted things out.

Later we visited a cigar factory which was quite interesting, and the National Art Gallery with its exhibits of Bahamian and African works of art.

An absurdly early flight the next morning in a Bahamasair Dash 8 propeller-driven aircraft flew us the 35 minutes, over the sandy Great Guana Cay, surrounded by shades of opal blue and green sea, to George Town Airport. The Tropic of Cancer runs through George Town, a town with a 15-mile-long harbour.

A small taxi took us to the Peace & Plenty Club & Beach Inn, a quaint pink clapboard building, named after an English trading ship which, in 1783, had sailed to the cotton plantation located on Exuma Island. Its grounds are planted with palms, crotons and bougainvillea.

*

Great Exuma is about forty miles long and seven miles wide at its widest part. The Exuma islands are amongst the friendliest islands in The Bahamas and the people are delighted to welcome visitors. They grow much of their own food, including cassava, onions, cabbages and pigeon peas, guavas, mangoes and avocados, where previously their ancestors had worked as slaves.

We had contacted Judy Hurlock of Dillycrab Reality, an estate agent, before we left home, and she came over to our hotel and drove us in her Jeep to view Bahama Sound, which was situated in the centre of the narrowest part of the island.

The developers had built roads, but several of them were overgrown with vegetation and there were very few completed houses, but several part-built. Apparently, locals who owned plots would commence building, then cease until they had earned some more money, then resume building until their funds ran out, cease again, and repeat this cycle over several years.

We felt our corner site had potential, with views of the sea from two sides, but none of our family were particularly interested in owning a bungalow so far from home in the UK, which they would rarely visit, so we considered selling the plot.

We had arranged to stay for a few days and hired a small car, for about sixty Bahamian dollars a day. The Bahamian dollar was at par with the US dollar.

*

The commonest surname in Exuma is Rolle. Lord Rolle owned most of the cotton plantations in the 18th century, but never set foot on the island. He is reported to have given land to some of the slaves, and following emancipation in 1843 many families took the name Rolle.

An elderly woman wearing a florid-coloured Bahamas Mama t-shirt, sitting in front of her little shanty, stated, "*You are born a Rolle, all your cousins are called Rolle, you marry a Rolle and have children called Rolle, and all the mourners at your funeral, related or not, are called Rolle.*"

*

We drove down the pretty coastal road to the southernmost tip of Great Exuma and crossed the 200-yard-long bridge to the small island of Little Exuma.

On the island we visited the Hermitage, the last surviving example of the erstwhile numerous cotton plantations. In 1806 it was offered for sale and the advertisement read, "970 acres more or less, with 160 hands," referring to the slaves.

On returning to the Peace and Plenty for supper, we found ourselves in the middle of the village fête, with many stalls, bands and dancers.

Next morning, we took a ferry from Elizabeth Harbour to Stocking Island with its beautiful white sand beaches. There were numerous people snorkelling and scuba diving and some walking along the sands seeking seashells – "shelling."

We drove to Bahama Sound and took photos of the land and its vicinity, and after lunch in Ting'um restaurant in the Four Seasons Hotel, contacted Judy in the Dillycrab office and asked her to list the site for sale for US$ 60,000.

Several months later, Judy informed us that she had found a local purchaser, and we agreed to sell the land for $ 50,000.

*

Early the next morning a taxi took us to the airport and Bahamas Air flew us back to Nassau Airport. We checked in with US immigration, in International departures, and after a two-hour wait, flew American Airlines to Fort Lauderdale in Florida, where we stayed in the Hyatt Regency Hotel.

*

Florida was first colonised by the Spanish in the 16th century and, following the introduction of European illnesses, the native population died out over the course of several years. The English defeated the Spaniards in 1763 and Andrew Jackson took ownership of Florida in 1820.

*

Fort Lauderdale, known as the Venice of America, has 165 miles of inland waterways, and with its extensive marina on the Atlantic coast it is the yachting capital of the world.

We found the marina to be absolutely fascinating with many large luxurious boats moored there, which we could view whilst seated for a drink in the Pelican bar.

One could travel to most parts of the city by water bus, a cheap and frequent service.

Close to the outskirts of the city is the subtropical freshwater wilderness known as the Everglades, where one can see many American crocodiles, occasional manatees and, if lucky, Florida panthers.

Travel on the Everglades, with a guide, is by airboat, a flat-bottomed craft propelled by an aircraft propeller and powered by an aircraft or automobile engine. We discovered to our surprise that Alexander Graham Bell, who in 1876 designed the first telephone, was also the designer of the first airboat. Airboats, in Russian *aerosanis*, were widely used in many parts of the world, including Siberia in the Soviet Union

*

After three days we caught an American Airlines Boeing 757 to Los Angeles and spent 10 days there seeing many members of Nahid's family, my cousin Annette, who lived there, and Riga Pemba, my Tibetan friend Tsewang's eldest son, who was a Medical Practitioner in LA.

*

ICHARM 2007

I was liaising with Professor of Epidemiology Dave Leon, from the London School of Hygiene and Tropical Medicine, who for some years had been researching the causes of sudden death in young men in the town of Izhevsk, in the West Urals mountains in Russia.

Looking for funding for our ICHARM project, I was introduced to Frank Flowers and we met at the Institute of Directors to discuss ways of promoting and presenting the project to potential funders. He, in conjunction with Ian Wilson, a corporate financial adviser, eventually came up with a business plan.

Richard and I had met with Brook Horovitz, CEO of the International Business Leaders Forum, IBLF, in his office in the basement of a beautiful Nash terrace house in Regent's Park. Brook would be a very helpful source of contacts.

The IBLF had been set up by Charles, Prince of Wales in 1990 with the objective of promoting economic development in emerging markets.

Richard and I, having given much thought to health care problems in Russia, had decided to try to help them reduce early mortality, particularly amongst Russian men. The initial name of the project was to be "Reducing Early Mortality in the Russian Federation", with the acronym REMRF. However, we later decided to change it to ICHARM, "International Cardiac Healthcare and RiskFactor Modification."

London visit

In May 2007, a four-day visit to London was arranged by the Trust for a delegation from the Institute of Paediatrics and Children's Surgery, Moscow, Professor Larisa Baleva, and Professor Ismail Osmanov and his son Alan Asmanov, a final year medical student. Unfortunately, Professor Alexander Tsaregorodtsev was unable to come. Accommodation was arranged in Domus Medica, located on the first floor of the original Royal Society of Medicine building in the heart of the medical quarter surrounding Harley Street.

They met their colleagues in the Institute of Child Health GOSH and University College Hospital London and undertook an intensive medically orientated programme. Future joint cooperation was initiated.

A reception in the boardroom of GOSH, hosted by Baroness Cox, was held in their honour. We had contacted Jamie Lowther-Pinkerton, Private Secretary to the Princes William and Harry, to ascertain whether Prince William could honour us by his presence, but due to prior commitments, he was not free to attend.

*

Leonardo da Vinci

Leonardo da Vinci had written in the 15th century "*Health is a gift, the greatest one, and those who take this gift for granted just don't deserve it.*"

Heart disease and related circulatory illnesses such as stroke were, arguably, the single largest threat to Russia's economic well-being and its political future, which it would have to face in the 21st century. Fortunately, they were problems that could, with appropriate measures, be controlled relatively easily - or so we thought.

Cardiovascular disease was not a new problem. Deaths from heart disease in the Soviet Union doubled between 1965 and 1989, and Russia's population was declining at the rate of 700,000 people per year, over 4 per cent annually. Population size fell by 6 million during the 10 years up to 2003, and it was estimated that by 2050, the population will have fallen by a further 40 million to about 100 million, from an existing level of 150 million.

Life expectancy for Russian men was almost 20 years less than in Britain. Over half of all early deaths in Russia were caused by heart and circulatory diseases, with 1.25 million Russian men dying from heart disease every year before they reached retirement age.

Some of the factors that increased the risk, and likelihood of developing heart and circulatory disease, such as genetic predisposition, severe stress and some infections, could not be significantly modified. However, the good news was that many of the risk factors are related to lifestyle and were potentially modifiable. These included diet, obesity and levels of physical activity, smoking and excessive alcohol consumption, particularly "binge drinking."

ICHARM's aim was to reduce incidence of heart disease and stroke by 2 per cent each year, largely by modifying lifestyle factors.

Our "Bible" was the World Bank publication, *Dying too Young*, prepared for the

World Bank by Patricio Marquez, Lead Health Specialist Europe and Central Asia region, with whom we developed a close association.

*

President Vladimir Putin at a State of the Nation address in 2005 had stated, *"I am deeply convinced that the success of our policy in all spheres of life is closely linked to the solution of our most acute demographic problems. Many of the current mortality factors can be remedied and we should implement a whole range of measures to overcome them. Our work must result in the young generation recognising the need for a healthy lifestyle and physical exercise. Each young person must realise that a healthy lifestyle means success, his or her personal success."*

At the national level, the Russian economy was experiencing serious losses as a result of early death and illness. Their total gross domestic product, GDP, had fallen by about 1 per cent. The World Bank had estimated, in 2005, that by 2015 this loss would have increased to 5 per cent of their GDP. There would be increasing medical costs, reduced productivity and tax revenues, decreased savings, increased absenteeism from work, fewer healthy workers, increased disparities in regional population, fewer military conscripts and increased risks of potential political instability.

At the personal level, individuals and families were experiencing illness, disability and early mortality which contributed to increased personal family stress, depression and alcoholism, with destabilisation of the family units and reduced income.

*

Our scholars that year were Nina, mother of two children, who was a radiologist from Moscow; her family name, Koroleva, when translated into English means "queen", and Natalia, a Paediatric Surgeon from Nizhny Novgorod, which translates into Lower New Town, known in Soviet times as Gorki after the Russian author Maxim Gorki, was the city where Andrei Sakharov, the dissident physicist, was exiled.

*

Platonov

The Maly Drama Theatre based in St Petersburg had brought its magnificent production of Chekhov's early untitled play *Platonov* to the Barbican Theatre. Directed by Lev Dodin and presented in London with subtitles.

it tells the story of a provincial schoolmaster, Platonov, who believes society was without ideas and principles and, having an amorous nature, has affairs with many women. Eventually his wife, Sonya, shoots him. He has been likened to a mixture of Hamlet and Don Juan.

*

ICHARM pilot project

We proposed introducing a five-year pilot project, later amended to three years, to be called "Reducing Early Mortality in the Russian Federation", REMRF, in a Russian city with a population of more than 1 million people. There were 12 such cities in the Russian Federation. The chosen city would need to be wealthy enough to be able to afford to participate in the project and, most importantly, be willing to undertake it.

I had kept Nelli Naigovzina closely informed regarding the project's progress, and Professor Rafael Oganov, Director of the National Research Centre for Preventive Medicine Moscow, agreed to be Project Director for the Russian Federation.

In the UK, Professor Philip Poole-Wilson, National Heart & Lung Institute London, Professor Janet Grant, Open University Centre for Education in Medicine UK and Professor Rifat Atun, International Health Management Tanaka Business School Imperial College London, would all be involved in advisory capacities.

The project had also been discussed with several members of Parliament, including Sir Malcolm Rifkind, who had been Foreign Secretary at the time of the dissolution of the former Yugoslavia, and had a keen interest in affairs in Eastern Europe and Russia.

The pilot project would be implemented via a carefully prepared programme of assessment, evaluation, awareness, training and monitoring.

There would be tailored, short, intensive postgraduate educational programmes for Russian polyclinic doctors and nurses, and training programmes for Public Health workers. Training programs would be based on simple diagnostic and treatment algorithms.

Individuals would be risk assessed for heart disease in polyclinics and given appropriate advice and medication.

Intensive and comprehensive long-term public awareness campaigns would be organised throughout the local target area.

Doctors, nurses and Public Health workers involved in the project would be regularly monitored, and there would be ongoing analysis of demographic surveys throughout the duration of the pilot project.

The total funding required for a three-year pilot project was estimated to be approximately £5 million.

The ultimate objective would be to roll out similar schemes throughout the Russian Federation, which could of course also be applied anywhere in the developed or developing world.

Vedomosty, "The Bulletin", a Russian financial newspaper which was closely associated with the *Financial Times* and the *Wall Street Journal*, agreed to publish an article about the project.

*

REMRF seminar

We launched the project with an introductory seminar titled "Reducing Early Mortality in the Russian Federation" held in Pushkin House, London, organised by the Russo- British Chamber of Commerce and sponsored by The Russia House travel agency.

Sir Rodric Braithwaite opened the seminar and Harald Lipman explained the background causes of early mortality in the RF, and the part which our project could play in assisting with resolving the problem. Richard Wyse spoke about the experience learned from other health care systems, and Rifat Atun spoke about health administrative reform. Olga Alexeeva, formerly Administrator, Charity Aid Foundation, CAF, Russia, spoke of Russian corporate giving, and Frank Flower, Chairman, The Russia House, raised the question of British corporate participation.

The World Service of the BBC covered the seminar, which Edward Ochagavia later broadcast. Subsequently under the title of "Russia's Broken Heart", an article was published in the English language paper, *Moscow Times*.

*

A salutary thought

A woman walks up to an old man sitting in a chair on his porch. *"I couldn't help but notice how happy you look,"* she said. *What's your secret for a long, happy life?"*

"I smoke three packs a day, drink a case of beer, eat fatty foods, and never, ever exercise," he replied..

"Wow, that's amazing," she said. *"How old are you?"*

"Twenty-six."*

CEELBAS/BEARR conference

I took every possible opportunity to publicise the ICHARM project by attending meetings and conferences such as the CEELBAS/BEARR conference "Opportunities and challenges for NGOs in the Health Field" and IAPOS, International Association of Physicians for the Overseas Services.

*

Zhenya

I had been introduced to Dr Zhenya Alexeeva with a view to engaging her to organise and run a public awareness campaign in Russia.

This would form an essential part of the whole project and we estimated would require 10 trained Public Health workers. The campaign would need to be intensive and continue for the full three years of the initial project. It would focus on lifestyle risk factors – alcohol, tobacco, diet and obesity, physical activity, raised cholesterol, raised blood pressure and diabetes. Families, schools, institutes and work places would be targeted.

Zhenya was the Director of Focus Media, a Public Health and Social Development Foundation which had been granted funds from the UN Global Health Fund to help counter HIV and AIDS.

She became very interested in our project and offered to act, on a voluntary basis, as our representative in Russia.

*

Blair/Brown

In 2007 Tony Blair resigned as Prime Minister and Chancellor of the Exchequer, Gordon Brown, succeeded him as PM, having waited for eight years.

It is widely believed that the two met in the restaurant Granita in Islington, London, in 1994, following the unexpected death of the Labour leader John Smith on 12 May of that year, and that Brown agreed to not stand in the forthcoming Labour leadership election so as to allow Blair a better chance of easy victory.

It is also widely believed that Blair agreed that, if he were appointed Prime Minister, to stay in the job for only two terms and then resign in Brown's favour.

*

Scholarship Selection Board

By chance, the Scholarship Selection Board was due to be held in Moscow, just before the WHO/World Bank meeting.

I wasn't able on that occasion to spend much time with the Board, but two excellent Scholars were selected. One, Ekaterina Budaeva, from Ulan Ude in the republic known as Buryatia near Lake Baikal, whose interest was Neonatal Intensive Care and diagnostic ultrasound, and the other Viktoriya Karaeva, an Endoscopist from Vladikavkaz in North Ossetia in the Caucasus.

Ekaterina was an ethnic Buryat, and she was a practising Buddhist. Buryats formed approximately 30 per cent of the population of Buryatia. In addition to orthodox medicine, *shamans* in Buryatia practised a form of traditional medicine based upon nature, spirits and magic.

Viktoriya was staying in the flat of a young doctor, Rebecca Flower, who worked at the Royal Free Hospital in Hampstead. Her accommodation had been arranged for us by an organisation called Doctor in the House. Viktoriya's mother was Head of the English department in Vladikavkaz University, and had insisted Viktoriya learn to speak English from an early age.

Viktoriya told us fascinating tales of life in the Caucasus on the border with Georgia, and having a lovely signing voice entertained us with traditional songs when she and Ekaterina came to supper in our house.

*

CEELBAS

Roderic Lyne had introduced me to Robin Hazelwood, Director of UCL School of Slavonic and East European Studies, SSEES, who invited me to attend their launch conference of a Centre for East European Language-based Area Studies, CEELBAS. This could be an opportunity for me to spread details of the project International Cardiac Healthcare & RiskFactor Modification, ICHARM, as REMRF was now called, to a potentially interested audience.

Moscow World Bank meeting

The World Bank invited me to participate in a WHO/World Bank meeting held in Moscow, in conjunction with the Ministry of Health and Social Development of the Russian Federation, to discuss "Strategy for the Prevention and Control of Noncommunicable Diseases in the Russian Federation."

The scope and purpose of the meeting was to help Russia face a demographic challenge fuelled by low fertility and high mortality. Noncommunicable diseases, including heart disease, cancer, trauma mainly due to road traffic accidents and suicide were the leading causes of death in Russia, with mortality rates between three and five times higher than in EU countries.

I was staying in the Pekin Hotel and the traffic noise was so loud that I put earplugs in both ears and didn't hear the alarm the next morning.

I had arranged to meet Zhenya, who was going to come with me to the meeting, on the platform in Kitai Gorod metro station. It was an established Russian custom to arrange to meet someone on a specific platform in a specific metro station. I had a rushed breakfast, and then fitted in a very useful meeting with Rafael Oganov before meeting Zhenya.

The next morning, the meeting, which was held in the conference room of the Metropol Hotel, with about thirty-five participants including representatives from Russia, Canada, the UK and Finland, had very useful discussions, followed by a networking reception in the evening.

The following day, there were further discussions including issues such as priority setting, effective tools and strategies, process, timelines and sequence of events, stakeholders' involvement, WHO and international support.

I made many very useful contacts, including Veronika Skvortsova, then Director of the Federal Stroke Institute, who later would become the Minister of Health of the Russian Federation.

Nahid telephoned me to tell me that Amanda would be starting a second course of chemotherapy shortly, so I cancelled my other appointments in Moscow and returned home. Nahid and I had arranged to make a trip to Jordan, but this also had to be cancelled.

BEARR Seminar

Jill Braithwaite's charity, The BEARR Trust, had organised a seminar on "The Demographic Challenge in Russia and Eurasia: What Role for Civil Society?" and asked me to speak on "Reducing Early Mortality in Russia."

In my opening remarks, I quoted Lenin's query: *shto delat?* – "what is to be done?"

"*This is a worldwide problem. Seventeen million people die annually from CVD, cardiovascular disease. The problem is widely recognised, the causes are known and many of the answers are known. It is time that measures to reduce Russian male mortality were implemented.*"

I ended my short talk with the words *vot nasha programma* – "here is our programme."

"What Is to Be Done?" – *Что делать?* – was a political pamphlet written by Vladimir Lenin. Its title was inspired by the novel of the same name by the 19th-century Russian revolutionary Nikolai Chernyshevsky. To convert the working class to Marxism, Lenin insisted that Marxists should form a political party to spread Marxist political ideas amongst the workers.

*

Project funding

We knew that if we were to proceed with our project, we needed to find sources of funding, preferably both in the UK and Russia. It was never easy to find funders, but it was particularly difficult at that time when the world was in a state of economic uncertainty, at the start of what was later to be known as the Great Recession. It would certainly be an extremely difficult task.

*

Peter Hambro

Still actively seeking funding for the ICHARM project, I was introduced to Peter Hambro, Chairman of Petropavlovsk, an Anglo–Russian venture established in the 1990s which mined gold in the Amur region in southeast Siberia near the Chinese border.

We had several very useful discussions; however, for a variety of reasons, these were ultimately non-productive. However, he did introduce me to Dr Andrew Nicolaides who had developed a system of using ultrasound to determine the likelihood and severity of heart disease and stroke by assessing the degree of narrowing of major blood vessels.

*

Prague 2007

Our first visit to Prague in 1990, before the downfall of the Communist regime, was when we were driving our new Merc from West Germany to Moscow.

On this occasion in 2007, we were participating in a week of painting, sculpture, filmmaking and culture in Prague, arranged by Artbreak.

We flew EasyJet on a Saturday to Prague and stayed in the small comfortable Art hotel. The week's course was well planned, very comprehensive and interesting.

On Sunday afternoon, we met a group of five other participants, and after dinner together we all went to the Festival of Modern Dance, in the Divadio Ponec theatre, and saw a performance of Dagmar Chaloupkova's *Gradina*.

The following day we sat in on a class in Life Drawing and Painting, and in the evening had a wine and cheese tasting in the Monarch Vinoteka, followed by a performance of Tchaikovsky's *Swan Lake* in the Statni Opera house.

We attended an uninteresting class on Collage and then paid a visit to the Martin Mainer exhibition. He was a contemporary artist who worked in acrylic with a very modernistic approach. Some of his paintings were very colourful and some, such as *Budda*, rather grotesque and frightening.

Following this class we then travelled by taxi to the Bertramka Villa for a recital by soprano Ivana Broukova accompanied by Petra Matejova on the clavichord, playing pieces by Mozart, Haydn, Josef Steffa, Jiri Benda, Jan Vorisek and Leopold Kozeluh.

The performance had been preceded by a visit to the Mozart Museum, containing many Mozart memorabilia, including two of his pianos. In 1787 he had completed his opera *Don Giovanni*, whilst residing in his friend, the Dusek's, house.

After breakfast in the hotel next morning, we departed for Muddum by tram and attended a course in Ceramics and Sculpture. In the afternoon, after lunch in U Slepe Kocicky restaurant, we were taken on a walking tour of the Old Town and Jewish Quarter. That evening we went to a gig at the AghaRTA Jazz Club where an excellent quartet Lubos Arndst Group was playing.

*

The best was yet to come. The following day, we attended a fascinating class called Film Animation where we were asked to make small figures in clay based on *Swan Lake*. These were then filmed, recorded on a DVD and later the soundtrack of part of *Swan Lake* was added. It was great fun. This DVD we have in our possession until this day.

*

"*Where the bee sucks there suck I,*
In the cowslip's bell I lie,
There I couch when owls do cry,
On the bat's back I do fly after summer merrily,
Merrily, merrily shall I live now,
Under the blossom that hangs on the bough"

A production of Shakespeare's *The Tempest* was staged, in Czech, in the open-air theatre in the grounds of Prague Castle. It was a moderately good production, but it was interesting to hear and see it presented in a foreign language.

Friday would be our last day and plenty remained to be done.

After breakfast we spent the morning in Letna Park painting and sketching *en plein air*.

The afternoon was spent at the Jan Zrzavy exhibition, then a farewell dinner at Hergetova Cibelna restaurant, followed by the Czech Philharmonic Choir singing Orff's rousing "*Carmina Burana*."

Jan Zrzavy was part of the modernism movement in the early part of the 20th century and was strongly influenced by European Medieval Art.

Chapter 23

Great Recession

Great Recession 2007–2013, RCP Global Health, WHO World Bank Geneva, Knees injury, Georgia/Russia, Scholars' reunion 2008, Barack Obama, Ann Liebeck recital, Bloomberg tobacco reduction initiative, Swine fever

Great Recession 2007–2013

In 2007 there was a worldwide economic decline stemming from the collapse of the US property market, in large part due to granting enormous numbers of "bad loans". As a result of this there was a global credit crunch as banks' lending fell, leading to a loss of confidence amongst consumers and businesses. Many of the effects of the recession would still be felt for the next six or seven years.

*

2008 RCP Global Health

The Royal College of Physicians London had organised a Conference to discuss "Global Health: Current Issues, Future Trends and Foreign Policy", which I attended and raised the specific demographic problems relating to the Russian Federation. One of the speakers was Dr Shanti Mendis, Senior Adviser Cardiovascular Diseases WHO, who would be very helpful to ICHARM in the future.

*

WHO World Bank Geneva

WHO/World Bank organised a further meeting in Geneva to discuss the progress relating to the "Challenge of NCDs and Injuries in the CIS Countries", which I was due to attend. However, fate determined otherwise.

Knees injury

Nahid and I were visiting Los Angeles to see her family, and on the day we were due to return to the UK on an overnight flight, the US Independence Day 4th July and my brother-in-law's birthday, we had been invited for brunch on a Sealine T-46 twin prop cruiser. We departed from Marina del Rey and had a most enjoyable cruise to Malibu, and an excellent brunch.

On returning to Marina del Rey, I decided to assist with mooring the boat to the quay as they were docking.

As I jumped down, the ocean swell lifted the boat so that I fell from a height of about twelve feet onto the hard stone quay, struck it hard and found that I was unable to bend or straighten my knees.

An ambulance was called, which came very quickly, and took me to the recently opened UCLA Ronald Reagan Medical Centre. Speaking with the ambulance crew, who were very helpful and attentive, I discovered that it was a requirement for ambulance crew to be trained members of the City Fire Department.

The doctors in the Medical Centre were very caring and concluded that I had ruptured the quadriceps tendons, which attach the thigh muscle to the kneecap, in both knees. They had never previously seen a bilateral rupture, and asked if I minded if some junior doctors could come in to see if they could diagnose the problem. After I was fitted with knee supports, we returned to Nahid's sister's home and cancelled our London flights.

Following numerous phone calls later to Amanda, Marc and our travel insurers, a nurse called Rebecca flew out from the UK and accompanied us in Club class back to Heathrow. Most of the night on the plane I listened to Beethoven and Vivaldi, and the only real problem was when I needed to go to the loo. However, it was certainly much easier and quicker passing through the airports in a wheelchair rather than walking.

Marc had arranged an Orthopaedic Surgeon and hospital admission, and without too much difficulty the ambulance took me to the Wellington Hospital. A couple of days later, the torn tendons were cobbled together and I was fitted with leg braces.

In the 16th century, Mary the First, Queen of England, was said to have had *Calais* engraved on her heart. Under somewhat different circumstances, five centuries later, I have *Marina del Rey* engraved on my knees.

I wore the braces for about three months and had intensive physiotherapy at home, and then hydrotherapy in the pool. With the aid of two elbow crutches, I gradually regained full mobility and seven months after the accident I was able to ski again. Since that time, I have exercised at home every morning before breakfast and attended a local gym three times a week.

*

Sadly, whilst I was partially immobilised, two very good friends, Noel Marshall and Jill Braithwaite, died, and I was unable to travel to their funerals.

*

The Olympics were taking place in Beijing, and I watched on TV Usain Bolt winning the 200 metres sprint race.

*

Our two Scholars, Victorya and Ekaterina, who we had not seen as much as we would have liked to because of my accident, came to a farewell supper in our house before they returned home.

I continued to make progress and managed to go to the OpenAir Theatre in Regent's Park to see a production of *Gigi* with Amanda, Hugh, the grandchildren and Marc, which unfortunately was interrupted by rain.

*

The Great Recession was taking its toll – Lehman Brothers, a giant US investment bank, filed for bankruptcy, the largest in history.

Russia was suffering a financial crisis which was compounded by political fears after the war with Georgia and by the plummeting price of Urals's heavy crude oil.

*

Georgia/Russia

In 1991, Georgia had declared independence from the former Soviet Union. By 2008 there were worsening diplomatic relations between Russia and Georgia, and South Ossetia, the area in Georgia bordering Russia, was effectively under Russian control. In western Georgia, Abkhazia, which borders the Black Sea, similarly had a powerful separatist group supported by Russia.

When fighting broke out between South Ossetia, Abkhazia and Georgia, Russia undertook a so-called "peace enforcement operation." Eventually, the EU negotiated a ceasefire, but subsequently South Ossetia and Abkhazia declared independence and aligned themselves with Russia.

Viktoriya, our Scholar, wrote to us about the tragic situation in South Ossetia and Georgia and the effect it had on Vladikavkaz, her hometown. Patients fit enough had been discharged from the local hospitals, and the doctors were organised into teams to accept injured children and adults who would be transferred from the war zones. However, none arrived and they were informed that many of the injured including children and pregnant women were deliberately killed by the Georgian soldiers and mercenaries.

Some of their doctors were working in a town called Tskhinvali, and they had witnessed people being locked in barns which were set alight, and others crushed by tanks. A 28-year-old cousin of Viktorya's, who went to assist the Ossetians, and many other innocent young people were killed in battle.

She commented that, *"the most outrageous thing in the situation was the disinformation in the mass media which had blamed Russia for unleashing the war."*

Valeri Gergiev, conductor and artistic director of the Marinsky Theatre St Petersburg, himself by origin Ossetian, during a visit to the UK publicly declared the "true" facts.

*

Scholars' reunion 2008

I was still using one crutch from time to time, but felt under an obligation to visit Moscow for the Scholarship Selection Board and our second Scholars' reunion.

Again, we stayed in the Pekin Hotel and attended part of the Paediatric Congress in the Cosmos Hotel, where we held the Selection Board. Two Scholarships were awarded: one to Rezida Galimova, a Neurosurgeon from Ufa, and the other to Anton Zadoya, an Anaesthetist from Yekaterinburg. Later, I shall tell you more about our involvement with Rezida, and quite separately, about a visit to Yekaterinburg.

The Scholars' reunion, on this occasion, was held in the Filatov Childrens' Hospital, with which Olga Crawford had close ties. By this time, the Trust had awarded 18 Scholarships, but for a variety of reasons only 10 past Scholars were able to attend.

The British Ambassador, Dame Anne Pringle, kindly hosted a reception in the temporary residency in Vakhtangova. After the reception, Nelli Naigovzina invited several of us to dinner in her apartment.

Ekaterina Budaeva from Ulan Ude was amongst the Scholars who attended the reunion, and she told us that financing for hospitals and doctors' salaries had been cut and they were desperately looking for other sources of income for the Neonatal department.

A new modern British Embassy had been built on Smolenskaya Embankment and had been officially opened there in 2000 by Anne, The Princess Royal. In 2002, the Embassy moved there, but the original Embassy building, on what was now called Sofiskaya Embankment, was to be in part internally reformatted and refurbished, and would house a considerably larger Ambassador's residency and various offices.

Whilst this construction work was being undertaken, the Ambassador resided in temporary accommodation in Vakhtangova Street.

The following day, on arriving at Domodedovo Airport for our flight back to the UK, we found there was no record of flights having been booked for us.

*

2009 Barack Obama

Barack Obama was inaugurated as the first black American President and many people anticipated, quite unrealistically, that this heralded a new "dawn" for America and American diplomacy.

*

Ann Liebeck recital

Fortunately, life wasn't solely full of problems. Mary Murphy, who we knew from our time in Moscow, had a sister, Ann Liebeck, who was an accomplished opera singer with a beautiful soprano voice. Ann very kindly offered to give a fundraising recital of works by Handel, Debussy, Richard Strauss and Tchaikovsky at Burgh House in Hampstead, accompanied by a pianist, Neil Kelly.

This raised a considerable sum which certainly helped to offset some of the Trust's increasingly high expenses.

*

Bloomberg tobacco reduction initiative

With the aim of reducing tobacco usage worldwide, WHO had announced criteria which should be applied: monitor usage, protect people, offer help to quit, make people aware of the dangers, enforce bans on smoking and raise taxes on tobacco.

Michael Bloomberg, a wealthy former Mayor of New York, had declared that during his lifetime he would give away the bulk of his fortune through Bloomberg Philanthropies.

In 2007, he had donated $1 billion to a tobacco reduction fund seeking tobacco usage reduction by policy change and increased public awareness.

The first round of an International competition for the Reduce Tobacco Use Grant, funded by Bloomberg, had been announced, and we decided to submit an application.

As you can imagine, competition was intense and we were unsuccessful on this occasion and on three later occasions during the next three years.

*

Swine fever

In 2009 a new variation of the flu virus, H1N1, probably originating in pigs in Mexico, spread to the United States and subsequently to approximately sixty countries worldwide. A total of 6 million people contracted the illness and there were 19,000 fatalities. In the UK, in the region of 29,000 people became ill, of whom 450 died. The Russian comparable figures reportedly were 25,000 ill with 600 deaths.

*

I had by then retired from the Foreign Office and was working for two or three sessions a week in Dr Charlie Easmon's travel clinic, Number One Health. I had known Charlie professionally for several years since we had first met when he was working in the Medical and Welfare department of the FCO.

Amongst many individual clients, business organisations and some foreign Embassies, there was a great demand at that time for advice regarding precautions to be taken to protect against the risk of acquiring the swine flu. We were, when appropriate, prescribing an anti-viral drug, Tamiflu, which rapidly became in short supply.

Chapter 24

Tushinskaya Trust

Sri Lanka, Russian–Sri Lankan relations, Tushinskaya Trust, Raisa Gorbachev Foundation, Eurasian National Resources Corporation, Rezida's wedding, Lord Mayor, Ufa ICHARM project, Kazakh Scholarships, Ufa project, RGF developments, Burnt by the Sun, Rasul and Alan, UK news, Russian lessons

Sri Lanka

Nahid and I had been invited to a literary festival in Galle in Sri Lanka by a Sri Lankan friend. The very traumatic civil war between the Sri Lankan government and the Tamil Tigers had finally ended, with a ceasefire a few months previously.

We flew via Bombay, visiting some of our close friends there, Humayan and Mickey, whom we had known since their student days in London in the 1960s, staying in the Taj Mahal Palace Hotel, opposite the Gateway to India, and Mickey's beautiful villa in Kandella in the hills, and then travelled on to Colombo.

Tara Coomaraswamy, Nahid's friend from the Commonwealth Secretariat based in London, had made all the arrangements for hotels, dinners, a fascinating tour of Sri Lanka and our visit to the Galle Literary Festival.

*

The Commonwealth Secretariat

The Commonwealth Secretariat is the intergovernmental organisation that supports member countries that wish to achieve the Commonwealth's aims of development, democracy and peace.

"The establishment of the Commonwealth Secretariat in 1965 emphasised the equality of all members, and gave final discouragement to the lingering sentiment that one member had a right to some predominance over others. It has enabled the Commonwealth to develop along independent lines in accordance with the interest of all its members." Julius Nyerere, President of Tanzania (1973).

*

A car took us to the Galle Face Hotel, very pleasantly sited by the sea, and in the evening we dined with Tara and some of her many friends and family in the Cinnamon Grand Hotel.

A visit to Parliament had been arranged for the next morning, then lunch in a lovely house, time for some shopping, drinks at Tara and her husband Inderjit's house and dinner at Tintagel, the Bandaranaike residence.

Colombo was on high security alert as an election was scheduled for the next day and trouble was expected.

This was far from our minds as we drove to visit an elephant orphanage at Pinnawala to see the tiny elephants squirting water at one another down their little trunks. This was followed by a visit to the Dambulla Caves to see the Buddha statues in the Golden Temple.

That night we stayed in the Kandalama Hotel, designed by Sri Lanka's renowned architect Geoffrey Bawa, which is built into the hillside with wonderful views over the lake.

During the next three days we visited Sigiriya Rock Fortress, known as the Eighth Wonder of the World, with many steps and wall paintings, the Temple of the Sacred Tooth in Kandy and a herb and spice garden near Matale, where we had lunch in Ena's house. We then had an interesting and intriguing visit to an Ayurvedic medicine centre, where treatment is based on a natural and holistic approach using plant derivatives, and then to a small batik factory. Lunch was in Helga's Folly, with its unique décor.

Driving past tea plantations, we stopped for lunch at the Kitulgala Rest House, where the film *Bridge on the River Kwai* had been filmed in 1957, and then returned to Colombo.

Next day, election day, the streets were surprisingly quiet, with short queues outside polling stations and little obvious security.

We had been introduced to Dr Prem, who had founded a school in Kalutara for disadvantaged children. She was a close friend of Tara and accompanied us on our visit to Galle, 70 miles south of Colombo.

En route, we stopped for lunch at Lunuganga Estate, the country home of Geoffrey Bawa. The garden there led Bawa, a Lawyer called to the Bar at the Inner Temple, London in 1940, to decide to become an Architect. The garden at the estate remained his first muse and experimental laboratory for new ideas.

In Galle we stayed at the beautifully located hotel by the beach, Fortress Hotel. Sadly, the mother of one of our party, Mary, had died and she had to return to the UK.

There was a torrential rainstorm, and it was announced on the radio that Mahinda Rajapaksa of the United People's Freedom Alliance had won the Presidential election, obtaining 57 per cent of the votes. I spent most of the day reading David Lodge's *Deaf Sentence*.

We had been invited by the literary festival committee to an evening reception in Galle, and we were intrigued to hear it would be held in the grounds of The Dutch House, which is the name of our house in Hampstead, so we felt very much "at home." Michael Frayn, Claire Tomalin, Ric Freeman, an Evangelist American pastor and author, and Michelle de Kretser, Sri Lankan author of *The Hamilton Case*, were all there.

We went to many talks and discussions, breakfasts, lunches and dinners with well-known, and less well-known, authors, from many lands.

One in particular, Artemis Cooper, granddaughter of the diplomat Duff Cooper, spoke about Patrick Leigh Fermor, the traveller and author, who had requested that her biography of him be published only after his death.

As we sat in a café, I had ordered their house speciality, a type of dessert, and she and her husband, the historian Antony Beevor, were seated at the adjacent table. Artemis ordered the same dessert, but was told by the waiter that they had run out of them. I gallantly passed mine over to her. I often wonder if she recollects the occasion.

*

In the UK, the Iraq Inquiry had commenced, and Tony Blair was appearing before it for questioning. One of the participants in the inquiry was our good friend from Moscow, Sir Roderic Lyne.

The Iraq Inquiry, also referred to as the Chilcot Inquiry after its Chairman, Sir John Chilcot, was a British public inquiry into the nation's role in the Iraq War. The inquiry was announced in 2009 by Prime Minister Gordon Brown and published in 2016 with a public statement by Chilcot.

*

On the last evening of the literary festival, we all attended a recital by the Colombo Chamber Music Society.

Returning by car to Colombo, we bade farewell to Tara and were very appreciative of the wonderful, exciting and informative programme she had organised for us. We spent the night in a hotel and the next morning flew back in a Sri Lanka Airline Airbus to Bombay, Mumbai, where we experienced very tight security.

The following morning, BA flew us very comfortably back to a cold and damp London.

A most excellent and enjoyable trip.

*

Russian–Sri Lankan relations

In the 1950s the USSR and Sri Lanka had established diplomatic relations, and during Communist times there was a considerable degree of economic and technical cooperation. Post-Communism, the Russian Federation had provided training for the Sri Lankan army during their Civil War, but, in collaboration with China, vetoed the UN resolution for a ceasefire in 2009.

*

Tushinskaya Trust

We were concerned about the future of the Trust as funds were running low, and we would only have enough to cover Scholarships until 2011. Ismail Osmanov offered to seek funding from the Russian Ministry of Health and Social Development, and commercial or philanthropic Russian sources.

He was hopeful that a Russian businessman from Dagestan, Abdullah Magramov, would offer to donate funding. Although we met him and dined with him in his restaurant, political problems in the Caucasus prevented him proceeding with this offer.

By absolute chance, two completely unconnected developments occurred which would resolve the funding problem.

*

Raisa Gorbachev Foundation

Whilst attending a networking meeting of the Russian British Chamber of Commerce, RBCC, held in the Westbury Hotel, I was introduced to Marcus Beale, Director of the Raisa Gorbachev Foundation, RGF.

This Foundation was considering establishing Scholarships for young Russian

Paediatric Oncologists and, following detailed discussions, the Trust was invited to organise and administer the Scholarships, which would be funded by RGF. As part of the agreement, RGF would donate an agreed unallocated sum of money to Tushinskaya Trust, part of which could be used to fund Diana Memorial Scholarships.

Raisa Gorbacheva, wife of Mikhail Gorbachev, had studied philosophy and helped humanise the image of the Soviet Union. Her dream was to pave the way towards the eradication of childhood cancer, and she raised large sums of money which were used to try to achieve this aim. She died from leukaemia in 1999, and in 2006 an oligarch, Alexander Lebedev, and his son, Evgeny, established the foundation in her name, with Mikhail Gorbachev as Patron.

The Raisa Gorbacheva Institute for Treatment of Childhood Cancer was opened in St Petersburg, and in the UK the foundation worked in conjunction with Marie Curie Cancer Care. The foundation also gave grants to the palliative care team in Great Ormond Street Hospital and the Louis Dundas Centre which undertook evidence-based research into paediatric palliative care.

The Foundation Trustees, Alexander Lebedev, Geordie Greig, then editor of the Evening Standard, Jonathan Rutherford-Best, an event organiser, and the Honourable Robert Hanson, a financier, later invited me to become the Medical Adviser to the foundation.

*

ENRC

Great Ormond Street Hospital was building a new department on its site, and Morgan Stanley was arranging the funding. A Kazakh company, ENRC, Eurasian National Resources Corporation, was considering funding the building which, when completed, would be named after it, and when they heard of the Diana Memorial Scholarships they requested that Tushinskaya Trust organise similar Scholarships for young Kazakh Paediatricians.

*

Russian scholars & Rezida's wedding

Rezida Galimova and Anton Zadoya arrived in London, and after supper we took Rezida to St Dorothy's Convent and Anton to Dima, Nataly Duddington's grandson's flat, where he would initally be staying until his room with a family in Highgate became available.

We saw a lot of both our Scholars and grew particularly close to Rezida, who told us she was due to marry shortly after her return home to Ufa and invited us to her wedding.

Hugh's father, Dermot, who we were very fond of, had sadly died and his funeral in Winterslow near Salisbury took place on the day we were due to fly to Ufa. We travelled by train to Salisbury and, following the service and burial in the cemetery and a reception in the Old Manor House, returned home by early evening.

A car took us in a torrential downpour to Heathrow, and en route we were delayed by a lorry accident. By the skin of our teeth we arrived at the airport just in time to catch the BA flight, and three and a half hours later arrived in Domodedovo Airport Moscow. Moscow time is three hours ahead of London.

Following a two-hour wait at the airport, we boarded the S7 Airbus for a two-hour flight to Ufa. When we arrived, exhausted having flown across another two time zones, Rezida and her husband-to-be, Igor, were waiting for us with a car and took us to the President Hotel. What a long, sad and tiring day.

Ufa, with a population of over 1 million, the capital of the Republic of Bashkortostan, previously known as Bashkiria, lies at the confluence of the Belaya and Ufa rivers, near the foothills of the southwestern Ural Mountains.

It is an important industrial centre and transport hub with large oil fields close by. The population of the republic is approximate 50 per cent Russian, 25 per cent Bashkiri and 20 per cent Tartar.

The Bashkiri are of Muslim Turkic origin, and their language is closely related to the Tartar and Kazakh languages.

Notable inhabitants of Ufa include the artist Nesterov, the renowned ballet dancer Nureyev and the remarkable basso-profundo Chaliapin.

We overslept the following morning and Igor came to collect Nahid to take her to the hairdresser. I stayed in the hotel preparing the speech I would have to give in Russian at the wedding reception.

Igor, who became a very close friend of ours and later my Russian partner in the ICHARM project, was a brilliant young Cardiologist specialising in interventional diagnostic and clinical procedures which were performed by inserting a catheter into the blood vessels that supply the heart. He was also a fitness fanatic who spent a lot of time in the gym assisting with training others, and played the guitar in a jazz combo. His father, at that time, was Head of the department in which Igor worked. Later, Igor was to succeed his father in that position.

Rezida, a skilled Neurosurgeon, later became head of the Neurosurgical department in her hospital.

The wedding ceremony was to be held in the open air, in the garden of a restaurant. Overnight and during the early morning there had been heavy rain falls, but, as Rezida's open car appeared, the sun came out and shone throughout the ceremony.

It truly was a fabulous occasion. All their many friends and brothers and sisters had participated in the preparation of both the food and the decorations, and played a large part in entertaining the company after we had finished feasting and drinking. My short congratulatory speech had been well received, and Igor's jazz combo entertained us. Everyone was very welcoming to the strangers from abroad and many of them spoke some English.

The short civil ceremony was held on the lawn in the gardens surrounded by flower beds of multicoloured scented roses in full bloom. A female Registrar officiated, and vows and wedding rings were exchanged.

Next day a dozen of us accompanied the newlyweds on a river trip and we barbecued in the rain. Clambering down to the boat, we passed a junkyard in which we saw a bust of Stalin lying on its side. What *lese-majesty*. Then in the evening, Rezida and Igor took us to a jazz club run by an Ophthalmic Surgeon, Bulat. Another late night but very enjoyable.

Rezida had arranged for her deputy, Rasul Khasanov, to look after us during our stay. He was full of charm and a lovely person and told us that next year he hoped to apply for a Diana, Princess of Wales Tushinskaya Memorial Scholarship in his speciality, Endoscopic Surgery. Nahid advised him that he must improve his English and said that she would phone him every night at about 3 a.m. Bashkiri time in order to ensure that he was practising the language.

Rasul collected us from the hotel and took us to visit their hospital, the Republican Children's Clinical Hospital, where, amongst other staff members, we met his father and viewed the hospital, and then we were invited to lunch with them.

Rasul's father greatly admired Princess Diana and asked us whether we had ever shaken hands with her. When we told him that we had, he said that he would never wash his hands again, as his hand had touched ours, which had touched the Princess's.

We were then taken to Minzdrav to meet the Minister of Health, Andrei Evsukov, and had a long discussion with him regarding our ICHARM project.

Ufa ticked all the boxes and satisfied all our criteria for a city in which we could set up the pilot project, and Andrei agreed to participate. Later in the year, we received the authorisation of the Prime Minister of Bashkortostan, Rail Sarbayev, to proceed with the project.

Of course, Ufa is in Russia and in Russia things rarely happen as you would expect them to.

After viewing the Salavat monument, set in a public space on a mound in the heart of Ufa with views of the city and surrounding countryside, we had supper in a Bashkiri restaurant with Rezida's sisters, Elizabeth, Venus and her partner Alexei.

All next day, Rasul kindly accompanied us, first to the Cardiovascular Centre with its very impressive facilities, where Igor introduced us to the Director, Irina Karamova, a very charming person.

Then after lunch in an Uzbeki restaurant, to the National Museum and the Nestorov Gallery. We also viewed three well-stocked supermarkets, and met Rezida and two friends for supper.

Bashkortostan is famed for its honey, and rightly so – it is excellent. When we left the following morning, we were given several rather heavy jars of honey as presents.

The flight to Moscow departed one hour late, and, on arrival there, we found that one of our bags hadn't been tagged at the check-in desk, and Nahid's exit visa slip was missing from her passport. Eventually, we managed to sort all this out and still had time in hand to catch the BA flight back to Heathrow. Over the years we had learnt how to deal with Russian bureaucracy.

A very interesting and hopefully, fingers crossed, successful trip.

*

Lord Mayor

I met the Lord Mayor of London, Nick Anstee, at an RBCC reception, and he told me he was paying an official visit to Russia in the near future and requested I let him have a brief regarding Russian health care. He was the only Lord Mayor in modern times who refused to accept an honour, namely a Knighthood, on his retirement.

*

Ufa ICHARM project

We had translated the proposed CVD reduction in the Bashkortostan Republic project into Russian and forwarded a copy to Professor Veronika Skvortsova, who was now the deputy Minister of Health and Social Development of the Russian Federation, and Nelli Naigovzina, Head of the Department of Social Development of the RF, and arranged to meet and discuss it with them when I would be in Moscow for the next Scholarship Selection Board in October.

Zhenya and I visited Veronika Skvortsova in her office and discussed the project in detail with her and Oleg Chestnov and Elena Bulgova of the International Department of Minzdrav. They were very cooperative, and we felt we were "pushing at open doors."

The Selection Board selected Alan Asmanov, Ismail's son, now a very bright ENT surgeon, and Rasul Khasanov from Ufa, who had taken Nahid's advice and diligently studied English.

We all managed to find time to visit the Tretyakov Gallery and see *Rigoletto* at the Novaya Opera, built in the Art Nouveau style in 1997 during the mayoral reign of Yuri Luzhkov.

*

Kazakh Scholarships

Following numerous discussions, with Great Ormond Street acting as intermediary, we eventually managed to hammer out a draft agreement with ENRC. The Trust would organise and administer two Scholarships annually for a five-year period. ENRC would donate a lump sum of £250,000, which would include a secretary's salary and an unrestricted annual sum of £10,000 which the Trust could apply to funding the Diana Memorial Scholarships.

Members of the Trust would be invited as guests to Astana, the capital of Kazakhstan, to see the medical facilities, establish contacts with the KZ authorities and doctors and meet the ENRC board.

Joint British–Kazakh selection boards would be held in Astana annually. Over the course of the next five years, we awarded 13 scholarships to Kazakh Paediatricians.

Scholars came from various parts of the country including Astana, Almaty, Akmola and Ust-Kamemogorosk. Their specialities covered Oncology, Neurology, Anaesthetics, Cardiology, Neonatology, Neonatal surgery, Cardiac surgery and Gastroenterology.

*

Ufa project

In parallel with the discussions regarding the Trust Scholarships, I commenced discussions relating to the ICHARM project with the Department of Primary Care and Population Health attached to UCL Medical School, based in the Royal Free Hospital. Professor Irwin Nazareth was the Director of this department and I met with him and some of his colleagues including Joe Rosenthal, Tamar Koch and Richard Meakin, with whom at a later date I would closely collaborate.

*

RGF developments

My discussions with Marcus Beale of the Raisa Gorbachev Foundation were progressing well, and by the end of the year we were able to sign an agreed two-year contract, based on similar terms as those of the ENRC contract, to select two young Russian Paediatric Oncologists annually for attachment as Clinical Observers to GOSH. The contract was later extended for a further two-year period.

RGF Scholarship applicants were interviewed in Moscow at the Diana, Princess of Wales Tushinskaya Memorial Scholarship Selection Board meetings, and over the next five years, ten RGF Scholarships were awarded.

In fact, we found when we came to the end of both the ENRC and the RGF contracts there were still funds available enabling us to offer further additional Scholarships.

Eventually a total of 13 ENRC, 10 RGF and 33 Diana Memorial Scholarships were awarded.

*

Burnt by the Sun

The National Theatre was presenting an excellent stage adaptation, directed by Howard Davies, of Mikhailov's award winning film *Burnt by the Sun* – Утомлённые солнцем, *Utomlyonnye solntsem* – literally "Wearied by the Sun." The story of one day in the life of a Soviet General and his family during Stalin's Great Purge in the late 1930s.

*

Rasul and Alan

Our Scholars, Rasul and Alan, stayed in Netherhall House, and although in many ways they had very different personalities, they established a close ongoing friendship.

One of the highlights of their stay in London was bungee jumping from a 160ft-high crane sited outside the O2 Arena. It really made their adrenaline pump, and whenever we saw them in the future we reminded them of this event.

Rasul's final report was a bound detailed account of the Scholarship and the hospital full of colour photographs. Truly to this day, the most impressive of any of the reports prepared by our Scholars.

Alan's report read: *"The experiences of this three-month scholarship in the greatest hospital, the Great Ormond Street Hospital, has changed my entire life and the new way my life will impact upon the welfare of children throughout this world and the health care delivery system in Russia."*

*

UK news

Following the UK general election, resulting in a "hung" Parliament, the Conservative and Liberal Democrat parties had formed a coalition, the first since the end of the Second World War.

*

At the Lyttelton Theatre, we saw a production of Bulgakov's *The White Guard*, directed by Howard Davies. The plot relates to a family called the Turbins who lived in Kiev at the time of the 1917 revolution. It was, rather surprisingly, one of Stalin's favourite plays and he wrote, *"The Turbins has become another Seagull for the new generation."*

*

Russian lessons

Recognising that my spoken Russian was getting rather rusty, I enrolled in Pushkin House for a course of weekly Russian language lessons which, although entailing a fair amount of homework, I found to be very useful.

Chapter 25

Russian Bill Gates

Russian Bill Gates, Ufa progress, Russian journalist, Moscow, Astana visit, Astana, Charity football match, December 2010

Russian Bill Gates

In 2010 Pravda published an article titled "Russian Billionaires Double Their Wealth". The estimated total wealth of the top 10 Russian oligarchs totalled US$139 billion. Private philanthropy was becoming accepted in Russia, and several of the oligarchs, such as Potanin, Prokhorov, Vekselberg and Lebedev, had established foundations with philanthropic aims. The benefactors included the arts, churches, education, sport and, to a very limited extent, health.

I decided to stimulate discussion in Russia regarding setting up a Russian organisation equivalent to the Bill and Melinda Gates Foundation, which in the field of health care largely concentrated on communicable diseases such as malaria, tuberculosis and HIV. I suggested that a Russian foundation could concentrate on noncommunicable diseases.

If the 10 richest Russians were to donate 5 per cent of their wealth, they could create a fund worth US$7 billion, which could generate US$350 million annually of which, net of expenses, US$280 million would be available for grants for low-and-middle income countries. Not an inconsiderable sum. Obviously, all the dealings would have to be 100 per cent transparent.

My article "Where is the Russian Bill Gates?" was published in English and Russian in the Russo-British Chamber of Commerce Bulletin, on the Charities Aid Foundation Philanthropy website and in Novoy Vremya – The New Times – a Russian language magazine published in Russia.

*

Ufa project progress

Our Ufa project was progressing, and this entailed several conference calls with

AstraZeneca Moscow and with Igor Buzaev, Rezida's husband, as we had decided to arrange a teaching videoconference prior to commencing the project.

*

Russian journalist

A young Russian journalist, Maria Lobanova, contacted me and asked if she could interview me regarding our Ufa project and Tushinskaya Trust. I arranged to meet her for coffee in the Royal Society of Medicine, RSM. When she eventually turned up late for the meeting, a common Russian trait, I found she was quite a decorative young woman who apparently was editor of a Russian magazine called *Sex and the City* and was actually fishing for information about the oligarch Alexander Lebedev.

*

Selection Board, Moscow, Astana visit

We were holding our Scholarship Selection Board in Moscow, and then had arranged to travel on to Astana to finalise arrangements for the Kazakh scholarships.

At that time, Brits required visas to visit Kazakhstan, although a couple of years later, this requirement was waived. The Kazakh consulate was then situated in a building opposite the Victoria and Albert Museum, where we personally had to attend to apply for and receive our visas.

Michael, Quen, Susan and I stayed in Moscow in the Cosmos Hotel, where we interviewed six candidates and selected two scholars. Whilst we were in Moscow, I was able to take the opportunity of meeting Astra Zeneca, accompanied by Zhenya.

We took a late-night three-hour flight with Transaero to Astana, having spent two hours in the heavy traffic travelling from the Cosmos Hotel to the airport. Then, crossing another two time zones in flight, it was breakfast time when we arrived at the Radisson Hotel in Astana. Rising late from our beds, we were met by Alima from ENRC, and an excellent interpreter, Talgat, who accompanied us throughout our stay in Astana.

*

Astana

In 1997, the capital of Kazakhstan was moved from Almaty to Astana (the name means 'capital city'), which lies at the geographical centre of the country. The move from Almaty was apparently made because of the risk of earthquakes in Almaty, and because Almaty is close to the Chinese border. The president, Nursultan Nazarbayev, also wished to spread the country's wealth around the country.

Astana, the most modernised city in central Asia, lies on the banks of the Ishim River. It was constructed on the basis of a master plan devised by a Japanese architect, Kisho Kurokawa, with many futuristic buildings, hotels and skyscrapers. My first impression was to liken it to Gotham City with its unique architecture – the city where the comic book character Batman lived.

Talgat took us first of all to Astana City Health Administration, where we had a useful meeting, and all parties agreed to cooperate. After lunch, with an excellent shashlik – Kazakhis eat a lot of meat including horseflesh which is a delicacy – we visited the City Paediatric Hospital. It was clean, well-equipped with a pleasant staff, but few patients. Then we were taken to the Educational Clinical Centre, which was responsible for the government-supported Bolashak International Scholarships. These granted Kazakh graduate nationals the sum of €1,250 a month for up to three years' study in an overseas university.

We also visited City Paediatric Hospital No 2, and met the British Council representative, Ancer.

On Sunday, Alima, Assiya and Mawlin on her birthday had arranged to take us on a three-hour journey north of Astana to Borovoye in the eastern foothills of the Kokshe Mountains, in the region known as Kazakhstan's "Switzerland."

In Borovoye lies the "holy lake", surrounded by pine forests, with a small mushroom-shaped island called Zhumbaktas, meaning "Sphinx", sited in its clear still waters.

The Kazakh poet Saken Seifulin wrote:

"Burabay water's more limpid than dew
One cannot withhold admiration its view.
Its shore's overgrown with glorious trees
Magnificent pines, white birches make scenery splendid indeed."

En-route, we stopped at Ablai Khan glade, the historical site where in the 18th century, with the agreement of ambassadors from Russia, China and Bukhara, Ablai Khan merged three districts forming a single state, now known as Kazakhstan. In the museum one can see the sacred white-stone throne on which he sat, and which traditionally one should walk around seven times.

It was indeed a memorable day, and not solely because we had sat in a car for six hours.

I had forgotten to set my alarm, and Michael woke me at 9 a.m. Following a rushed breakfast, we visited the Neurosurgical Research Centre and the Mother and Childhealth Research Centre, and after lunch we visited Minzdrav where we discussed the Diana Memorial Scholarships, Raisa Gorbachev Scholarships and ICHARM.

The next day was another very busy day, visiting the well-equipped State Diagnostic Centre, the remarkable Children's Rehabilitation Centre and the Paediatric Cardiac Clinic.

In the afternoon, at ENRC offices we met and had long discussions with their CEO, Felix Vulis. At supper we had arranged to meet Aida Omarova, who would be our direct link with Minzdrav and act on the Trust's behalf in Kazakhstan.

Next morning, up at the ungodly hour of 3 a.m., too early to have breakfast, we flew Transaero to Moscow, and following a delayed transfer, caught a flight back to Heathrow. It had been a very interesting and useful trip.

*

Charity football match

Natalia Davydova and her husband Yuri were visiting London, and lunched with us in the RSM to discuss a possible charity football match between a British and Russian team to be held in London with the objective of raising funds for GOSH. Later I had a meeting with Natalia and representatives from GOSH, but they were rather cool about the idea.

We also discussed holding a roundtable conference in Moscow, with a view to establishing a Russian "Bill Gates-style" fundraising foundation.

*

December 2010

As usual on Christmas Day, all our little family gathered in our house and enjoyed Nahid's excellent cooking. After Santa had handed out the presents from under the Christmas tree, Rachel played for us on her guitar, singing some of the songs she had composed. Little did we know then that this would be the last Christmas we would all celebrate together.

Chapter 26

Amanda

Skiing, ICHARM UCL Ufa videoconference, Moscow Selection Board RGF, Street demonstrations, Amanda's 50th birthday, AstraZeneca, Alternative vote, Europrevent conference 2011, WHO Global Forum Moscow, First global ministerial conference, Moscow Declaration, Sequel to Moscow meetings, Amanda's party, Andrei Kozlov, Amanda

Skiing

From very early ages we had taken our children, Amanda and Marc, and then later our grandchildren, skiing each year. In February 2011, the grandchildren's half term, we all went to Zell am See in Austria and had an enjoyable time. Amanda, although not well, still skied, but sadly we would never again all ski together.

*

ICHARM UCL Ufa videoconference

As a preliminary to the commencement of the CVD reduction project, we arranged a videoconference with both the Republican Cardiological Centre Ufa and UCL participating, to introduce and discuss aspects of Preventive Cardiology.

I chaired and introduced the conference in London, and Professor Irina Karamova chaired in Ufa. Consecutive translation was undertaken in London by Inessa Ray and Marina Dalziel, and in Ufa by Rezida Galimova.

Professor Robert West, Director of Tobacco Studies at Cancer Research UK and Head of Health Behaviour Unit UCL, spoke of the risks of tobacco smoking. Professor Richard Morris, Head of Medical Statistics and Epidemiology UCL, presented the risks of excessive alcohol consumption. My colleague Richard Wyse explained cardiac risk assessment and the use of statins. Dr Joe Rosenthal, Senior Lecturer of Primary Care and Population Health UCL Medical School, introduced the ICHARM Educational Training Course in Preventive Cardiology which he and his colleagues were designing and would eventually teach in Ufa.

Professor Irina Karamova explained the measures which were already in use in Ufa to control and reduce the risk of CVD.

The Bashkortostan Minister of Health was unfortunately unable to attend due to other commitments, but the Director of Ufa Medical College and the head of Cardiology Ufa University were present at the conference.

Numerous questions were raised by members of the Ufa audience.

The two-hour videoconference was held in the Pearson Building UCL, and, after initial problems coordinating the different software systems used in Russia and in the UK, proceeded remarkably smoothly with very few problems.

All in all, it was felt both in Ufa and London that the effort entailed had been well worthwhile, and that hopefully future similar events could be arranged.

*

Moscow Selection Board RGF

For this first Selection Board, at which we would choose both Diana Memorial and Raisa Gorbachev Scholars, we had invited Peppy Brock, a consultant Paediatric Oncologist from GOSH, to accompany us. She had studied paediatrics in Louvain University in Belgium, and then became Head of Haematology and Oncology in the University before returning to GOSH. Her special interest was in neuroblastoma – a type of brain tumour.

Our first Raisa Gorbachev Foundation Scholar, Timur Valiev, a Paediatric Oncologist from the Blokhin Cancer Research Centre in Moscow, was selected. He was born in and graduated from Ulyanovsk, Lenin's birthplace. His main interest was in the diagnosis and treatment of leukaemia. His Scholarship would commence in September 2011.

In his final report he wrote, "*I would like to express my special regards to Dr Harald Lipman and Nahid Lipman who made these experiences unbelievable for me. From the moment of my arrival, they made me feel at home. Their hospitality was very warm, friendly and my scholarship smooth. I will never forget their warm reception, my birthday celebration, which was organised by them for me, an interesting tour around the centre of London and the delicious meals prepared for me.*"

Street demonstrations

There was a small public demonstration in Triumphalnaya Square in Moscow, and this was the forerunner of much larger demonstrations in several Russian cities later in the year, with demands for Prime Minister Putin to stand down. Reports circulated that the Parliamentary elections for the Duma had been rigged, and Vladimir Putin had announced that at the coming Presidential elections he would stand for election as President.

Some saw this as a rerun of the demonstrations in the 1990s, which eventually led to the downfall of the Communist regime. This was wishful thinking on their part.

*

Amanda's 50th birthday

We celebrated Amanda's 50th birthday in Cinquocento, an Italian restaurant in Archway. This would be our last birthday all together as a family.

*

AstraZeneca

I heard from Simon Greaves that AstraZeneca had agreed to sponsor the doctors' Preventive Cardiology Training Course in Ufa.

*

Alternative vote

In the UK a referendum had been held at the LibDem's instigation to introduce an alternative vote system in Parliament, replacing the existing "first past the post" method. This had been rejected by a large majority.

*

Europrevent conference 2011

In 2011 Europrevent, a section of the European Society of Cardiology, held its annual two-day conference in the Centre International de Conferences Geneva, CICG, situated close to the United Nations office in Place des Nations. There was easy access by tram from the Hotel Kempinski where Nahid and I were staying.

I attended some very interesting sessions, including one on cardiovascular disease in Russia, presented by Professors Raphael Oganov and Sergei Boytsov, both of whom I knew well. Professor Shanti Mendis, from the WHO, spoke on Global Health and NCDs, and Professor Pekka Pushka, the Finnish doyen of preventive cardiology, spoke of his experience in practically applying preventive cardiology measures in Finland.

Somewhat surprisingly, the opening ceremony was held in the late afternoon, followed by a fascinating talk on the Mediterranean diet, a musical performance and a reception, all of which Nahid and I attended.

The following day, there were discussions related to CVD prevention around the world, risk assessment and smoking bans.

Nahid and I took the opportunity to walk along the lakeside and through the interesting old city. Before departing for Geneva Airport, we attended the final morning session of the conference, which I had found to be very useful as it related so closely to the ICHARM project.

A couple of days after our return, we had a farewell dinner for David Ratford, our retiring Chairman, when all the Trustees gathered in the Isola Bella restaurant not far from GOSH.

*

WHO Global Forum Moscow

Dr Ala Alwan, Assistant Director-General Noncommunicable Diseases and Mental Health WHO, invited me to attend a global forum in Moscow titled "Addressing the Challenge of Noncommunicable Diseases" to be chaired by Professor Margaret Chan, Director-General WHO. The event was organised in collaboration with the Ministry of Health Russian Federation.

This would be followed by the First Global Ministerial Conference on "Healthy Lifestyles and Noncommunicable Diseases Control." I arranged for Zhenya Alexeeva to be formally invited to accompany me to the meetings.

Representatives from NGOs involved with various aspects of Noncommunicable Diseases from approximately sixty countries attended the Global Forum held in the World Trade Centre in the Mezhdunarodnaya Hotel.

Following the opening plenary welcome and scene-setting meeting, the attendants divided into six separate concurrent breakout sessions, each one with its own moderator. Zhenya and I attended the Health Professionals and Health Services session.

Lunch was followed by the six rapporteurs reporting back on the outcomes of the morning discussions in a plenary session, and then a final plenary meeting with an overall summary of findings and the main messages from the day.

In her final summing up, Margaret Chan emphasised that to achieve any significant reduction in NCDs, it was necessary to mobilise all aspects of society. She further made the point that if one educated young girls, they in turn would educate their mothers, and thus empower women.

Following the forum, I was interviewed by a reporter from a Russian medical Journal, *Zdorove Natsee* – "Healthy Nation."

At a reception in the evening held in the hotel, we all had an opportunity to network, meet old friends and colleagues, and make some new acquaintances.

*

First Global Ministerial Conference

On the following two days, the First Global Ministerial Conference on Healthy Lifestyles and Noncommunicable Diseases Control was held in the World Trade Centre in Moscow. Delegations from 160 countries attended, the majority led by their Minister of Health or deputy Minister of Health. Rather surprisingly, the UK delegation was led by a somewhat junior-ranking Parliamentary Undersecretary for Public Health at the Department of Health.

Approximately fifty non-governmental organisations involved in health care, including International Cardiac Healthcare & RiskFactor Modification, ICHARM, had been invited as collaborators.

I travelled from my hotel to the conference venue by metro and this entailed two changes of trains. When I arrived at the World Trade Centre there were long queues waiting outside as security was tight.

I joined one of the queues, then saw Oleg Chestnov from the International Department of Minzdrav standing by the entrance and went over to speak with him. As I was speaking with him, I noticed that people were requested to show their ID to the security guards at the entrance, who checked them against a rather voluminous list of names. Feeling inside my zipped jacket pocket, I realised to my horror that I had forgotten to bring my passport with me.

I hurriedly excused myself to Oleg, ran to the nearest metro and returned to the hotel. Fortunately, in Moscow metro trains are both very frequent and fast. Retrieving my passport from my room, I rushed back to the conference centre.

By then there were very few people arriving and effectively no queues. As I handed my passport to the security guard, he laboriously thumbed through the registered list of names and said "*Vee zdess net*" – you're not here. I knew that I had registered the previous day, and replied "*Mozhno posmotreet*" – may I look at it. I went through the alphabetical list of names and did not see Harald Lipman, but noticed a much slimmer and shorter list on his desk, which I picked up. There, lo and behold, in all its glory, was my name.

Following the opening ceremony and welcoming remarks by Professor Tatyana Golikova, Minister of Health and Social Development Russian Federation, there were Keynote addresses on the "State of the NCD epidemic", "Economic realities and political priorities" and "Strategies and best buys." Professor Margaret Chan was present, and a declaration from Ban Ki-moon, Secretary-General United Nations, who had been unable to attend, was read out.

A high-level panel discussed Challenges and Opportunities for Multisectoral Action to prevent NCDs.

It was announced that President Vladimir Putin would be speaking to the conference, and eventually when he arrived, he gave a somewhat dry and not very inspiring prepared talk about the problems of noncommunicable diseases in the Russian Federation. He did however invite questions from the participants in the auditorium, and then came to life giving considered responses couched in a humane and humanitarian manner.

Following a lunch break, four roundtable discussions were held on tobacco control, food and nutrition, harmful use of alcohol, physical activity, sports and transport. I attended and participated in the tobacco control roundtable.

I was due to return to the UK the following afternoon as Amanda was unwell, but I had time in the morning to attend the second plenary session on international cooperation and coordination, and the roundtable for "Bridging the Implementation Gap."

Unfortunately, I missed sessions on monitoring NCDs and their determinants, NCDs and socio-economic development, innovative options for health financing, primary care, essential medicines and technology, civil society and social mobilisation, and discussion regarding the coming high-level meeting of the United Nations General Assembly on NCDs.

The closing session was designated as Moving Forward. Looking at short and long routes to addressing NCDs and uniting around a common NCD agenda, to be known as The Moscow Declaration. Over lunch I had useful discussions with Patricio Marquez, Sergei Boytsov and Nina Pogosova of the State Scientific Research Centre for Preventive Medicine, and all agreed to collaborate on the ICHARM project in Ufa.

I travelled by metro back to the hotel to pick up my luggage, and caught a car to the airport. On a large TV screen on the foyer wall in the hotel whilst waiting for the car, I watched the Royal wedding of Prince William and Kate Middleton.

A very interesting and worthwhile trip.

*

Moscow Declaration

The Moscow Declaration was a five-page document which recognised the right of everyone worldwide to the enjoyment of the highest attainable standard of physical and mental health, but this could not be achieved without greater measures to prevent and control NCDs as major causes of mortality and disability at global and national levels.

It stated that NCDs have serious negative impacts on human development with the potential to significantly impede progress of the UN's millennium development goals (MDGs).

At the international level, coordinating the contributions of a diverse range of stakeholders' efforts towards achieving the objectives of NCD prevention and control worldwide, and highlighting the pivotal role of the WHO.

At a Ministry of Health level, strengthening health information systems and public health systems at the country level, and integrating NCD-related services and primary health care are national priorities. Facilitating and supporting the key roles of civil society and private sector stakeholders and local governments as resources and partners in the response to NCDs must be given a high priority.

A reconfiguration of health systems and health policies and a shift from disease-centred to people-centred approaches and population health measures was necessary.

Evidence-based and cost-effective interventions, such as measures to control tobacco usage, reduction in the harmful use of alcohol and reduction in salt intake, could have profound health, social and economic benefits across the globe. Particular attention should be paid to the promotion of healthy diet and increased physical activity.

Effective NCD prevention, control and management requires concerted whole-of-government action across a number of sectors such as health, education, energy, agriculture, sports, transport and urban planning, environment, industry and trade, and finance and economic development.

At government, Ministry of Health and international level, multisectoral detailed public policies that create equitable health-promoting environments and promote healthy lifestyles for individuals, families and communities must be developed.

With a view to securing an ambitious and sustainable outcome, the declaration stated, we commit to actively engaging with all relevant sectors of government, on the basis of this Moscow Declaration, in the preparation of and the follow-up to the United Nations General Assembly high-level meeting on the Prevention and Control of NCDs in September 2011 in New York.

*

Sequel to Moscow meetings

From the pronouncements made at the two Moscow meetings by Tatyana Golikova and Veronika Skvortsova, who later became Health Minister, it was quite obvious that the Russians had now started implementing most of the proposals initially put forward by ICHARM. This was very gratifying, but it would entail considerable modification of the project we were hoping to introduce in Ufa.

*

Amanda's party

To celebrate Hugh's birthday and their wedding anniversary, Amanda, although unwell, had organised a large party for their friends and relatives in her house. Perhaps she had a premonition that this could be the last time she would see them all together.

*

We were due to visit Berlin with IAPOS for the first time since our visit in 1989, and we were looking forward to it. However, as Amanda was unwell, and I had a stiff neck due to sitting in on so many meetings, we cancelled the trip.

*

Dave Leon of the London School of Hygiene and Tropical Medicine had invited me to participate in a project he was planning in Russia, related to non-arteriosclerotic myocardial infarct – heart attacks not caused by narrowing of the arteries.

*

Our Russian Scholar, Anastasia Nosko, a Paediatric Neurologist from Moscow, who we were very fond of, was experiencing problems with obtaining a visa extension, and also problems in St Dorothy's Convent where she stayed. We managed to sort out her visa extension for a further six weeks, but the additional charge was £550. As I shall relate later, we began to have serious problems with obtaining visas for our Scholars.

Anastasia wrote in her final report: "*I want to thank members of Tushinskaya Trust for organising this remarkable scholarship, for their support, hospitality, kindness and patience. It was a real and very important support for me, which was so necessary to complete my studies successfully. I also want to thank all members of Tushinskaya Trust for showing me London as one of the most many-sided, cultural and democratic cities in the world.*"

*

We were expecting our first two RGF Scholars, Timur Valiev, a Paediatric Oncologist from Moscow, and Andrei Kozlov, a Paediatric Oncologist from St Petersburg. A couple of days before they were due to arrive, Andrei contacted us to tell us that whilst playing football he had ruptured an Achilles tendon and would be unable to take up the Scholarship this year.

Nahid arranged a birthday supper in our house for Timur where several members of the Trust joined us for the celebrations.

*

Hugh drove down to Cornwall with Rachael, and Isabella and Jacob accompanied Amanda by train. A friend of Rasul's, Timur, an IT specialist from Ufa, visited us for lunch.

*

We saw quite a good production of *The Cherry Orchard* in the Olivier Theatre with Zoe Wanamaker playing the part of Mme Ranyevskaya. Critiques were ambivalent: "*While this production strenuously avoids sentimental cliché and a deeply English vein of romantic nostalgia, it also misses something of the play's elusive poetry: it is highly intelligent and richly detailed, but it doesn't eclipse memories of past productions.*"

*

Amanda

The news from Amanda was not good and, on Rachel's 16th birthday, Amanda had to return to London from Cornwall by train, accompanied by Jacob. We met them at Paddington and took them both to our house, where she saw Marc's new car, and then later to her house, arriving just as Hugh, Rachel and Bella returned.

Two days later, she was admitted to the Royal Marsden Hospital where there was some initial improvement in her condition for a couple of days.

We were called at five thirty in the morning of 11 June by the hospital ward to say she was sinking, and a few hours later whilst we were all gathered around her bed, our beloved lovely daughter died. On her last conscious day, she had written in her diary, *"Gratitude that I can stay relatively positive in the face of all this – and the drs feeling that I am on the final road."*

Five days later, after a touching humanist celebration of her life conducted by a wonderful celebrant, Pippa Willcox, and attended by 250 friends and relatives, our darling Manda was cremated.

Our two Scholars, Anastasia and Timur, attended the ceremony.

Hugh, Rachel, Jacob and Bella scattered her ashes in our Hampstead garden, outside the house in Highgate where she had grown up, her garden, Queen Mary's Garden Regents Park which she was very fond of, and Clissold Memorial Park, where she used to walk her children.

We announced her death in *The Telegraph*, where fifty years earlier we had announced her birth. Donations from colleagues and friends were sent to The Haven in Fulham, a centre for breast cancer sufferers, where Amanda had received much psychological and social support over the years, and a flower was inscribed with her name on the hand-painted Tree of Life on their stairwell.

An obituary was published in *Sight & Sound*, to which she regularly contributed film reviews. It stated that, *"Her writing was marked by an incisive yet humane intelligence, which served her well in her subsequent career as a psychotherapist at the Terence Higgins Trust."*

Hackney Choir, which she had sang in for many years, held a memorial recital of Mozart's "Requiem" in her memory. Amanda would have enjoyed singing in it.

Some months later, a plaque with the inscription *Amanda Zohreh Lipman* was laid at the base of the beautiful bird-like Isis sculpture, next to the Serpentine in Hyde Park and adjacent to the Memorial Fountain to Princess Diana. A very peaceful setting which we visit each June. Manda loved walking in Hyde Park.

The sculpture was created by Simon Gudgeon in 2009 to raise money for the Isis Education Centre where young people can learn about wildlife and nature.

Isis was the ancient Egyptian goddess of motherhood, magic and fertility, protector of the dead and goddess of children. Ancient Egyptians believed that the Nile flooded each year because of her tears of sorrow for her dead husband, Osiris.

Our life had to go on.

Chapter 27

Life goes on

St Petersburg and Moscow Selection Board, Raisa Gorbachev Gala reception, Dechert LLP, Nina, Françoise memorial service, Tsewang Pemba, My 80th birthday

St Petersburg and Moscow Selection Board

We had decided that we would visit St Petersburg in 2012 prior to holding the Selection Board in Moscow, and we would organise a Scholars reunion in Moscow. Michael unfortunately had developed a problem with his foot and would be unable to accompany us.

This would give us the opportunity to visit the Raisa Gorbacheva Centre for Childrens' Haematology and Marrow Transplant in St Petersburg and meet the Director, Professor Boris Afanasyev.

He showed us around the Institute, which appeared to be coping with quite a heavy workload. His relationship with the staff was good and the Institute impressive, but possibly over equipped. We were however rather surprised that it looked after both adults and children.

We met all three Scholarship candidates, and they kindly accompanied us on a visit to Petropavlovskaya Krepost, which in Tsarist times was a prison for political opponents of the regime such as Dostoevsky, Gorky, Trotsky and later Tito.

Only two of these candidates attended for interview in Moscow, and unfortunately neither of them had enough experience or adequate English to be offered Scholarships. The third candidate had been unable to obtain a train ticket, and we informed her that we were prepared to interview her in Moscow the following day if she could get there.

Neither of the two Moscow candidates from the Blokhin Institute attended the interview, and when I spoke with Yuri Mentkevich on the telephone he stated that they had not been advised of the date, time and location of the interview. Our Russian partner Ismail Osmanov informed us that all candidates had been sent details. We offered to interview them in Yuri's office the following day.

All three attended for interview, but the candidate from St Petersburg informed us she would only be able to attend the Scholarship for one month. One of the Blokhin candidates, Natalia Subbotina, was offered a Scholarship subject to passing the IELTS examination at the required level. We also offered a Diana, Princess of Wales Tushinskaya Memorial Scholarship to Ilya Korsunsky, a Paediatric Immunologist from Moscow.

I met with Alexander Moseev of AstraZeneca Russia, and he offered on their behalf to donate US$40,000 towards the cost of the ICHARM project in Ufa.

*

Raisa Gorbachev Foundation gala reception

Nahid and I were invited to the Raisa Gorbachev Foundation Gala Reception, an annual fundraising event, which was held in the gardens of The Stud House, Alexander Lebedev's house, situated in the grounds of Hampton Court Palace.

The guest of honour would be Mikhail Gorbachev who had recently celebrated his 80th birthday, but unfortunately on this occasion he was unwell and unable to undertake the flight to London.

The Gala organising committee were Alexander Lebedev, Baroness Thatcher, Geordie Greig and Vanessa Redgrave, Evgeny Lebedev, Graydon Carter, Editor of the magazine *Vanity Fair*, and Colin Firth. They would all be present at the reception and gala dinner.

The ticket price for guests was £1,500, and a fundraising auction would be held. Lots included works of art by Andy Warhol, Tracey Emin, Sir Peter Blake, Anthony Gormley, football with Hugh Grant, cricket with Stephen Fry, a Botswana safari, and a holiday in India including a dinner hosted by the Maharaja of Jodhpur. Similar fundraising RGF galas over the preceding five years had raised more than £10 million. This year, however, a serious problem had arisen.

A Russian company called Gorby 80 Ltd had organised an extravagant birthday celebration for Mikhail Gorbachev on his 80th birthday, which was held in the Royal Albert Hall. The cost of the concert was estimated to be between £2 million and £3 million, and they hoped to raise £5 million for charities.

Kevin Spacey and Sharon Stone hosted the evening, and Bryan Ferry, Welsh mezzo-soprano Katherine Jenkins, ex-Spice Girl Melanie C as well as the London Symphony Orchestra with legendary conductor Valery Gergiev and Russian baritone Dmitry Khvorostovsky all participated. Arnold Schwarzenegger, the

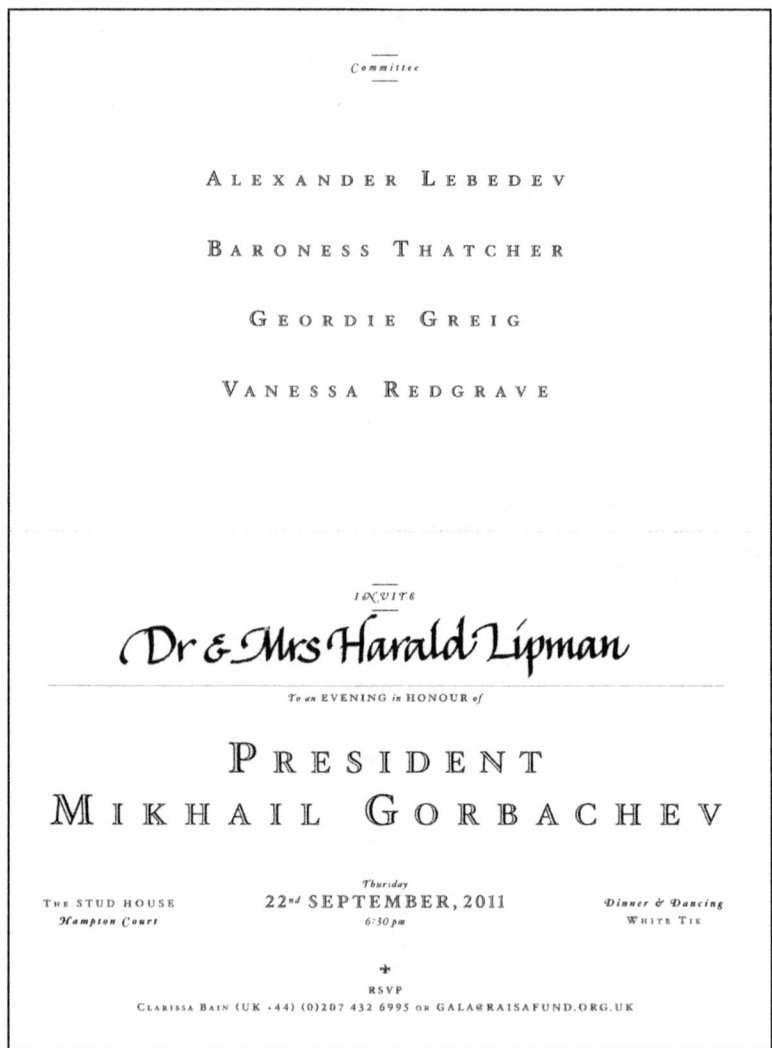

The Raisa Gorbachev Foundation gala

former Governor of California, Lech Walesa, the former Polish President, and actresses Goldie Hawn and Milla Jovovich were amongst stars who made a red-carpet entrance to the event.

The effect of this concert on the annual RGF gala was dire. Both attendance and donations received were significantly reduced, compared with previous years. The gala raised only 50 per cent of the expected sum.

In light of this, Marcus Beale, the RGF Director, decided to resign, all funds promised to charitable organisations were distibruted to them, and subsequently in 2015, The Raisa Gorbachev Foundation was dissolved.

Fortunately, although we were saddened by the news, the Tushinskaya Trust was not adversely financially affected by this decision as it had received in advance, in two tranches, the funding granted to cover four years' Scholarships. As we had husbanded our resources, we were in fact able to grant RGF Scholarships for a total of five years.

Our last RGF Scholar, in 2016, would be Anna Krasatseva, a Paediatric Oncologist from Moscow.

*

Dechert LLP

At an RBCC meeting, I was introduced to Doug Getter, a Director of Dechert LLP, an International American law firm which had a Moscow office, who subsequently offered to act on a pro bono basis as our adviser for drawing up the complicated AstraZeneca contract with ICHARM.

*

Nina

Nina Koraleva, a past Scholar, and her young son Nikita, were visiting the UK and came to see us in our house in Hampstead. Nina was a radiologist from Moscow. Koraleva in English means "Queen", and this word is included in her email address.

We took her to see an excellent evocative film in the Curzon cinema called *A Room and a Half*, directed by Khzanovsky. This is the story of the dissident poet Joseph Brodsky, who in Stalinist days was exiled. The plot imagines his return in post-Communist times to St Petersburg, and recalls his early days living with his parents in a communal flat in Leningrad.

*

Françoise memorial service

Françoise, a very good friend of mine from the age of 15, had died in hospital, and her daughter Laurance telephoned us to tell us that there would be a memorial service in Paris.

On our return home from Paris, we received more bad news: our very, very good friend, Tsewang Pemba, had died. The year 2011 had truly been an *annus horribilis*.

Tsewang Pemba

In his last letter to me, my dear friend Tsewang, who I had known since first entering UCL Medical School in 1949, had written Omar Khayyam's memorable verse.

"*Ah moon of my delight, that knowest no wane... how oft rising shall she look, through this same garden after me... in vain!*" and "*When thyself with shining foot shall pass... over the same spot where I made one, turn down an empty glass!*" On 26 November 2011, Tsewang "turned down an empty glass."

Tsewang was a highly intelligent secular non-practising Tibetan Buddhist, with an enormous appetite for absorbing knowledge and a great interest in philosophy and religion.

*

My 80th birthday

For my 80th birthday we had erected a marquee in the garden of our house, where the sixty or so guests enjoyed a Persian luncheon party. In my diary I wrote, "*So sad no Manda.*"

What a sad, sad year.

Chapter 28

Sequelae 2012

Darjeeling, Russia–Tibet relationships, Healthy Russia programme, ICHARM amended project, Russian Presidential election, KZ Selection Board, UK recession, EACRP conference Dublin, Natalia Davydova football match

Darjeeling

According to Tibetan Buddhist beliefs, following a death the soul transmigrates and passes to another realm within 49 days. There are six realms – heavenly, demigod, human, animal, ghosts and hell. Their destination is determined according to merit earned during their lifetime. Every seven days, prayers are recited by monks at religious services, and on the 49th day the monks officiate over the final service.

Marc and I decided to travel to Darjeeling to be present with Tsewang's wife Tsering and the family on the 49th day. This entailed a flight to Delhi and an overnight stay there.

Next morning, we were flown by Jet Air to Bagdogra Airport, and then took a car and driver up the circuitous steep and bumpy mountain road, with several traffic diversions, on the three-hour drive to Darjeeling.

Darjeeling, located at a height of 2,000 metres in the Lesser Himalayas in West Bengal, in the time of the British Raj, was a hill-station were the Brits living in Calcutta would stay during the Summer months. They built a sanatorium, a British public school, and established a military depot in the town. Tea plantations were developed, and the town is full of shops selling the distinctive flavoured Darjeeling tea.

The name originates from the Tibetan words *Dorje*, meaning "thunderbolt", and *ling*, meaning "place."

Marc and I stayed in the Windamere Hotel, which had changed little since it opened in the 19th century. Now it was owned and run by a Tibetan couple. From the garden there were fabulous views of Kangchenjunga, the third-highest mountain in the Himalayas.

Brothers and sisters, sons and daughters, uncles and aunts, nieces and nephews, friends and colleagues were all so happy to see us and welcomed us with open arms and open hearts. Many of them we had known over the years, and some of them we had seen grow from childhood to adulthood.

Tsewang's house was immediately next to a monastery where for many years he had looked after the medical problems of the monks. One room in the house was a prayer room, and laid out in front of the Buddhist altar on a table was a portrait of Tsewang, numerous candles, incense burners, flowers, fruit and an image of the Buddha.

Prayer room, Tsewang's house

Six to eight robed monks arrived at the house and for several hours prayed and recited the King of Prayers, chanting mantras, such as *Om Mani Padme Hum* – "the Jewel in the Lotus" – banged drums and clashed cymbals.

Following a lunch, where monks and non-monks mixed together, the service continued.

> "*The Buddha said,*
> *Life is a journey.*
> *Death is a return to earth.*
> *The universe is like an inn.*
> *The passing years are like dust.*
> *Regard this phantom world*
> *As a star at dawn, a bubble in a stream,*
> *A flash of lightning in a summer cloud,*
> *A flickering lamp – a phantom – and a dream.*"

*

Up at 4 a.m., a car drove us down the circuitous road, accompanied by Tsewang's daughter Lhamo, to Bagdogra Airport, where following a two-hour delay, we caught a Jet Air Boeing 737 to Delhi. Staying again in the Taj Hotel, we supped with Lhamo and the sister of an Indian friend of Marc's, Maryam.

We were so pleased that we had been able to bid a final farewell to our very good friend Tsewang, who I had known since my first day in Medical school in 1949.

*

Russia–Tibet relationships

Imperial Russia maintained diplomatic contact with Tibet. During the early years following the Bolshevik revolution, the Soviet Union tried to establish a relationship with the Dalai Lama, with the ultimate political intention of invading India via Afghanistan.

Following the demise of the Soviet Union, a Tibet Culture and Information Centre was opened in Moscow, and the Dalai Lama was invited by the Russian Parliament, the Duma, to visit Moscow.

However, in the early 2000s, Moscow and Beijing established closer cooperation and thus Russia accepted that Tibet was a Chinese province, and Putin stated that *"China is Russia's strategic partner",* although deep mistrust remains between the two powers.

*

Healthy Russia programme

In 2009, in large part as a response to the recommendations proposed by ICHARM, more than five hundred health centres for adults and two hundred centres for children were opened throughout Russia, based upon existing health care facilities and new preventive clinics.

The main objectives were to create a responsible attitude for one's own health and encourage people to give up their "bad" habits. To achieve these results, they were screened for lifestyle risk factors, including blood cholesterol, and were advised about the risks of tobacco, alcohol, unhealthy diet, inadequate physical activities and mental health.

A Healthy Russia telephone hotline was set up to provide professional advice on nutrition and stopping smoking.

"Healthy Hearts" – *Zdorove Sertse* – developed action programmes in 23 of the largest Russian cities, including Ufa. The project aimed to persuade the city administrators of the importance of health promotion, to improve the professional skills of doctors in preventive medicine, raise awareness amongst the population and evaluate risk factors for heart disease and stroke.

On World Health Day in 2010, 500 members of the Russian Parliament, the State *Duma,* were screened for cardiovascular risk factors.

*

ICHARM amended project

In light of these positive developments, we decided that the ICHARM project in Ufa would concentrate on devising a teaching programme on Preventive Cardiology for health professionals which, hopefully, would later be applied throughout the Russian Federation.

The Department of Primary Care and Population Health, University College London, was engaged to undertake the preparation of this teaching programme in conjunction with and under the guidance of myself.

Dr Joe Rosenthal, Senior Lecturer, Dr Richard Meakin, Senior Clinical Lecturer and Dr Tamar Koch, Senior Clinical Research Associate, all active general practitioners, agreed to undertake this task.

It involved much discussion and amendment, but eventually a satisfactory ten-session course was devised which could be presented in PowerPoint. Each session would last approximately three hours, as it was necessary to allow for contemporaneous translation into Russian. My Russian Cardiologist colleague, Rezida's husband, Igor Buzaev, participated in the discussions and advised how best to present the course to Russian doctors.

I found an excellent medically trained Russian translator, Dr Elena Vvedenskaya, who lived in Nizhny Novgorod, and she undertook the translation of the PowerPoint presentation into Russian.

All we needed now was the authorisation from the Bashkortostan government to teach the course in Ufa, and funding to cover the cost of engaging two of the medical authors to accompany me for a week's stay in Ufa and teach the course.

If you read on you will see how this was eventually achieved.

*

Russian Presidential election

Standing for election as President of Russia for a third term, Vladimir Putin was elected for a six-year term – his United Party receiving 64 per cent of the votes cast. One of the oligarchs, Mikhail Prokhorov, with remarkably liberal policies, achieved 8 per cent of the votes in the election.

*

KZ Selection Board

Having received our visas from the Kazakhstan Consulate, then situated opposite the V&A Museum in London, following a somewhat laborious procedure, Nahid, Marc, Michael and I departed for our first scholars Selection Board in Astana.

Very few airlines flew direct flights to Astana, and on this occasion we flew Lufthansa via Frankfurt. A five-hour flight, and on arrival a further five hours' time difference. We checked in to the very comfortable Rixos President Hotel.

Marc had arranged to fly for the day to Almaty to meet Kazakh colleagues and discuss TB at the National Respiratory Research Institute, whilst we visited the British Ambassador, David Moran, and updated him on Scholarship developments. Quen and Susan arrived, having flown on a later flight due to prior commitments, and met up with us in the hotel.

The next morning, in ENRC's office, which was a short walk from our hotel, we interviewed 15 applicants, five of whom we provisionally selected, subject to passing the IELTS examination. Professor Nurgul Khamzina, Director of the Department of Research and Human Resources, and Professor Alma Syzdykova, Director of the Department of Science and Education, represented Kazakhstan.

The following morning, we were up at 2 a.m. to catch the Lufthansa flight to Frankfurt and then transfer to the London flight.

*

UK recession

It was formally announced that the UK was in a double-dip recession following two consecutive months during which the UK economy had shrunk. This certainly would make it even more difficult to find funds for the Ufa teaching course.

EACRP conference Dublin

Nahid and I flew Aer Lingus to Dublin to attend the European Association of Cardiac Rehabilitation and Prevention, EACRP, conference. We took a taxi from the airport with a very talkative and amusing Irish driver. Nahid asked him, "*How large is the population of Dublin?*" He thought a little, and then replied in his rich Irish brogue, "*Ah begorah to be sure, there is myself, my wife, her brother and sister, my four sisters and two of them have husbands, then there is their children and my cousins. To be sure there's a lot of people in Dublin.*"

The new European Society of Cardiology, ESC, guidelines titled "Prevention of CVD" had just been published. I suggested that the ESC should prepare undergraduate and postgraduate teaching courses in Preventive Cardiology.

I was pleased to see that two Russian colleagues, Raphael Oganov and Nana Pogasova, from Moscow were attending the conference.

Whilst we were in Dublin, Nahid and I watched a very melodramatic production of Daphne du Maurier's *My Cousin Rachel* at the Gate Theatre.

*

Meanwhile, in the UK there had been large Labour gains in the council elections, and Boris Johnson had been re-elected as Mayor of London.

In France, François Hollande had won the Presidential election, and in the Greek elections there had been an inconclusive impasse.

Following Vladimir Putin's election to his third term as President, Dmitry Medvedev became Prime Minister, and Veronika Skvortsova became the Minister of Health. The Duma announced that in future, NGOs in the Russian Federation would be looked upon as "foreign agents." Fortunately, this did not affect either Tushinskaya Trust or ICHARM as they were based, and spent their funds, outside the Federation.

*

Natalia Davydova football match

Ismail Osmanov had introduced us to Natalia Davydova who had launched a children's charity in Russia in 2005, known as "Under the Flag of Kindness" – *Pod Flagom Dobra*.

The charity was extremely well endowed, with an organising committee including the First Deputy Chairman of the State Duma, the Deputy Mayor of Moscow, the Deputy Head of the Expert Department of the Russian President, and was supported by leading Russian statesmen and women, politicians, actors, athletes and journalists.

The goal of the programme was to provide targeted assistance to critically ill children who were in need of costly treatment. By 2012 more than 1,800 children had been helped by the project.

Natalia invited Nahid and I, as guests of their charity, to attend a football match between a Russian and an English team to be held in the Luznikhi Stadium in Moscow.

The stadium was crowded; in the grounds there were a roundabout and swings for the children and a carnival atmosphere. We met Ismail, Alan and Dasha and were introduced to some of the people attending the match.

The Russian team was a mixture of politicians and musicians, and the British consisted entirely of musicians. The Russians were victorious, and our Ambassador, Tim Barrow, presented them with a cup. The joint Russian and British musicians played a short programme of pop music, and I was then invited to give a short speech. Following this, the children, who had been selected to be presented with vouchers with a monetary value to cover the cost of their treatment, filed past.

Following a press conference, which I was invited to, we were taken to a local restaurant for a supper party.

The next day, we visited Tushinskaya Hospital where Ismail, who was now the Medical Director, told us of the enormous problems he was experiencing both with the staff and the Moscow authorities. Later that day we lunched with Nelli, her husband Dima and son Kiril and had some useful discussions.

At the Institute of Preventive Medicine in Moscow, I met with Sergei Boytsov, who had now succeeded Rafael Oganov, and Nana Pogosova, and had productive talks regarding the ICHARM project.

Chapter 29

Problems and pleasures

Scholars' passports, London Olympics, Scholars' baggage, Astana, Moscow, Alan's wedding

Scholars' passports

Our two Scholars, Ilya and Natalia, had applied for a six-week extension of their business visas as originally they had only been granted six-week visas, and they submitted their passports, as requested, to the UK Passport Agency.

When they were due to return home at the end of their Scholarships, they had not yet had their passports returned to them, meaning they would be unable to travel. I spoke with the Passport Agency, but to no avail, and we were forced to cancel their flights. This caused a lot of problems for them as they had family commitments at home, and their hospitals were expecting them back to resume their duties.

I formally wrote a letter to the then Minister of State for Immigration, Damian Green, explaining the problem and requesting that in future our Clinical Observer Scholars could apply for general visas, which were valid for up to six months, rather than business visas.

The response was rather noncommittal, but suggested the Scholars should go down to the UK Border Agency office in Croydon to withdraw their applications for visa extensions and retrieve their passports.

Our two Scholars from Kazakhstan, Ainur Akhmetkaliyeva and Jabrail Pogorov, later experienced similar problems, and eventually I had to go down to Croydon with them to sort the matter out.

We were getting fed up with this hassle and I decided to involve the Department of Health, as according to the Home Office, it was they who had proposed that Clinical Observers should be granted a six-week initial visa.

The Department of Health informed me that only the "workforce" team based in Leeds could look into the issue and arranged a teleconference between myself and them.

Eventually, the workforce team did intervene and several months later I was informed that the Home Office had changed the Imigration rules to allow medical graduates to undertake an unpaid Clinical Observer attachment for an initial period of three months.

Phew! What a lot of hard work, but fortunately I eventually achieved a satisfactory result from which many visiting postgraduates benefited.

*

London Olympics

The London Olympics opening ceremony, choreographed by Danny Boyle, was quite a remarkable, impressive event in which Great Ormond Street Hospital played a significant part.

The Russian Federation won a total of 24 gold medals and Anastasia Davydova won five golds in synchronised swimming. However, 26 track and field athletes failed doping tests.

*

Scholars' baggage

Our first two Scholars from Kazakhstan were due to arrive.

Ainur Akhmetkaliyea, a married 26-year-old oncologist, who during her Scholarship was offered the post of Head of the Oncological Department following her return home.

Kazakhstan had a great shortage of adequately trained specialists, and thus appointed relatively junior people, and in some cases those with limited experience, to senior positions.

She stated in her final report: *"This scholarship is given for me my lucky ticket for the future."*

Jabrail Pogorov, a Neurologist from Akmola, close to Astana, who had flown via Moscow from Astana to London, rang from Heathrow to say that he had had problems with Immigration and had lost his luggage. We spoke on the phone with Immigration, arranged for a car to bring him to our house, had lunch and then I drove him back to the airport. With some considerable difficulty I managed to sort the matter out, as by then his bag had arrived from Moscow.

In 1997 Akmola replaced Almaty as the capital of Kazakhstan. The following year it was renamed Astana.

*

Astana, Moscow

We were due to visit Astana and Moscow for the Scholarship Selection Boards and it turned out to be a most eventful trip.

Nahid, Michael, Quen, Susan and I arrived at Heathrow in good time for the Lufthansa flight to Frankfurt, and then from there we would take the ongoing connection to Astana. The incoming Lufthansa light was delayed, and we were advised that we would miss the connection in Frankfurt. The airline then arranged for us to fly by Turkish Airlines to Istanbul, where we would catch a connecting flight to Astana.

For some unexplained reason, Turkish Airlines flight left London two and a half hours late, and when we arrived in Istanbul we found our connecting flight had already departed. The airline offered us vouchers to purchase food in the airport restaurant, but, as we discovered, this entailed passing through Immigration as the restaurant was in the waiting area. We had no Turkish visas, but eventually we managed to persuade the Immigration officers to let us pass. The restaurant was crowded and the food was awful.

Cramped seats had been arranged for us on an Air Astana plane, and four and a half hours later we arrived at Astana Airport.

We had risen at 5 a.m., left home just after 7 a.m., journeyed for 15 hours and on arrival at Astana Airport found that our luggage had not been loaded onto the plane from London. Astana time was five hours ahead of London, so on arrival at the Rixos Hotel, tired and weary and dishevelled, we had breakfast.

With the help of the Guest Relations Officer in the hotel, and our London travel agents, Russia House, the bags were eventually located in Istanbul, and we were advised we could collect them at the airport when we left for our flight to Moscow two days later.

At the interviews, the following day, we selected two good candidates, one of whom was Baglan Baizakova, an Oncologist and Nephrologist, who later withdrew for personal reasons.

We had little sleep that night as the Moscow flight departed at 3 a.m. the following day, and prior to that we had to find and collect our baggage at the airport. Aida kindly accompanied us to the airport and traced our luggage. There was only one problem: everybody's bags were there except mine. I would need to try and sort that out when we arrived in Moscow.

*

Nahid and I spent the whole afternoon and following morning shopping for clothes for me in Moscow – an interesting experience. I purchased a suit, a jacket and trousers, a couple of shirts, ties, underwear, socks and shoes, as well as pyjamas.

We had a very busy schedule in Moscow, as in addition to the Selection Board we had arranged a Scholars' reunion, with a reception in the British Embassy, and we also had been invited to attend Alan and Dasha's wedding.

Professor Alexander Rumyantsev welcomed us to the Dimitry Rogachev National Medical Research Centre of Paediatric Haematology, Oncology and Immunity which had opened the previous year.

Dimitry Rogachev, a young child with leukaemia, had by chance met President Putin, and the President decided to endow a clinical and diagnostic centre in Moscow. The modern centre was remarkably well planned, equipped and staffed with the creme de la creme of Russia's paediatric specialists.

Dr Anthony Mikalski, a Paediatric Oncologist from GOSH, known to everyone as "Ski", joined us in Moscow and sat with us on the Selection Board held in Tushinskaya Hospital. We awarded Scholarships to three RGF Scholars; two from the Rogachev and one from St Petersburg, and two Diana Memorial Scholars, one of whom was our first Russian nurse.

At the Scholars' reunion, Nina, Natalia, Rasul and Anastasia gave PowerPoint presentations detailing aspects of their working lives to other past Scholars who were attending the reunion, and this was followed by a tour of Tushinskaya Hospital.

We were pleased to see many parents helping to look after their sick children and the staff, who all seemed content, caring for them holistically, and importantly, preventing spread of infection by washing their hands between each procedure.

Rather surprisingly, on return to the hotel, I found that my suitcase had arrived.

In our Embassy that evening, the Ambassador, Sir Tim Barrow, who I had known whilst posted in Moscow in the early 80s, hosted an excellent reception for the Scholars with about 40 guests, including the oligarch Alexander Lebedev, who I knew through my association with the Raisa Gorbachev Foundation.

*

We took a taxi to the Sokolniki OX Hotel where a magnificent reception had been arranged for Alan and Dasha's wedding. There must have been a couple of hundred guests, naturally almost entirely Russian apart from our small group from the Trust, and an American couple and an Italian couple who were friends of Ismail.

Alan and Dasha dancing

A sumptuous feast starting with zakuski, followed by numerous Russian and Dagestan dishes, accompanied by much vodka and Georgian wines.

The cabaret consisted of groups of Russian and Dagestan dancers in traditional embroidered colourful costumes performing traditional dances.

Dasha, now Alan's wife, wore a beautiful white gown with a long train, and she and Alan took to the floor to perform an excellently choreographed dance. Everyone joined them on the dance floor, and then the men and women lined up facing one another whilst Dasha turned her back and threw her bouquet over her shoulder. By chance Rasul caught the bouquet, and this signified that he would shortly be married. Which indeed he was.

I had a long talk with an elderly Russian gentleman from the Bolshoi Ballet who was seated at our table, and we spoke of the great Russian ballerinas Ulanova and Plisetskaya, and about food on Aeroflot flights – invariably chicken tabaka.

In the Russian tradition there were several overlong speeches, and I was invited to speak. In my best Russian, I reminded Alan of the occasion several months previously when he and Rasul, whilst in London, had bungee jumped. I didn't know the Russian word for bungee jumping but most people seemed to understand what I was talking about.

We all truly felt that we had attended a remarkable and unforgettable event.

The next morning, we left for London from Vnukovo Airport which was just being developed as Moscow's third International airport.

Chapter 30

Progress

Preventive cardiology teaching manual, Scholars, Russian Ambassador, Astana/ Moscow Selection Board, Chemical weapons ban, Trade delegation Ufa, Bilbao, Funding teaching course, RBCC reception, Apothecaries dinner

Preventative cardiology teaching manual

Based on the Preventive Cardiology course which we proposed to teach in Russia, with the consent of the authors, Joe, Richard and Tamar, I edited the seminars and added other relevant details, formatting them as a book: *Preventive Cardiology: How can we reduce CVD risk?*

Professor Shanti Mendis, WHO Global Coordinator Prevention and Management of Noncommunicable Diseases, kindly wrote the foreword.

*

Scholars

Anastasia, a Neonatal Surgeon from Ekaterinburg, and Liana, our first and only nurse, a radiological nurse from Moscow, had had no difficulties obtaining three-month visas in Moscow and had safely arrived in London and were staying at St Dorothy's Hostel.

Liana, commented in her report, "*I believe that teaching parents holistic approach to treating sick children, IPC measures such as proper hand hygiene and antiseptic techniques can have many positive outcomes without having to expend large financial resources.*"

Anastasia told us, "*It was a great honour to be invited to have tea with Baroness Cox in Parliament House. We were so delighted to be there, to have tea and an engaging conversation with one of the greatest women in the history of the United Kingdom. She told us about one of her fields of interest in politics and was so kind to guide us through the House of Parliament and we had a chance to observe the discussion in the House of Lords which was quite impressive.*"

Poor Baglan, an Oncologist from Almaty, however, had experienced all sorts of problems both with obtaining her visa and with her flights. Eventually, following a 35-hour journey from her home in Almaty, we met her at Victoria railway station.

Baglan's woes were not yet over. It was our custom to take the Scholars out to a restaurant for a farewell dinner a few days before they were due to depart. It was a mild Summer's evening. We were all sitting around a table next to the open French windows in Carluccio's restaurant in Hampstead enjoying the meal and conversation, and taking many photographs on our iPhones.

A man walked in through the French windows and went from table to table offering small packs of pictures for sale. He placed a couple of the packs on the table but no one, sadly for him, wanted to buy them. He picked the packs up from the table and walked out through the open French window. Immediately Baglan said, "*Oh, he has taken my mobile.*" She had placed the mobile on the table, and obviously the man had covered it with his packs of pictures and then picked up the whole lot together.

We went outside into the street but could see no sign of him. Hurriedly paying the bill, we drove to the nearest police station and reported the incident, finally getting to bed by 1 a.m. Apparently similar events in Hampstead had been reported to the police.

On her departure she stated, "*In conclusion, the clinical attachment to Great Ormond Street Hospital was a valuable experience. I think that all my aims set before the scholarship are achieved. It helped me to reassess my own point of view not only in oncology also in the whole of medicine. It is my hope that my clinical attachment will contribute to improving oncology service in my country.*"

*

Bolshoi reception Russian Embassy

To mark the 50th anniversary year of the first Bolshoi production presented on the London stage, they had arranged a season in the UK and the Russian Ambassador held a reception to launch the season. Talking at the reception with Melvyn Bragg, the presenter of the discussion radio programme *In Our Time*, he told me that he was considering producing a programme related to Russian ballet.

*

Russian Ambassador

His Excellency Alexander Yakovenko, Russian Ambassador to the UK, previously the deputy Foreign Minister of the Ministry of Foreign Affairs, invited me to an intimate lunch with him in the Embassy.

*

Scholars

With Scholars from three separate sources, RGF, Kazakhstan and Diana Memorial, we decided to have two or three Scholars twice a year. This of course meant that for a considerable part of the year we were having to spend our time either arranging their visits or mentoring them during their stay in London.

Yulia Skvortsova, an Oncologist from Moscow whose specific interest was bone marrow transplant, applied for a 12-week visa and was granted one lasting only six weeks. This entailed my contacting Tim Barrow, our Ambassador in Moscow, and requesting his assistance in sorting the problem out.

Yulia's comprehensive report clearly showed her understanding of the differences between management of hospitals in the UK and Russia, and highlighted many areas which hopefully could be translated to Russian health care.

"I was impressed by the impact of nurses in the health care system of Great Britain, and particularly in GOSH life. They exist parallel to doctors and play a great role in children's care. Most of them are devoted to their profession, very enthusiastic and highly qualified. The areas of their work very often concern those time-consuming actions which doctors do in Russia themselves – primary patient's examination, catheter-associated care, tissue-repairing care, analyses reporting, management et cetera. Such implementation is completely impossible for the nurses in Russia, and I am looking forward to seeing how it could be possible to transfer our nursing structure up to that level."

Another RGF Oncologist from St Petersburg, Sergei Shriaev, commented, *"Many hours I spent in library that has free access to all databases. I found a lot of cutting-edge information that is extremely informative and useful. I want to make special mention to informativeness of this observership. I received priceless knowledge and experience in oncology and bone marrow transplant units. That would be impossible without kindness and friendship of consultants, associate specialists, fellows and nurses."*

Raisa Oganesyan, a Paediatric Surgeon from the Rogachev Hospital in Moscow, with a special interest in Oncology wrote, *"I appreciate that on my arrival before the beginning of my job, Susan MacQueen and Dr Quen Mok took care of me and two other scholars and showed us the way to the hospital and structure for the hospital, explained many different aspects of the organisation of the work in hospital and even made a tour around the hospital.*

Then we began with two-day introduction course (mostly for those who started their postgraduate education), but interesting for us as well, included lectures about organisation, the clinical work in the hospital and electronic system of making medical records, some specific topics on antibiotics and blood transfusion policies and even industrial safety in case of fire. One of the most interesting lectures for me was the lecture about extravasation injuries and their management. Further, it was a good opportunity to get accustomed to the British accent."

*

Astana/Moscow Selection Board

Quen, Susan and I flew to Astana via Moscow with a four-hour transfer wait in Moscow.

We interviewed 13 applicants in the ENRC office and selected three Scholars and two reserves. During our short visit we were very happy to have the opportunity of meeting Bota, Baglan and Ainur, who was now Head of the Oncology department in her institute.

When we arrived back in Moscow, having flown from Astana, we were joined by Olga Crawford, and Nina Koroleva and her son dropped in to visit us in the Pekin Hotel.

I visited the British Embassy to update them on developments regarding the Trust and the ICHARM project, and also was able to speak with Zhenya about these matters.

Through a friend of Olga's, we had managed to obtain tickets for a concert in the splendid new International Concert Hall. Vladimir Spivakov conducted the National Philharmonic Orchestra of Russia in pieces by Wagner, Mahler and Shostakovich. A very enjoyable evening.

At the Selection Board held in Tushinskaya Hospital we awarded two Diana Memorial Scholarships and two RGF Scholarships. That evening we all supped at Alan and Dasha's new flat.

*

In our small family, Mr Fish, one of the two goldfish given to us by our youngest granddaughter Isabella, sadly died. My attempts to treat her with minute doses of Paracetamol had been to no avail.

*

US Russia–Syria agreement

The US and Russia signed an agreement regarding banning the use of chemical weapons by the Syrian army in its fight against opponents of the Syrian regime.

*

Trade delegation Ufa

UK Trade and Investment based in the British Consulate in Yekaterinburg invited me to join a Trade Delegation to Ufa in November 2013.

I flew Aeroflot to the new International terminal at Sheremetyevo, Moscow, and then transferred to the domestic terminal. Through some misunderstanding, I missed the connection to Ufa and had to arrange to fly later that afternoon. Fortunately, I managed to contact Igor in Ufa and he met me at the airport on arrival.

Igor took me to my hotel, the Azimut, and later to supper with Irina Karamova, previously Chief Cardiologist of the Bashkortostan Republic, and her young daughter, to discuss the ICHARM cardiology teaching course.

Next morning, after breakfast in the hotel, we went to Igor's flat to see Rezida and Michael, for his years a very advanced young 'man', and then to meet Professor Irina Nikolaeva, recently appointed Chief Cardiologist of the Republic.

The three-day conference was being held in the conference room of the Azimut Hotel, and 16 organisations including ICHARM were attending. Other attendants included Deloitte & Touche; Ernst & Young; GlaxoSmithKline; KPMG; EBRD, the European Bank for Research and Development; and Alan Thompson, the Russia Director of the Russo British Chamber of Commerce.

I attended the Russian–British roundtable on cooperation in the field of biotechnology and bioscience. There, amongst many others, I met Dmitry Sharonov, deputy Prime Minister of the Government of the Republic of Bashkortostan, and Alexander Afanasiev, deputy Head of the Ministry of Health of the Republic.

I briefly explained to all the 50 attendants at this roundtable the aim of the ICHARM project, namely to reduce heart disease and stroke in the Republic, and gave some details of the proposed Preventive Cardiology teaching course.

That evening, Neil Semple, the British Consulate General in Ekaterinburg, hosted an informal welcome reception in the hotel.

The following day, meetings had been arranged with the President of the Republic, Rustem Khamitov, whose background was aircraft engineering and specifically automated control systems.

I spoke with the President, briefly detailed the ICHARM project and told him that on behalf of the United Kingdom, ICHARM wished to assist Bashkortostan by gifting and teaching Preventive Cardiology courses in the Republic. He welcomed this proposal and endorsed the project.

Before departure for London, I had further meetings with Sharonov, Afanasiev and Irina Nikolaeva, all of whom agreed that we should proceed with the project in March or April in the coming year.

A very interesting and fruitful visit.

*

Bilbao

Flying out to Bilbao, Nahid and I met up with Rezida, Igor and their seven-month-old very bright son Michael. We spent a most enjoyable three days together, exploring the Guggenheim Museum, admiring Jeff Koon's giant 40-foot-high dog called Puppy covered with planted seasonal flowers, walking in the city and discussing every possible subject you could think of.

*

Funding teaching course

We were now left with the problem of finding funding to teach the Preventive Cardiology course in Ufa. Many possible funders both in the UK and Russia were approached, but for a variety of reasons were unable to offer funds. Eventually we found a donor who was prepared to undertake the entire funding of the training course, but wished to remain anonymous.

*

RBCC reception

The Russo Britain Chamber of Commerce, RBCC, had arranged a seminar and reception hosted by Prince Michael of Kent entitled "Building Bridges."

I had received a call from Aysilu Aletdin, who had been the Iinvestment Business Development Manager in Ufa when I had attended the Trade Mission and had very helpfully assisted me with interpreting. She was now employed in Dmitry Sharonov's office, would be accompanying him to London, and they would be attending the RBCC seminar.

I introduced him to several people who were attending the seminar.

*

Apothecaries dinner

I invited the Russian Ambassador HE Alexander Yakovenko as my guest to a Livery dinner held at the Apothecaries Hall in January 2014. As he was the guest of honour, we both sat at the head table.

Following the established tradition, the other 120 Liverymen and guests, after a short reception, had taken their seats at the tables. The Ambassador and I then accompanied the berobed Master, past Master and Chairman of the Trustees with their spouses in procession into the hall, accompanied by the clapping of the hands of the standing guests - as was the custom.

Following a short grace, a three-course dinner accompanied by excellent wine from the Society's cellar and the passing of the port and Madeira, we undertook the rose water ceremony.

An ornamented silver Armada bowl filled with rosewater is passed from guest to guest in a clockwise direction. The corner of one's table napkin is dipped into the rosewater and patted behind one's ears, stimulating a branch of the vagus nerve, known as the Alderman's nerve, and thus soothing the digestive organs.

Shortly after this, the traditional ceremony of the Loving Cup is performed.

This dates back to Anglo-Saxon times. King Edward the Martyr was stabbed in the back at the command of Queen Elfrida, his stepmother, whilst drinking a toast from the two-handed goblet that she offered him. To prevent this happening again, during the passing of the Loving Cup, the back of the drinker is guarded by their next-door neighbour. This is known as the "pledge."

The contents of the Loving Cup are made according to an old Apothecaries' recipe and are a closely guarded secret.

Then, the "Queen" is toasted by the Master, followed by a toast to "Prince Philip Duke of Edinburgh, the Prince of Wales, the Duchess of Cornwall and other members of the Royal family", and then a toast to the "Lord Mayor and the City of London Corporation."

The Junior Warden toasts the "guests" and one of the guests responds.

Finally, the Master's toast is recited: *"The Worshipful Society of the Art and Mystery of Apothecaries of the City of London, may it flourish root and branch – bringing help to all – till time ceases."*

Following the final toast, artistes from the Guildhall School of Music and Drama presented a short musical recital.

In the adjacent reception room, those who wish can mingle and enjoy a "stirrup cup" before their carriages arrive.

The Ambassador was delighted to have had the opportunity of attending a traditional Livery Company dinner.

Chapter 31

A preventable war

Ukraine crisis, Letter Ban Ki-Moon, Ban Ki-Moon, Malaysian airliner, Dave Leon project, Moscow launch, ENRC scholars, Ufa PC teaching course, RGF scholars, Selection Board Moscow/Astana

Ukraine crisis

In 2014, the president of Ukraine, Viktor Yanukovych, suspended preparations for the implementation of an agreement of association with the European Union, sparking mass protests in the streets, possibly with covert assistance from the Western powers, and he was subsequently ousted.

Putin saw an opportunity to regain the largely Russian-speaking Crimea, sent in troops, and following a "referendum" the majority of the population apparently voted to rejoin the Russian Federation.

Political unrest in eastern Ukraine bordering Russia evolved into an insurrection, supported by Russia, against the post-Yanukovitch Ukrainian Government.

Letter Ban Ki-moon

From an early stage, I had a foreboding that this matter would escalate rapidly, and with my interest in and considerable knowledge of politics in central and eastern Europe I decided to make a foray into International politics. I felt that a meeting should be called of all interested parties by an individual with International standing, with the objective of possible "Finlandisation" of Ukraine.

The term "Finlandisation" implies "to become like Finland", referring to the relationship between the Soviet Union and Finland during the Cold War.

In 1939, following a short savage war between Finland and the Soviet Union, Finland became a secure, politically neutral sovereign state. They did, however, lose part of Karelia – almost 10 per cent of their territory. Finland's sovereignty and security persists, for over 80 years to this day.

I proposed that NATO and the EU would not offer membership to Ukraine, and Ukraine would remain a sovereign state with no political affiliation either to the West or Russia. Gas supplies from Russia would be secured. Economically, Ukraine would be secured by grants from both the West and Russia.

Ukraine would retain its independence and remain politically neutral, and maintain close economic relations with both Russia and Western Europe.

Several years later, I discovered that Henry Kissinger, then US Secretary of State, and Noam Chomsky, renowned American intellectual, the father of modern linguistics, philosopher, cognitive scientist, historian, social critic, and political activist, had both separately made similar proposals.

*

Ban Ki-moon

In an attempt to set up this meeting I contacted Ban Ki-moon, Secretary General of the United Nations, the UK Foreign Office, the EU, the American State Department, the Russian Ambassador and the then Ukrainian Prime Minister, Arseniy Yatsenyuk.

Most of them had reservations and, rather surprisingly, the only positive response came from the Russians.

Over the course of the next few months, my worst expectations became true. My feelings remain that if Yanukovytch had not been toppled, Russia would not have had the opportunity of reoccupying Crimea.

Subsequently, both the US and the EU introduced sanctions against Russia.

*

Malaysian airliner

A scheduled passenger flight by a Malaysian Airlines Boeing 777, en route from Amsterdam to Kuala Lumpur, was shot down over eastern Ukraine, probably by the Russian-backed Ukrainian separatists, with the death of all the passengers and crew.

*

Dave Leon project

Professor Dave Leon of the London School of Hygiene and Tropical Medicine contacted me and invited me to join in a project which he was launching in Moscow, which was looking at the burden of alcohol-induced non-atherosclerotic heart disease. That is, cardiovascular disease not caused by narrowing of the blood vessels supplying the heart muscle. In previous studies he had undertaken in Russia, he had shown that alcohol was the cause of more than half of all male Russian deaths between the ages of 15 and 54 years.

*

It was proposed that studies would be undertaken in three Russian cities: Archangelsk, Chelyabinsk and Novosibirsk. He wondered whether it might be possible to collaborate with ICHARM in Ufa.

Moscow launch

For the two-day launch of the project, I flew Transaero to Moscow and stayed with the rest of the group in the Holiday Inn, where I met up with Dave Leon and Professor Martin McKee, who I knew well.

I had introduced Dave to Sergei Boytsov, and the project launch was being held in the National Research Centre for Preventive Medicine. There I met David Zaridze, who I had last seen 25 years previously whilst we were posted in Moscow, and Vladimir Shkolnikov, Maria's husband.

During the two days, there were very many interesting, informative and useful talks and discussions regarding the problems of cardiovascular disease in the Russian Federation. It had been a very useful and worthwhile trip.

*

ENRC Scholars

That year we had some excellent Scholars from Kazakhstan: Kuanysh Karibayev, Head of the Department of Paediatric Anaesthesiology in Almaty Regional Children's Hospital; Assel Tulebayeva, a Paediatric Cardiologist also from Almaty, who later was offered a research Scholarship in Cambridge; and Bota Kuanova, an Oncologist from Astana, who worked with Ainur and who succeeded her as Head of department during Ainur's maternity leave.

Kuanysh, during his Scholarship, was able to observe lots of cardiac and general surgery including different types of anaesthetic techniques. He was particularly impressed by the separate anaesthetic room in the operation theatres, and also commented that he would miss Nahid's dinners and sweet desserts.

Bota, as a little girl, had thought that no child should have to suffer the agony of cancer. As the years passed, her biggest concern became the 350 to 400 children in the Paediatric Oncology department of the National Scientific Centre of Maternity and Childhood in Astana. During her three months training in GOSH, she had been able to realise her dream.

At the beginning of Assel's Observership in Great Ormond Street, she had made a list of interesting and important things which she wanted to study and see. Her main goal was to improve her knowledge in Paediatric Cardiology and especially develop her skills in cardiac imaging and echocardiography.

*

PC teaching course

In preparation for the Paediatric Cardiology teaching course in Ufa, I flew out a couple of days before Joe and Richard. The BA flight to Moscow left at 6 a.m, and I checked my baggage through all the way to Ufa.

On arrival at Domodedovo Airport, I found there was a rather complicated route to the domestic departures, and the S7 flight eventually departed two hours late. When I arrived in Ufa at 11 p.m. there was no sign of my baggage. Igor kindly met me on arrival and drove me to the Azimut Hotel.

A not very auspicious start. I texted Joe and Richard to warn them of potential problems and advised them how to get from the International arrivals to domestic departures in Moscow.

However, all was not lost. The hotel reception ascertained that my suitcase was at the airport in Moscow, but for various regulatory reasons they would not be able to forward it to Ufa.

By good fortune, next morning, Alexy, the partner of Rezida's sister Venus, was at Domodedovo Airport in Moscow seeing his mother off on a flight. Igor contacted him, sent him the baggage tag details, and asked him to try and retrieve my bag.

Alexy was a very determined person, and after three or four hours had managed to locate the bag, convince the airport authorities that they should release it to him, meet Joe and Richard on arrival at the airport from London and pass the bag to them. They then checked it in on their S7 flight and eventually it was reunited with me when they arrived in Ufa.

Igor and I met Joe and Richard at the airport and during the course of the day took them to see the Republican Children's Cardiology Centre where the teaching course would be held, and showed them various sights in the city.

The following morning, we introduced them to Irina Nikolaeva and Professor Valentin Pavlov, Dean of the Bashkiri Medical School.

Over a hundred and twenty doctors and nurses attended the first seminar. In the afternoon, during the second seminar, they were introduced to the concept of interactive teaching, role playing, small discussion groups and questions and answers. These were teaching methods they had never previously experienced, and after a slow start all those participating became very enthusiastic.

The British teachers on their laptops had English versions of the PowerPoint course, and on the screen in the lecture hall the audience viewed Russian versions. We also had engaged an excellent professional translator, Albina Nazerova, who translated very accurately and consecutively.

We asked for volunteers from the participants to teach the course to their colleagues when they returned to their home regions. Eventually we had 18 doctors, and following the final seminar we taught them how to teach interactively and gave each one a copy of the PowerPoint course.

Following each seminar and at the end of the five-day course, all attendants were asked to complete questionnaires, comment on the course and rate it on a scale of one to five.

The local press and television in Ufa interviewed us and gave good coverage to the Preventive Cardiology course, and the fact that it was being taught by doctors from the UK.

I took the opportunity of meeting with Sharonov and Aysilu, who were very supportive and, of course, discussed the course in detail with Irina Nikolaeva and broached the possibility of Bashkortostan funding a follow-up course the following year.

Professor Pavlov had invited us to give a presentation to the doctors and students in the Bashkiri Medical School, where he was the director, and Joe fortunately had brought with him an instructive video produced by UCL.

Not all our time was spent teaching. Igor had arranged for us to visit his gym where we all enjoyed a workout, and Professor Pavlov invited us to his dacha on an island in a lake near Pavlovka, 90 minutes' drive outside Ufa. A boat journey took us to the island, and there we met his friends, Farid and Venera, who had prepared a very tasty lunch with lots of vodka. After lunch we swam in the lake and then spent some time in their sauna.

When the final two seminars had been presented on Friday, following closing speeches certificates were handed out to all the participants. Everyone felt it had been a very successful course and expressed the hope that further teaching would be continued by the local doctors under the supervision of the Republican Cardiological Children's Centre.

Igor, Rezida and Michael drove us to the airport the following day and on arrival at Domodedovo in Moscow found that BA had upgraded us to Club class.

We all felt this had been a very worthwhile exercise which hopefully would bring long-term benefit to the whole of Bashkortostan, and ultimately to other parts of the Russian Federation

*

RGF Scholars

Olga Tatarinova, a Paediatric Oncologist from the Rogachev Research Clinical Centre, noted that she was impressed by the organisation of work and how effective their teams were in GOSH with perfect collaboration between immunology, haematology, oncology, metabolic diseases units, pre-bone marrow transplant, inpatient and post-transplant periods of patient care. She stated: *"I would like to use these ideas in our hospital in Moscow."*

A Paediatric Oncologist from the Raisa Gorbachev Memorial Institute of Child Oncology in St Petersburg, Asmik Gevorgian, commented very favourably on the weekly oncology, haematology and morphology teaching meetings and also her visits to Oxford, Cambridge and Edinburgh. She wrote *"had the opportunity to see the gorgeous musical The Lion King and it was fantastic!"*

*

Selection Board Moscow/Astana

That year, when we arrived in Moscow to interview Scholarship candidates, we were very surprised and upset to hear that Moscow Health Department had changed the hospital's name from Tushinskaya to Balsheva. The Trust had spent years helping to improve the facilities of the hospital and assist the medical staff, and the Russians hadn't had the courtesy to consult us before arbitrarily changing the hospital's name.

We informed Ismail that we would continue to refer to the hospital as Tushinskaya. He fully understood our feelings and explained that the decision had been made solely on the order of Moscow City Council.

Having selected one DMS scholar, Artem Burkin, a Urologist, and one RGF scholar, Olga Slesarchuk, an Oncologist, we departed the following day for Astana, flying Air Astana via Almaty.

Until 1997, Almaty, previously known as Alma Ata, had been the capital city of Kazakhstan. In the Kazhak language the name means "father of apples" and the region remains famous for its apples.

During the 15th and 16th centuries it lay on the Silk Road and is still the major commercial and cultural centre of Kazakhstan. Lying in the foothills of the Altai mountains, it experiences hot summers and cold winters with heavy snowfalls, and a ski resort, Shimbulak, is within easy reach by mountain railway.

Following the Selection Board, where we selected Dyar, a Cardiac Surgeon, and Zarip, a Neonatal Surgeon, we were interviewed by a newspaper journalist working for the *Express K*, a socio-political newspaper.

We took Almira and Aida, who was now pregnant, out to supper and at 3 a.m. caught the flight to Vnukovo Airport, Moscow

Chapter 32

Kazakhstan

Our scholars, SHOUT, 2015 KZ scholars' reunion in Almaty, EAPC poster, Moscow reunion, Ski's visit Astana, Scholars

Our scholars

Artem Burkin, a Paediatric Urologist who spoke excellent English and whose wife worked in the Moscow office of accountants Grant Thornton, was later to be appointed Head of the Urology department in Tushinskaya Hospital.

In his report he wrote, *"I have spent three wonderful months in the Great Ormond Street Hospital. I had the opportunity to see a lot and learn a lot. It is not only the work of the most prominent surgeons in the world I have observed, not just a lot of complex cases as I saw, but I also learnt about something very practical and useful – the structure and organisation of the National Health Services in the United Kingdom. I believe the knowledge which I obtained during this scholarship will help me to optimise and to improve the work of the hospital where I work in Russia. I became familiar with the structure of the nursing services and this might help me to make the corporation between the doctors and the nurses in my hospital more effective and smooth. In my opinion the protocol for pre- and post-operative patient management is very important and if designed well can be safely relied upon."*

Olga Slesarchuk, an RGF scholar from St Petersburg whose specialist interest was bone marrow transplant, made the observation that *"in the BMT unit there is a useful rotation not only of clinical fellows, but also of consultants. It helps to avoid psychological overload of the staff, helps to share responsibility and to treat patients as a team."*

*

SHOUT

After a 10-year wait, Gordon Brown finally succeeded Tony Blair as Prime Minister. Having shortly after his appointment missed an opportunity to call an election, which he might have won, he eventually called one in 2010.

The Conservatives, led by David Cameron, became the largest single party, but rather than govern with a "hung Parliament", they formed a coalition with the Liberal Democrats, led by Nick Clegg, and Gordon Brown resigned.

In the ensuing Labour leadership election, Ed Milliband, younger brother of David Milliband, who had previously been Foreign Secretary and was the favourite candidate, narrowly won. Many felt he had stabbed his elder brother in the back.

Prior to the election due in 2015, the first to be held following the introduction of a fixed five-year term of government rule, the Labour party declared they would introduce a "Mansion Tax", ostensibly to raise revenue for additional funding of the NHS.

This annual levy would be charged on all properties valued at £2 million or more. They aimed to raise a total of £1.2 billion annually. To achieve that sum, owners with properties valued over £3 million would have to make an annual average payment of £20,000 each.

This appeared to me to be a very unfair tax, which would largely and seriously affect the 30,000 people who were *"asset rich and cash poor."* I decided to set up a non-partisan organisation which would campaign against the introduction of this unfair tax.

A committee of eight like-minded individuals with a wide range of experience in a variety of relevant fields, including accountancy, the law, property and health care, was set up with the aim of seeking to stop the mansion tax.

We developed a website making the case for opposing the establishment of the tax, and we changed the name of the campaign from Stop Mansion Tax to Stop Home Owners Unfair Tax – SHOUT.

We engaged an independent public affairs consultancy, Central Lobby Consultants. We held several meetings in different venues and obtained coverage in local newspapers, such as the *Ham & High* and national papers including the *Evening Standard*.

Our counterarguments were based on the unfairness and inequitability of the new annual tax on non-cash-generating sources, and the fact that a small proportion of the population would be funding national public services.

As those who were unable to pay would be forced to move to cheaper areas, the super-rich would be able to buy properties at "knock-down" prices. Local businesses would suffer due to homeowners reduced spendable income and overseas buyers would spend less on investing in the UK.

Charitable donations would be reduced, and perhaps most importantly the asset rich/cash poor would experience humanitarian problems.

I made the opening introductory speech at one of our meetings held in the Holy Trinity Church in Sloane Street, having just returned from skiing in the Dolomites where, trying to avoid a child, I had fallen and struck my face on a ski stick. The audience must have been very surprised to see my black eye. I reassured the audience that I had not been assaulted in the street by those who disagreed with our views.

Every member of Parliament and many Peers were contacted. Many business firms, the Church of England and the Royal Borough of Chelsea & Westminster all offered their support.

There was a remarkably good response and we eventually received donations from several thousand individual supporters from across the political parties.

There is little doubt that our media coverage and intensive lobbying played a significant part in withdrawal of the unfair proposed tax.

*

2015 KZ Scholars' reunion in Almaty

ENRC had offered to arrange a reunion and reception for our Kazakh Scholars when we next held a Selection Board in Astana, and we had decided on the same trip to visit Almaty and meet some of our Scholars and visit their Institutes.

We would take a seven-and-a-half-hour Premium Economy direct flight to Almaty, then transfer to Astana on an Air Astana flight. On our return to Almaty, we would stay there for a few days.

Michael at that time had a back problem and decided, at his own expense, to fly Club class with a flatbed. Unfortunately, the day before our flight, his back worsened and he decided that it would be better not to accompany us.

This decision had an unexpected sequel. During the long flight, Nahid developed cramp in her leg. I called the air stewardess and knowing that Michael had an unused Club class seat, requested that Nahid could move to that seat, which would be much more comfortable for her.

The air stewardess informed me that she would have to request the Captain's, the pilot's, permission for this transfer. He stated that this would not be possible unless I was prepared to pay for an upgrade. This I felt was a quite unreasonable demand in the circumstances, and subsequently I made a formal complaint to BA.

At Almaty Airport, following a four-hour transfer wait, we boarded the Air Astana flight to Astana, where on this occasion we stayed in the Hilton Garden Inn Hotel.

Aida had arranged tickets for us to see the ballet *Korsair* in the Opera House, and she came to the hotel for tea. She brought with her her baby son, Kasmirzhani, and her sister, to give us the tickets. It wasn't a bad production, but we had seen much better ones in Moscow.

During the night there was a false fire alarm, so we were a bit sleepy when we arrived in the ENRC office for the Selection Board. Due to other commitments, neither of our Kazakh colleagues, Nurgul and Alma, turned up but, in their absence we selected four Scholars and two reserves.

At the reception which was held in the Opera House, Ainur and her baby, Jabrail, Bota and Gulden attended. The British Embassy was represented by Simon Williams, Director of British Council Almaty.

We were welcomed by Yuriy Serebyako, Vice President ENRC, now called ERG, Eurasian Research Group. Quen Mok gave a PowerPoint presentation about GOSH, Harald Lipman spoke about Tushinskaya Trust, and all of our past Scholars who were present told us of their experiences and professional lives since completing their Scholarships in London.

Following refreshments, an excellent vocal recital was given by several members of the Astana Opera.

The following day, the UK members flew back to Almaty and stayed in the comfortable Rixos Hotel where we met Baglan and Assel, two of our past Scholars. Kuanysh was on night duty so we were unable to see him.

Whilst in Almaty we visited the Institute of Paediatrics and Paediatric Surgery and met the head of the Oncology department, Professor Bahram Malikkaidarovich. He very kindly drove us up into the foothills of the Altai Mountains, to a village where there was a long street full of shashlik restaurants. We all enjoyed an excellent supper.

Next day, Assel took us to see several of the sights in the city – the Panfilotsev Park and Second World War Memorial, the Resurrection Church and the fascinating Musical Instruments Museum. After lunch we were joined by Baglan and her mother, who took us by the gondola to the ski resort, Shymbulak.

We had arranged a tour to the frozen Big Almaty Lake, and in the evening Assel's parents had invited us to their house for dinner.

They had put on a magnificent traditional Kazakh meal and insisted that we must wear the Kazakh costume. I was dressed in a long black coat and gold thread-embroidered robe with a tall, black broad-brimmed hat on my head. The ladies wore simple long black dresses – much less impressive.

This sadly was to be Nahid's and my final trip to Kazakhstan. We still have fond memories of the visit and of the warmth and kindness of the Kazakh people. Four years later Assel visited us in London.

EAPC poster

I presented a poster at the EAPC, European Association of Preventive Cardiology, meeting in Lisbon detailing the Preventive Cardiology course which we had taught in Ufa.

The main points highlighted were:

There is no specific undergraduate teaching of Preventive Cardiology in the Russian Federation. ICHARM had engaged University College London to devise and write a ten-seminar introductory course in Preventive Cardiology. This was translated into Russian, and was taught over five days in July 2014 to doctors in Ufa, Republic of Bashkortostan, Russian Federation, by two of the British doctors who had prepared it.

During the teaching course, 18 of the attendants were trained to teach the course to their colleagues in the nine regions of Bashkortostan.

This was the first time that a course of Preventive Cardiology had been taught to Russian doctors in Russia by foreign doctors. The ten seminars were taught in an interactive manner, with frequent questions and answers, general and small group discussion, and role play. A novel approach to teaching in Russia and one which was widely welcomed by the attendants.

One hundred and twenty Russian doctors, all involved in either primary or secondary CVD prevention, from Ufa and the eight administrative regions attended. Evaluation forms were completed following each session and at the end of the course each attendant received a certificate of attendance. The majority of attendants rated content/presentation/value/ enjoyment as 4 or 5 on a scale 0–5. Based on samples of attendants' comments, we drew the following conclusions:

1. ICHARM/UCL Preventive Cardiology course is translational to other cultures. 2. Novel methods of teaching can be introduced in other cultures. 3. Training of trainers is essential if uniform approaches in Preventive Cardiology teaching are to be universally applied.

Moscow reunion

A reunion of Moscow hands who had served together in the Embassy in the 1980s was held in an Italian restaurant near Notting Hill Gate – Da Scalzo. It was such a pleasure to see and reminisce with so many old friends and comrades. How times had changed over the last 25 years.

*

Ski's visit Astana

Bota Kuanova, one of our ENRC Scholars who was now Head of Solid Tumour Oncology at the Astana National Research Centre for Maternal and Child Health, asked the Trust if they could arrange for an Oncologist from GOSH to visit her unit and advise.

With ENRC's consent we arranged for a GOSH consultant Oncologist, Dr Anthony Michalski, known as Ski, to visit Astana for five days.

He made a detailed assessment of the 45 bedded unit and its team of seven junior doctors who worked with paediatrically trained nurses and a psychologist. He reported: *"There was no formal rotation for the doctors and no structure for ongoing career progression and development. At night the hospital was staffed by a general paediatric and intensivist team and Bota dealt with any oncological emergencies."*

There was a separate Haematology unit, and a six-bed Bone Marrow Transplantation unit had just opened. Radiotherapy was delivered in a city hospital, but any child requiring anaesthesia or paediatric support for radiotherapy was treated in Almaty, 1,300 km away, a train journey of 13 hours.

Multidisciplinary team meetings were held to decide patient treatment, but were poorly attended by the overworked team.

A German team from Berlin's Charité Hospital visited four times a year, dealing largely with clinical problems, but did not appear to have a planned programme of ongoing academic and career development.

For his first three days in Astana, Ski was based on the Solid Tumour Oncology ward reviewing the care of current inpatients and a number of outpatients with difficult problems. He gave talks on diagnosing brain tumours, molecular biology of solid tumours and infants with brain tumours. He was also asked to give a talk on "burnout in paediatric oncology", which appeared very relevant to the young small medical team with its high workload.

For his final two days he was an invited expert at the VII International Conference of Paediatric Neurologists of Central Asian Countries, moderated all the Oncology sessions, and gave a talk on Paediatric Neuro-oncology in the UK, and modern investigation and treatment of medulloblastoma.

Before departure for the UK, he made several recommendations including increasing senior oncology presence and improved multidisciplinary team working. He also recommended that there should be a National Cancer Registry and a national network of paediatric cancer units with common protocols. Ongoing education and training of the senior oncology staff should be provided, and amongst other recommendations increased provision should be made for imaging and bone scanning. Additionally, provision should be made for key anti-cancer drugs usage, and protocols for radiotherapy treatment should be electronically available for radiotherapy centres.

This indeed was a very worthwhile visit from which hopefully future children in Kazakhstan will benefit.

*

Akbota Rakisheva, a Neonatal Surgeon from east Kazakhstan, who in her IELTS examination had achieved a very good score of 6.5, detailed after completion of her Scholarship, an extensive list of the main things she wished to implement in her hospital and share with her colleagues on her return home. These included, amongst others, *"parental visiting, team work, minimally invasive techniques, UK guidelines for neonatal care, peripherally inserted central lines, short-term paralysing in many surgical conditions, use of vacuum dressing, balloon dilatation of oesophageal strictures, sclerotherapy in lymphatic malformations, and research work in regenerative medicine."*

Gulden Ryspayeva, also a Neonatologist from Kazakhstan had a particular interest in neonatal reanimation as more than half of her patients were born prematurely. *"From the first visit to the hospital I was surprised of the local atmosphere: everybody is kind and ready to help at any time. All of the interior of the hospital was done to entertain kids and to make their staying in more comfortable and satisfies with the main motto of the hospital, 'The child first and always.'"*

Chapter 33

The last Tsar

Yekaterinburg, The last Tsar, REUR, Moscow, Future of the Scholarships, UK events, Our Scholars, , Dynasty, US Presidential election, Napoleon in Russia, Moscow to Cuba

Yekaterinburg

Marc had been invited to speak at the annual congress of the Thoracic Society of the Ural Region to be held in the Yekaterinburg, and invited me to come with him. In Soviet times, known as Sverdlovsk, it was a city closed to foreigners. As it was a city I had never visited, and from which we had had three Diana Memorial Scholars, I readily agreed.

In light of the worsening relationship between the UK and Russia, increasingly complex procedures had been introduced for those applying for visas. This involved personally attending the Russian Visa Centre, located near the Barbican, to record biometric data including fingerprints.

We flew Aeroflot to Sheremetyevo in Moscow, and there transferred to another two-hour flight to Yekaterinburg, crossing another two time zones, so on arrival we were five hours ahead of London time. We were very pleased on arrival to see that our baggage had arrived safely.

Fortunately, Hotel Angelo, where we would be staying and where the congress would be held, was only a short walk away.

Professor Igor Medvinsky, deputy Director of the Ural Research Institute of Phthysiopulmonology (Tuberculosis), had made all the arrangements for us and met us shortly after arrival. He had arranged for an interpreter, Elena, to accompany us throughout the congress.

Marc presented two papers on various aspects of tuberculosis at the congress and chaired one of the sessions. Everyone was very helpful and welcoming.

Following the final sessions on the second day of the congress, a dinner and dance had been arranged to celebrate the 85th anniversary of the opening of the Institute.

A visit had been arranged for the delegates to the Icon Museum, which had been founded and was run by the city Mayor, Evgeny Roizman, a very proactive person, who had opened a drug rehabilitation centre.

We were also taken to see the recently opened Boris Yeltsin Presidential Centre used for social, cultural and educational purposes. There were displays, photographs and videos detailing the contemporary political history of the Soviet Union and Russia and President Yeltsin's heritage. However, there appeared to be some distortion of some historical events. Boris Yeltsin was born in Yekaterinburg, in Soviet times known as Sverdlovsk.

The last Tsar

Yekaterinburg, located on the eastern side of the Urals in the 18th century, as it was a centre for trade and commerce, had been known as the "Window to Asia". From the time of Peter the Great, it was renowned for its iron-making plant.

Following the October Revolution in 1918, Tsar Nicolas II, his wife Alexandra and five children, Olga, Tatiana, Maria, Anastasia and Alexei, were exiled to Yekaterinburg and housed in the Ipatiev House, which was later demolished and on its site the Church of the Spilling Blood was built.

The Tsar's cousin, George V, refused on personal and diplomatic grounds, to offer him refuge in the UK, and all the family were murdered by the Bolsheviks. Their bodies were buried outside the city in a pit in a forest known as *Ganina Yama* where, in memory of this dreadful event, the Monastery of Holy Imperial Passion Bearers was erected.

*

Of our three Scholars, Anton Zadoya, an Anaesthetist, had emigrated to Australia five years previously and apparently was now well established there.

Anastasiia Nikitina, a neonatal Surgeon, now worked in a private clinic as a paediatric and adult Dermatologist and was studying family practice. On return to Yekaterinburg, following her Scholarship, she had become very disillusioned as the senior staff in her hospital would not agree to any of the changes she proposed. She felt the Scholarship had opened her eyes to another world.

Both she and her husband, Danila, were very kind to Marc and me and took us around the city. Having shown us some of the original machinery from the iron-making plant, they invited us to a restaurant for lunch, and then we visited the Stone Park and the Jewellery Museum as well as *Ganina Yama*.

Oleg Koshurnikov, a Urologist, was now head of the Department of Paediatric

Surgery at the Sverdlovsk Regional Paediatric Institute, looking after children aged two years to seventeen years. Every weekend he worked a 24-hour shift, and following one of these long shifts he came to visit us in our hotel. He was very appreciative of the help given to him by the Scholarship.

Marc and I flew from Yekaterinburg to Moscow on the same flight, where he caught another flight to London and I disembarked to spend a few days in Moscow, staying as usual at the Hotel Pekin.

*

REUR Retain EU Rights

I was woken at 7 a.m. on the morning of Friday 24 June 2016 to hear the BBC news announcing the result of the Brexit referendum. By a small margin, the Brexiteers had triumphed. I was devastated and felt as if there had been a death in the family.

With a turnout of 72.2 per cent of voters, 51.9 per cent had voted to leave the EU and 48.1 per cent to remain. A majority of 1,259,501 votes cast.

This vote was to have disorienting and serious political effects on both the UK and the EU.

David Cameron, fearful of losing votes at a general election to Nigel Farage's UKIP, had agreed to hold an ill-conceived referendum which Cameron had expected would result with the UK staying in the EU.

I decided to ascertain if the result could be challenged via the European Court of Justice and sought the advice of several experts in European law – Professor Catherine Barnard of Trinity College Cambridge, Karen Davies of Swansea University and Professor Derrick Wyatt QC, emeritus Professor EU law, Oxford.

They felt deprivation of UK nationals, EU citizenship and breach of their acquired rights was a weak case, as they were not being rendered stateless. Nevertheless, I felt that that this approach might be pursued if we could find a suitable applicant.

Initially this would have to be through the British courts, and if unsuccessful I could then as an EU citizen contact the European Court of Justice or the European Court of Human Rights.

I sought a young, professional, preferably academic British adult who was married with children and was working in or studying a research project in one of the EU countries other than the UK. He or she would need to be willing, capable and able to pursue legal proceedings.

His or her argument would be based on the loss of their right to hold an EU passport; loss of freedom to travel, reside, work or study in the EU; loss of reciprocal health care in the EU; loss of EU funding for research projects; loss of intellectual property rights in the EU; loss of entitlement to help from EU Embassies in any countries with no British Embassy; and loss of single-market benefits.

I thus sought a legal firm with experience in EU law and procedures and humanitarian issues, and on the advice of Jolyon Maugham QC chose Bindmans. I also sought a "top silk" barrister with similar interests.

All this would require funding, and so I began a long search for a funder.

In a letter to *The Times*, Chairmen and women and Chief Executives representing 1,200 businesses ranging from micro companies to FTSE 100 companies had stated that *"Britain leaving the EU would mean uncertainty for our firms, less trade with Europe and fewer jobs."*

Many of these firms I contacted and met seeking financial support for my REUR campaign. Roland Rudd, the City PR boss who had initiated the letter, gave me helpful advice, and Martin Sorrell, founder of WPP, the world's largest advertising and PR group, suggested I should contact Matthew Freud, founder of PR firm Freud Communications.

I knew Matthew as he had been a contemporary of my son Marc at Westminster School. His father was Clement Freud, a politician and writer, and his great-grandfather was Sigmund Freud.

We met on several occasions, and he felt we should take legal advice regarding the strength of our argument before embarking on a potentially prolonged legal challenge to Brexit.

By chance, the parents of a Director of his firm were very friendly with a member of the Supreme Court – I shall call him William Brown QC – and they sought his informal advice. He categorically stated that members of the Supreme Court would never oppose a government decision, and sadly Matthew felt that we should not proceed with our campaign.

As it happened, the Supreme Court later in 2019, after William Brown had retired from it, did oppose Boris Johnson's government decision to prorogue Parliament for five weeks, and stated it was unlawful and void.

Before our decision not to proceed, I had visited Cambridge and held a meeting with the Director of Communications in the University, with the objective of finding a suitable applicant who would be prepared to submit a case to the courts. Our grandson, Jacob, was at that time in his final year reading English at Fitzwilliam College and we met him and took him out to lunch and tea.

During the campaign I contacted every member of the cabinet and many MPs and Peers.

Who knows, but I still feel if we had proceeded with the campaign, it's possible Brexit could have been prevented.

*

Moscow

On my next visit to Moscow, Teatralny Square was decorated for the Easter spring festival and one could see preparations for the annual May Day parade.

We had had 12 scholars from Moscow. I met with three of them.

Anastasia Nosko was a Neurologist who was working in a private clinic, the European Medical Centre, two to three days a week, and teaching one day weekly in the Neurological department of the Neurological Institute located in Tushinskaya Hospital. She rehabilitated children with cerebral palsy, using botulin injections very effectively. She maintained close links with Jennifer Sargent in GOSH and had invited her to visit and speak in Moscow. Anastasia has a young daughter and her husband Igor was the head of a private medical clinic.

Artem Burkin, a Urologist, was head of Department of Urology and General Surgery (paediatric and adult) in Tushinskaya Hospital. The department was developing and expanding. He had a young son, and commuted daily to work from the outskirts of southwest Moscow. He felt that the Scholarship had been very beneficial for his career and was determined to do all he could to improve the services offered to his patients.

Alan Asmanov was now Head of the Ear, Nose and Throat department in the Veltischev Institute of Paediatric and Clinical Medicine, which had opened 12 months previously and was rapidly expanding its scope.

He wished to develop joint research projects with the Institute of Child Health London, and also to develop clinical aspects of his work and training of doctors and nurses, in conjunction with GOSH.

I also was very pleased to be able to meet again his wife Dasha, but sadly not their young daughter Elena as she was asleep.

Ismail Osmanov was gradually resolving the many problems he'd inherited in Tushinskaya Hospital. Medical staff were paid from Federal sources and in light of the economy's problems the health care budget had been reduced. However, nurses were paid by Moscow government, which remained relatively rich. The effect of this was that nurses' salaries in Moscow were now greater than junior doctors.

One of his major problems related to nursing. As nurses in Moscow received higher salaries than in the provinces, over 50 per cent of his nurses commuted for over three-hour journeys from outside Moscow. They then worked 24-hour shifts and as they were very tired, unhappy and not interested in the children, did not bother to look after them properly. They travelled home, had a further day at home looking after their house and their children, and returned to the hospital the next day.

Future of the Scholarships

We were considering closing the Scholarship programmes and trying to decide how best to use the remaining funds.

On a trial basis we asked Ismail to select one of his medical staff and offer him or her the opportunity of attachment to GOSH as a Clinical Observer for a period of two weeks.

He selected a young Cardiologist, Lev Krugly, and we arranged for him to stay in the Goodenough College International Students Hostel, within walking distance of GOSH. Artem, our Urologist Scholar, very kindly offered to mentor him and assist with introducing him to the procedures in the hospital.

We felt on balance that his visit had not been particularly successful, and this was a path which we would not follow in the future.

We also considered the possibility of secondment of medical or nursing staff from GOSH to Tushinskaya Hospital for limited periods, but GOSH didn't feel that this would be practical.

Perhaps we should resurrect the Diana School of Paediatric Nursing. It was not clear when and why it had ceased to function. The benefits to Tushinskaya would be the availability of specialised nurse Paediatric training and a locally based source of trained Paediatric nurses.

Subsequently, with the agreement of RGF and ERG, we decided to use the remaining funds to continue offering Diana Memorial scholarships for a further two or three years.

All in all, this had been a very interesting and useful trip.

*

UK events

Sadiq Khan had been elected to replace Boris Johnson as Mayor of London.
The Queen celebrated her 90th birthday.
Jo Cox, a Labour MP, was murdered in her constituency by a right-wing activist.

*

Our Scholars

With our two Kazakh Scholars, Dyar Beguzhinov and Zarip Mukhamedov, we visited the Wallace Collection located in Hertford House in Manchester Square London. The works of art collected in the 18th and 19th centuries by the Marquesses of Hertford and Richard Wallace, son of the fourth Marquess, were bequeathed to the nation by his widow in 1897.

We had considerable problems in finding accommodation for Dyar and Zarip as Netherhall House on this occasion was unable to accommodate them. Eventually, with the help of Britannia Student Services, at considerably increased expense, we found them ensuite self-catering rooms in Beaumont Court near King's Cross station, within walking distance from GOSH.

Zarip was informed that his visa had been refused and we had to try to sort this out. Eventually, we discovered that he had applied for the wrong type of visa as the regulations had recently been changed, and he was then able to reapply successfully.

Diyar was a Cardiac Surgeon, married with two young children, who came from east Kazakhstan, and Zarip, with an interest in children's Oncology, was a Neonatal Surgeon from Almaty.

We often invited them for meals in our house and on one occasion Zarip, who enjoyed cooking, cooked us all an excellent pilaf.

Diyar reported that the first day in hospital was the most difficult day in his trip. When visiting a new place like this, living overseas with people speaking a foreign language, the first week or so could be extremely difficult. However, by the time the Scholarship ended he was reporting that *"This is the most unforgettable and important experience in my entire life because it opened my mind."*

Zarip commented, *"The way everyone knows what they have to do in each time unit. Juniors and nurses are well educated, responsible and skilled, with a sense of self-esteem, and are a real support for physicians. As a doctor they are great joy to participate with."*

*

In September three new Scholars arrived, two from Kazakhstan – Assel Baimoldanova, a Neonatologist, married, with a two-year-old daughter who was staying with her grandparents in Ust-Kamenogorsk, and Assylzhan Messova, a Gastroenterologist with two young sons. They flew together from Moscow with Anna Krasatseva, an Oncologist from the Rogachev who would be our last RGF Scholar.

A few days after their arrival, by chance, it was Assel's birthday, and we arranged a small supper party in our house.

When we had selected Anna, she had asked if she could bring her husband and young baby daughter, Daria, with her for the duration of the Scholarship. We had advised her that, although we understood the reason for wishing to have them with her, this would not be practically possible as it would distract her from her studies.

Shortly after her arrival, even though she was speaking and seeing Daria on a daily basis on Skype, she asked if, at her own expense, she could return to Moscow for a few days each month. We agreed to this request, and in fact everything worked out quite smoothly and she missed very little time from her attachment in GOSH.

*

When Igor Medvinsky and his wife Elena from Yekaterinburg visited London, we took them for lunch to a restaurant in Hampstead, and Anna came with us to assist with interpreting.

Assel on departure commented, "*The feature which amazed me from my first day is the huge psychological support for patients and their families from the staff side and the hospital itself. The support is provided in the several different ways. The special room where parents can pray for their child, the entertainment rooms with many interesting toys for the stable patients where they can play and sometimes switch their mind from the disease, the rooms of parents where they can gather and communicate with each other, a lot of guidelines and books for the parents to better understand the disease of their child and sadly, but importantly, even the memory book which keeps the names of all patients who passed away in the Centre.*"

Assylzhan stated, "*For the first time in my life I had opportunity to do an internship abroad. When you work for many years in one place you do not know your mistakes and where you need to improve your knowledge. But when you get to another hospital, one of the best in the world, you realise how much you have yet to learn to provide assistance as a high level.*"

Anna appreciated so much that we had permitted her to make visits to see Daria. Her final report read, "*You do not only make my dream come true but help seriously ill children in Russia to be given the best care according to the world's best standards.*"

*

Geraldine Norman book launch

Geraldine Norman, an art historian who had uncovered the art forgeries of Tom

Keating, and was Chief Executive of Hermitage Foundation UK, had written a book called *Dynasty* about the Piotrovsky family, father Boris and son Mikhail, who had been and still were Directors of the Hermitage Museum in St Petersburg. The Russian Ambassador hosted her book launch in their Embassy.

*

US Presidential election

Against the odds, Donald Trump, although receiving almost 3 million votes fewer than Hillary Clinton, won the US Presidential election. Accusations were made that he was very close to Putin and had received Russian support by social media influencing the electorate to vote in his favour.

*

Napoleon in Russia

The Iranian Ambassador to the UK, Iraj Amini, at a meeting of the Iran Society, gave a most interesting talk entitled "Napoleon in Russia."

The relationship between Iran and Russia in the Caucasus, Georgia and Azerbaijan was very complex and very fluid. Napoleon, with a bid to counter British influence in the area, had formed a short-lived alliance with Fath-Ali Quajar, Shah of Iran, and when this broke down the Shah resolved to invade Tsarist Russia.

In 1812, Napoleon crossed the River Nieman into Russia, and initially after the battle of Borodino proceeded to occupy Moscow. However, the Russians employed a "scorched earth" policy which destroyed Napoleon's supply lines, and in conjunction with a very harsh winter he was forced to withdraw troops from Russian territory.

*

Jeanne Sutherland's memoirs

Nahid and I met many old friends from Moscow when we went to the launch of Jeanne Sutherland's memoirs, *From Moscow to Cuba and Beyond. A Diplomatic Memoir of the Cold War.* The book was based on Jeanne and her husband Iain's letters to Iain's parents, and following Iain's early death was based on Jeanne's diaries.

On the day of the event there was a heavy snowfall, and most of the roads to Highgate where she lived were impassable. We decided not to drive ourselves but engaged a minicab driver and hoped that somebody up above was looking after our welfare.

Chapter 34

Red star over Russia

Health of the Russian people, Alan and Dasha visit, UK election, Diana DVD, KZ scholars, Death of Stalin, Selection Board Almaty and Moscow, Crocus city, Russia and the EU, Scholars farewell, Red Star over Russia, Winter Olympics, Doping scandal, Michael, Three scholars

Health of the Russian people

In January 2017 the World Bank released an in-depth analysis of current economic conditions in Russia. The key messages were that the Russian workforce was ageing, premature mortality was high and access to public health services was glaringly inadequate.

However, improvements, such as a reduction in disease burden and mortality attributable to noncommunicable diseases had been made. But public spending on health care remained low and many of the reported health gains had occurred only in large cities and amongst more affluent Russians. Health outcomes for people living in rural areas were far worse than for those in urban settings.

*

Alan and Dasha visit

We were delighted to see Alan and Dasha when they paid a short visit to London. We introduced them to the Scholars and entertained them. They stayed with Dasha's uncle, the Russian Ambassador, in an Embassy flat.

*

UK election

Theresa May, the British Prime Minister, unexpectedly announced that a general election would be held in June 2017. The surprising result of the election was that her party lost their overall majority, but formed a minority government.

Diana DVD

The 20th anniversary of Princess Diana's tragic accident was on 31 August 2017. We had an amateur video taken by one of the staff at Tushinskaya Hospital when Diana visited in 1995. We edited it and made some copies on DVDs, which we forwarded to Kensington Palace to Miguel Head, Private Secretary to The Duke of Cambridge, Prince William, and Prince Henry of Wales, Prince Harry.

*

KZ Scholars

Aigerim Kamzina, a Neonatologist from Astana, our final official ERG, previously known as ENRC, Scholar, and Tatyana Li, had arrived in London from Kazakhstan.

Nahid had received a telephone call from what she thought was the local branch of Tesco informing her that they had found one of her credit cards in the store. When she went to the store to retrieve it, she was told that a customer had discovered it on the floor and handed it in.

Later that day, by chance, Nahid spoke with Aigerim who, to Nahid's surprise, asked her if she had retrieved her credit card from Tesco. Apparently, Aigerim had gone into the Tesco store shortly after Nahid had been there, discovered the card on the floor, noticed that Nahid's name was on, handed it to the cashier and then telephoned Nahid to tell her that she could collect the card from Tesco. A remarkable coincidence for which Nahid was extremely grateful.

During Aigerim's Scholarship, she was able to attend and participate in a course discussing new protocols for parenteral nutrition, that is intravenous feeding, held in Liverpool.

In her final report, Aigerim had recorded, *"During my stay here I had a chance to explore London and also I had yoga and Pilates classes. I lived in St Dorothy's residence which was comfortable and located in Hampstead known for its beautiful places, silence and safety."*

Tatyana Li, our first Diana Memorial Scholar from Kazakhstan, was specialising in Paediatric Emergency care, and on her departure mentioned her unique opportunity to self-study. *"I was allowed to read and copy all protocols and documents I wished. The library was a brilliant place to put one's thoughts to rest. Visiting a library is a pleasant time for me, there it is possible to find all modern and updated literature which I needed. It was very helpful for me because I am doing my PhD degree. During three months I have updated my review article on the topic of ARDS, acute respiratory distress syndrome, in children with BRD, bovine respiratory disease."*

She also prepared a comprehensive and very helpful list of the many acronyms used specifically in intensive care units.

*

Stalin

A film was released in the UK entitled *The Death of Stalin*, directed by Armando Iannucci, presenting as a black-comedy-political satire of the purported intrigues between Soviet leaders following his sudden death in 1953. It was banned in Russia, Kazakhstan and Kyrgyzstan because of its anti-Soviet theme.

*

Selection Board Almaty and Moscow

For the Trust's final Selection Boards in Kazakhstan and Russia, Quen and Susan would fly via Moscow to Almaty, where, on this occasion, we had arranged to interview the Kazakh Scholarship applicants. To break the long flight, they were booked into the Capsule Hotel at Sheremetyevo Airport Moscow, which was located airside so that they would not need to pass through immigration and would be able to have a few hours' sleep.

In fact, it didn't quite work out as planned, as on arrival at Sheremetyevo they were conducted to a different Capsule Hotel, which, as they discovered, was located landside.

By the time they had sorted out the matter with the Immigration officers and returned to the correct airside Capsule Hotel, there wasn't very much time to sleep as the Almaty flight departed at 8 a.m.

Fortunately, the next day in the comfortable Rixos Hotel in Almaty was a rest day and they relaxed, had a swim and saw a couple of our past Scholars.

The Selection Board had been arranged for the following morning in the Kazakh National Medical University Building. With Professor Rabiga Khozhamkul, Vice Dean of the School of General Medicine and Professor Kumiskul Umesheva, Docent of KazNMU, the Selection Board chose three good Scholars, one of whom later withdrew as she was due to marry.

A Russian *Docent* is equivalent to a British Reader, the academic level immediately below a Professor.

After lunch, Quen and Susan caught the Aeroflot flight to Moscow. Nahid and I had flown into Domodedovo that day and had arranged to meet Quen and Susan in the Pekin Hotel.

The next morning, Yulia Skvortsova, one of our Scholars, came to see us in the hotel and brought with her Maria, her two-year-old daughter.

To make up for all the travails that Quen and Susan had experienced, we had arranged to take them for lunch to an excellent restaurant, Shaler, on a small island on the lake at Chistoprudny.

In the evening, Nelli had invited us all to supper at the De Marco restaurant, and we all reminisced about events over the last 28 years.

Ismail had arranged a car and driver to take us to Tushinskaya Hospital where we interviewed 18 candidates, and eventually awarded three Scholarships and chose two reserves.

We were so pleased to see that the hospital had been remarkably transformed and all the concepts we had proposed 25 years previously had now been introduced, and we were looking at an extremely well-run modern children's hospital.

*

Ismail, Alan and Dasha entertained us in the evening at Nobu Restaurant in Crocus City.

Crocus City is a vast satellite in the city of Moscow, established in 2001, located at the intersection of Volokolamskoye Shosse and the Moscow Ring Road. It includes an International convention and exhibition centre, a concert hall seating up to 6,200 people, a hyper-market, a shopping and entertainment complex, a residential and business complex, a large hotel and several restaurants, with a metro station and parking for 20,000 vehicles.

On 22 March 2024, terrorists unexpectantly opened fire and detonated explosives in an attack at the Crocus City Hall music venue, killing over 133 people and injuring a hundred more. The Islamic State claimed responsibility.

*

Next morning it was snowing, and Quen and Susan left early for their return flight to London. Nahid and I had several friends who we wished to see and stayed on for another couple of days.

We met up with Galina, visited Olga and Sacha in their flat, and spent most of the day with Irina and Victor Solopov, who we hadn't seen for several years.

It had been an excellent, interesting and useful trip and possibly the last time we would visit Moscow. Who knows?

*

Russia and the EU

Quentin Peel, previously Moscow correspondent for the FT during our stay in Moscow in the 1980s, and later Fellow for the Europe Programme, Chatham House, spoke about relations between Russia and the EU.

He felt that Russia had used disproportionate force during the Georgian war the previous year, when they had breached the principles of sovereignty for South Ossetia and Abkhazia. The EU response of applying sanctions had adversely affected the Russian economy, and the disputes over the gas supply by Russia to the Ukraine, and issues over missile defence and NATO enlargement had significantly worsened the relationship between Russia and the EU.

*

Scholars' farewell

Before our two Scholars, Tatyana and Aigerim, departed we took them to see a musical show *American in Paris* and arranged a farewell dinner in a restaurant called Sarastro. In Mozart's opera *The Magic Flute*, based on Masonic rituals, Sarastro is the High Priest.

However, the buzzing, lavishly decorated restaurant with nightly vocal entertainers bore no resemblance to Mozart's opera. The food was good, and an excellent singer, Colin Ray, accompanying himself on his guitar, sang swing and Motown classics including songs of Sinatra, The Drifters and Lionel Richie, and it was most enjoyable.

*

Red Star over Russia

In 2017, to mark the centenary of the October Revolution, the Tate Modern gallery held an exhibition called *Red Star over Russia*. The exhibition's name was probably based upon Edgar Snow's *Red Star over China*, his 1937 account of Mao's Chinese Red Army "Long March" across China to the safety of Shaanxi in the northwest, following defeats by Chiang Kai Shek. The book had contained implicit criticism of Stalin.

The exhibition was a dramatic visual history of Russia and the Soviet Union from 1905 to the death of Stalin in 1953 – seen through the eyes of artists, designers and photographers.

Rebellion had brought hope, chaos, heroism and tragedy as the Russian Empire became the Soviet Union, endured revolutions, civil war, famine, dictatorship and Nazi invasion. A new visual culture arose and transformed the fabric of everyday life.

The core of the exhibition came from the extraordinary collection of photographer and graphic designer David King (1943–2016). He started his collection of over 250,000 items relating to this period whilst working for *The Sunday Times Magazine* in the 1970s.

The show displayed rare propaganda posters, prints and photographs – some bearing traces of state censorship, including works by El Lissitzky, Gustav Klutsis, Dmitri Moor, Aleksandr Deineka, Nina Vatolina and Yevgeny Khaldei.

*

Winter Olympics

A well-organised and very successful Winter Olympics Games was held in Sochi, situated in Russia near the Black Sea. Eighty-eight nations participated in the most expensive Olympics ever, and Russia was number one in the final medal table.

However, several of the participating Russians were later found guilty of taking medication to improve their performance and stripped of their medals.

*

Doping scandal

In Soviet times it was recognised many of the athletes and sportsmen and women owed their success to the illegal use of a variety of drugs and stimulants.

This continued during post-Soviet times, and in 2014 documents revealed that there was Russian State involvement in systemic doping. In excess of one thousand Russian competitors who had won medals in Summer, Winter and Paraplegic Olympics were disqualified from further competing, as their success was revealed to have been achieved by doping.

The IOC, International Olympics Committee, suspended the Moscow Anti-doping Centre and later suspended the Russian Olympic Committee.

*

2018 Michael

Michael Nicholls, my oldest and closest friend, a co-founder and Trustee of Tushinskaya Trust, sadly died. In my eulogy at his funeral, I spoke of our first meeting in 1950 across a dissecting table in the anatomy department of UCL. We remained close friends after graduating, and I told in Memories of Moscow, my previous memoir, of Michael and his wife Pam's visit to us in Moscow in the late 1980s. He thus was the obvious person to invite to be the first Trustee of Tushinskaya Trust and he remained so until his death.

He is sorely missed by all who knew him.

*

Three Scholars

Our three Diana Memorial Scholars arrived in March: Artur Sharaffutdinov, a Cardiac Surgeon from Ufa who worked closely with Igor Buzaev; Saniya Baiturova, an Oncologist from Astana; and Kuanysh Ongarbayev, Cardiac Surgeon from Almaty. Artur and Kuanysh would stay in Netherhall House, and Saniya in St Dorothy's hostel.

When they arrived at Heathrow, they were met by the taxi driver who told them that his car had broken down, and they had to wait at the airport until the hire firm had sent them another car and driver.

Artur had a seven-year-old daughter appropriately called Diana, and he spoke with her and his wife on Skype several times a week. Both Igor Buzaev and Irina Nikolaeva, Chief Medical Officer of the Republican Cardiology Centre, had highly recommended him and he certainly lived up to our expectations.

In his final report he wrote about a three-year-old boy with a rare congenital heart problem called Ebstein's anomaly. Artur was attending an international workshop on the treatment of children with this problem. The leading surgeon at the workshop, Prof Dearani from the Mayo Clinic, had stated: *"Cardiac surgery of congenital heart disease is like classical music – everything is written on notes and the surgery of Ebstein's anomaly is like jazz, you never really know how to do it, you have to make improvisations."*

Saniya was particularly interested in the treatment of a brain tumour called medulloblastoma, which apparently was seen quite frequently in her hospital.

Whilst in GOSH she spent a week observing in the Palliative Care Unit and noted, "*I found this field of medicine extremely useful because this service provides a seamless transition from hospital to home. I have an ambition to implement this type of service in my hometown hospital and share with my colleagues all the resources made available to me in GOSH.*"

Kuanysh was married and had three young children. He hoped whilst in London to obtain more knowledge about nurses' training, and on his return home to create a new course for nurses in his hospital.

He found living in Netherhall House a very instructive experience and made many friends who would discuss in the evenings after dinner a great variety of topics. At the weekends he played basketball, football and cricket, and on one occasion went to the countryside to play golf for the first time in his life.

His comments on Great Ormond Street Hospital were, "*I compare GOSH to Babylonian Tower. Highly qualified specialists from different countries work as one team that makes efforts in building the future, because the children are considered to be the future of humanity. Of course, it makes GOSH a unique therapeutic institution. This team includes specialists who share their knowledge and experience. They are always ready to do it with great pleasure.*"

For their farewell dinner we took them to Bel Canto restaurant where the waiters and waitresses were all young opera singers and the food was French cuisine.

During the meal they sang arias from the *La Traviata*, *Barber of Seville*, *Rigoletto*, *Romeo and Juliet*, *Cosi fan Tutte* and *Turandot* to the accompaniment of a pianist. A most enjoyable evening and certainly one the Scholars will never forget.

Chapter 35

Our Trust and Russia

Skripal, Russian propaganda talk, Atlantic Council, Trust's relationship with Russia, Football World Cup, Brexit, Scholars' farewell, Armageddon, Perspectives on 1989, Putin's Russia, The Final Scholars

Skripal

In March 2018, Sergei Skripal, a former Russian military officer and double agent working for the UK's intelligence services, and his daughter Yulia Skripal, who was visiting from Moscow, were poisoned in Salisbury, England, with a Russian-made nerve agent, Novichok.

In June, Dawn Sturgess and her partner Charlie Rowley were exposed to Novichok in nearby Amesbury after handling a contaminated perfume dispenser. Ms Sturgess died in hospital in July.

As a response to this, the UK expelled 23 Russian diplomats from their London Embassy, the US expelled 60 from the Russian Washington Embassy, and eventually there were a total of more than 150 expulsions from 27 countries.

On a tit-for-tat basis, Russia expelled 50 UK diplomats from Moscow and closed the British Consulate in St Petersburg and the British Council offices.

Additionally further sanctions were applied to certain Russian individuals.

*

Russian propaganda talk

I attended a talk given by Owen Matthews, a British writer, historian and journalist, co-sponsored by UCL and SSEES, School of Slavonic and Eastern Europe Studies, entitled "Through the Looking Glass – Inside the Kremlin's Propaganda Machine." He spoke about his experiences as a regular guest on Russian State TV with nightly live appearances on Rossiya 1's *60 Minute*, a top-rated slick political talk show.

The gist of the show was to convince viewers that the world, led by the US, was ganging up against Russia because they feared Russia's new might. The West had fomented a revolution in Ukraine and was aggressively surrounding Russia territorially, whilst Putin was bravely standing with those who resist Washington's global hegemony.

Owen had worked as *Newsweek*'s Moscow bureau chief, covered the second Chechen war and now lectured on Russian history and politics at Columbia university, Antony's College Oxford and the Journalism Faculty at Moscow State University.

A quite eye opening and worrying talk.

*

Atlantic Council

The Russian Ambassador invited me to a meeting to be held in the Russian Embassy to discuss "Global System on the Brink – Pathways Toward a New Normal." This was a joint study by the Atlantic Council's Strategic Foresight Initiative and the Russian Primakov Institute of World Economy and International Relations. Basically, it was an overview of the relationship between regions of the world and four possible scenarios for their future development.

Following a full discussion by experts in International affairs from several countries, including the United States, EU, UK and Russia, the Ambassador in his summing up expressed his feelings that a major factor in the increasingly difficult relationship was lack of trust on both sides.

We, in both the Trust and ICHARM, feel that our projects in a small way were assisting in developing "trust and understanding" between the peoples of the West and Russia.

*

Trust's relationship with Russia

Even though political differences between the UK and Russia were hardening, and many foreign NGOs working in Russia were experiencing difficulties, the Trust managed to maintain a completely apolitical stance and a good relationship with Russia and the Russian people.

*

Football World Cup

Russia hosted the football World Cup in 2018, and 32 teams played in 12 venues spread across western Russia, with France eventually becoming the World champion.

Prior to the commencement of the World Cup, Russia had had a very bad press in the British media, and fears were expressed of hooliganism, homophobia and physical attacks against visiting foreign fans in an alien environment. Fortunately, none of these anticipated problems occurred, and fans who went to Russia were impressed by the positive atmosphere.

There were street parties, lax police pressure, a good-natured welcome, and the visitors felt that Moscow was a normal place, and they saw the "fun side" of Russia. A remarkably positive result for Russia.

*

Brexit

In the UK, political and social divisions over the questions of leaving or not leaving the EU rumbled on. Brexit took up large chunks of Parliamentary time to the exclusion of many important decisions relating to other domestic problems.

Cabinet ministers, including Boris Johnson, the Foreign Secretary and David Davies, in charge of Brexit discussions came and went. Great Britain, mother of Parliamentary democracy, was fast becoming the laughing stock of the world.

*

Scholars' farewell

As was our usual practice, we mentored our Scholars socially as well as personally. We took them to a song recital in the Unitarian Chapel in Hampstead after supper in Carluccio's.

For their farewell dinner we decided to go again to the Bel Canto restaurant and invited Nataly Duddington, Olga Crawford and Inessa Ray to join us.

The menu was much the same as on our last visit six months previously, but the waiters and waitresses, that is the opera singers, had changed, as had their repertoire.

Again, a most enjoyable evening, and certainly one the Scholars will never forget.

*

Armageddon and Paranoia

At a Great Britain Russia Society meeting, Sir Rodric Braithwaite spoke about his recently published book titled *Armageddon and Paranoia*, which in light of the possession of nuclear weapons highlighted the ethical dilemmas and intelligence blunders that fuelled the Cold War.

*

Perspectives on 1989

I was invited to a launch at the Foreign Office of Documents on British Policy Overseas, "Britain and the Revolutions in Eastern Europe 1989". Lord Waldegrave, formerly Minister for Eastern Europe, Mischa Glenny, formerly BBC Central Europe correspondent and Sir John Birch, formerly Ambassador to Hungary, discussed events in Eastern Europe in 1989 which eventually led to the dissolution of the Soviet Union.

*

Putin's Russia

Shaun Walker, *The Guardian*'s Central and East European correspondent, spoke at a BEARR Trust meeting hosted by the EBRD on *"Putin's Russia and the Ghosts of the Past."* For 18 years he had been an observer of the Russian political scene.

Putin had stated that *"only a person without a heart would not mourn the loss of the Soviet Union – but only a person without a head would want to recreate it."* Putin felt that Russian myths and memories of victory in the Great Patriotic War were unifying ideas, so he harked back to those times.

Marcus Warren, head of EBRD Online, had introduced Shaun Walker and mentioned during his introduction that he himself was an old Moscow hand.

Reminiscing with Marcus at the reception after the talk, he told me that he had been posted in Moscow in the 1980s, at the time when HIV and AIDS had first been recognised there.

He also introduced me to a young woman, Anna, who was writing a thesis on HIV in the Soviet Union, and it turned out that she was the daughter of George Edgar, who I had last seen when I stayed with him and his family in the British Embassy in Skopje Macedonia in 2002. She and her sister I recollected had been very bright and lovely children.

A remarkably small world.

I arranged for Anna to come to our house so that I could give her further background detail about HIV in the Soviet Union. I was at that time writing the first volume of my memoirs and so had recently refreshed my memory about those events.

The Final Scholars

James Kirby and the Barbican Trio were playing in Conway Hall so we arranged to take Nastya and Sacha, our two Scholars who had recently arrived in London, and Sandra and Norma, our friends since we were all together in the Embassy in Moscow in 1983, to the recital. There we were delighted to see Barbara Hay, another friend from our Moscow days, who we had not seen for several years, and Helen Sharman, the British cosmonaut.

Anastasia Khudyakova, known as Nastya, from Moscow, was a Neonatologist, and Aleksandra Anikeenko, Sacha, from Kemerovo in eastern Siberia, was a Cardiologist. We had also awarded a third Scholarship to Nigmetzhanova Meruyert, a Neurologist who worked in the National Childs Rehabilitation Centre in Astana, but her hand had been requested in marriage, and she decided that she should forego the opportunity of a Scholarship in favour of marrying her fiancée.

Kemerovo is 3,000 km east of Moscow. Sacha had travelled by "fast train" and then plane from Moscow. The total journey to London had taken her almost three days.

In the early 1990s, two giant hairy creatures, possibly a mother and child, "Big Foot" or "Yeti" as they are called, had reportedly been seen in the vicinity of Kemerovo.

Sacha told us that in the winter, snowfalls in Kemerovo were so heavy that often one could not see through the windows or open the front door because the snow was piled so high. Shortly before she left for London, a fire in a shopping mall in Kemerovo had killed 60 people, but fortunately none of her family or friends were affected by it.

Before studying medicine, she had worked as a nurse in a paediatric department and also had a diploma in interpreting and translation.

She told us that one of the reasons for applying for a Scholarship was to learn about paediatric heart transplantation which was not performed on children in Russia as no donors were available.

In her final detailed report she stated, *"To sum up the scholarship was a fantastic experience and for me as a paediatric cardiologist extremely useful. We also had an opportunity to see The Lion King musical and A Christmas Carol and for me the most amazing visit was to the Harry Potter museum – it was my dream and I'm so happy it came true!"*

We also took them to an exhibition at the Tate Britain called *British Art over the Years*, as we felt that this would give them an overview of the changing art scene in Great Britain.

Pushkin House presented an exhibition of new works by British artist Laura Footes – illustrations and interpretations of scenes from Mikhail Bulgakov's *The Master and Margarita*. The works explored the artist's personal connection to the novel, having read it for the first time at the beginning of an ongoing battle with Crohn's disease. By immersing herself in Russian literature, Laura was able to transcend the physical and psychological constraints of chronic pain, escaping into Bulgakov's imaginary parallel universe.

Both Scholars of course knew *Master and Margarita* well and were delighted to find that people in England also knew of Bulgakov. We invited Quen to come with us, and after viewing the exhibition we all ate supper together in Olivelli's restaurant.

We had enjoyed our farewell supper in Bel Conto so much earlier in the year that as this would be our final Scholars farewell, we decided to eat there again.

On this occasion we invited Olga and Inessa, both of whom had done so much for the Trust over the years, as well as Mike and John, Quen's and Susan's husbands. This was an opportunity for all of us to drink a toast to Michael.

We had first met Nastya when we visited Tushinskaya Hospital, by then called Bashlyaeva Hospital, where she worked as a Neonatologist. It seemed fitting that one of our final Scholars should be closely associated with the children's hospital in Moscow which we had first visited 29 years ago and which we had assisted to develop into one of the best children's hospitals in the Russian Federation.

For three years, prior to studying medicine, she had been employed as a nurse in a Neonatal Intensive Care Unit. She had applied for a Diana, Princess of Wales Tushinskaya Memorial Scholarship as she wished to get to know the best practices of UK colleagues, which would definitely expand her knowledge and help her to become a better Neonatologist.

Whilst a medical student she had participated in an International student exchange programme in South Korea.

During her Scholarship she attended the SIGNEC (special interest group in necrotising enterocolitis) international conference which was held at Chelsea Football Club in London.

In her comprehensive final report she mentioned a fantastic lecture about fire safety given during the induction course: *"To be honest I have never heard those instructions given in such a creative and easy way although it is the most important information when you enter a new building. I reckon that an induction should be compulsory for every new member of every hospital. This is the first thing I would like to introduce in our hospital in Moscow."*

She also commented: *"I've noticed the importance of parents' presence at the bedside to create a more comfortable atmosphere in such stressful moments of being in NICU and gives them assurance they are doing all the best to help their child."*

She attended many varied courses including one about anger management where they had stated *"Keep calm and carry on."* A Second World War slogan.

Nastya's final acknowledgement was, *"I am grateful to all specialists in neonatal units in GOSH and UCLH for their help to my observership. It was a sheer pleasure to join those teams of professionals who explained to me everything and answered my all my questions."*

It was difficult for us to accept that Nastya and Sasha would be the last two Scholars in our ever-increasing Russian family.

Finale

What have we learnt?, Lepidopterists in Russia, Covid-19, War in Ukraine, Professorial chair

What have we learnt from our 35 years' association with Russia and the Russians? Certainly, in general, the Russian people are warm and welcoming and at a personal level are relatively easy to get on with.

At the national and International levels, however, the situation is very different. They are a very proud people with strong nationalistic feelings who suffered dreadfully in the Second World War, and more recently after the collapse of the Soviet Union when they were effectively demoted from being one of the two most powerful states in the world to a second- or third-class position.

Sadly, there is little understanding of Russian views by the West and of Western views by Russia. Certainly, there is a complete lack of trust in each other by both parties.

At a micro level, we feel that in a small way, organisations such as Tushinskaya Trust and ICHARM have played a part in establishing an understanding of and trust in Russia and the Russians by the UK, and Britain and the British by Russia.

The big question remains: how can this be achieved by nations at a macro level?

*

Lepidopterists in Russia

Let me enlarge upon the significance of butterflies in Russia and the Soviet Union.

As an honorary "benevolent lepidopterist" by adoption, I felt obliged to assess the historical role of lepidopterists in the USSR.

There are 540 species of butterfly in Russia. Peter the Great in the 18th century purchased a collection of butterflies for the newly established Kunstkamera Museum in St Petersburg.

Trotsky, when referring to the transfer of private property to the State, had commented *"that before becoming a butterfly, the caterpillar must pass through the stage of being a pupa. Myriads of pupae would perish without becoming butterflies."*

Khrushchev, on a State visit to the United States in 1959, had been observed to turn his head to watch a butterfly, *бабочка*, flutter by.

Lysenko, who rejected Mendelian genetic inheritance and claimed that environmental influences are inheritable, stated that geneticists researched useless things such as fruit flies and butterflies. He researched practical things – tomatoes, beets and wheat. Implementation, on Stalin's orders, of Lysenko's views by Soviet agriculture, views which conformed to the Communist ideals of creating *Homo Sovieticus*, Soviet man, had severely adversely affected Soviet agricultural output.

Nikolai Kuznetsov, a renowned Russian entomologist with a particular interest in the physiology of lepidoptera, had influenced and aroused the interest of the author Vladimir Nabokov, perhaps best known in the West for his novel *Lolita*, in the study of butterflies. A case of entomology influencing etymology.

*

Covid-19

In 2020, suddenly and unexpectedly, the whole world was turned upside down by a tiny virus, which came to be known as Covid-19. It was a distant mutated variation of the virus which had caused the SARS epidemic 18 years previously.

Those of you who have read *Memories of Moscow – Memoirs of a Medical Diplomat* may recall my reference to the "chaos" theory: "A butterfly flaps its wings in Brazil causing a tornado in Texas." Now we were seeing a tiny virus figuratively "flapping its wings" in China causing a worldwide "tsunami."

In logic and related fields such as mathematics and philosophy, if and only if (shortened to "iff") is a biconditional logical connective between statements, where either or both statements are true or both are false. It is perhaps too early to know iff the above statements are true or false.

The first cases of Covid, Coronavirus disease 2019, were reported in 2019 in Wuhan in China. It was thought to have originated from an animal source.

By March 2020, WHO had declared it a global pandemic. Since then, 670 million cases have been reported worldwide, with 6.8 million deaths.

The first reported case in Europe was diagnosed in Bordeaux in France in January 2020.

Measures to reduce the spread of the virus including handwashing, wearing masks and social distancing by a minimum two metres were introduced in several countries, including the UK.

Many countries, including the UK, introduced lockdowns, which involved working from home, closure of pubs, restaurants, leisure establishments, schools, and travel restrictions. Many jobs were lost, there were supply shortages of food and medications, education suffered and there was a vast increase in online shopping. The global economy was severely affected. People, where possible, were advised to work from home. Pubs were permitted to sell alcohol through a single open window.

From our windows, or on the rare occasion we went for a walk, it was very peaceful, with little noise other than frequent ambulance sirens, as there were few cars on the road and few people in the streets. It was a pleasure to hear the birds in the trees in our garden and the trees lining the streets chattering away together and doubtless conversing together.

We ordered food online from Waitrose, and they would deliver it to our house. Later, our son-in-law, Hugh, and some of our neighbours would buy food for us from a supermarket and deliver it to us.

The first lockdown was introduced in March 2020 and lasted several weeks. Due to further spikes in the numbers of cases and hospital admissions, in the run-up to Christmas 2020 a second lockdown was introduced, and the final one in early 2021.

There were daily press conferences on television, presented by members of the government, at which Chief Medical Officer Chris Whitty and Chief Scientific Adviser Sir Patrick Vallance frequently appeared. The slogan was "Stay at home, Protect the NHS, Save lives."

In the UK there were 24 million recorded cases of Covid and over 200,000 deaths. Russia, with its much larger population, recorded only 22 million cases and 395,000 deaths.

What a relief when eventually we could welcome friends and family into our house again, but life would never be the same. There was now a new norm.

*

War in Ukraine

The future of Europe's history and that of the whole world was about to be re-written, in large part due to serious lack of judgement by the West, following the Russian invasion and annexation of Crimea and eastern Ukraine in 2014.

In November 2021 the buildup of Russian troops near the Russian and Ukrainian border suggested that Russia might be preparing to invade Ukraine again. Shortly afterwards President Putin proposed that in order to prevent such an invasion Ukraine should be prohibited from joining NATO.

With further buildup of Russian troops, tensions heightened. Once again, as in 2014, I decided to attempt to persuade all interested parties to meet and discuss the possibility of holding a high-level meeting to discuss possible "Finlandisation" of

Ukraine. Ukraine would agree not to seek closer relationships with either Russia nor the EU, or NATO. Trade agreements would be made between Ukraine and all other involved parties, including agreements on gas supplies from Russia. Both the West and Russia would assist the Ukrainian economy by offering funds either as grants or loans.

I was, and still remain, convinced that Russia would never accept the admission of Ukraine to NATO. It was essential that a permanent solution be found which safeguarded Ukraine's security, political stability and economy. This solution would need to be underwritten by the US, EU, NATO, UK and Russia. Again, as in 2014, I contacted all these parties on 28 January 2022, but received no significant responses.

On 21 February, Russian troops were ordered to enter Ukraine, and the rebel-held areas of eastern Ukraine in Luhansk and Donetsk were recognised by Russia as "people's republics."

A "special military operation", as the war was called in Russia, formally commenced three days later, with the announced intentions of liberating and "denazifying" Ukraine.

Remarkably, Ukrainian troops successfully repelled Russian advances on Kyiv, the capital, and destroyed many Russian tanks and captured much military equipment, with significant losses of life on both sides.

Russia then changed its tactics and concentrated on shelling and bombing Ukrainian towns and cities, killing and injuring many civilians and destroying numerous non-military buildings in the process.

Russian airpower and available troops far exceeded that of Ukraine, and the war became bloodier and bloodier.

I felt that I must try to persuade all involved parties to bring the war to an end rapidly.

First, I had to convince the Ukranian President Zelensky that joining NATO was an impossible pipe dream, and regaining Crimea and occupied parts of the Donbas would be very unlikely to succeed.

To this end I started corresponding in early March with the President in English.

My first letter read as follows.

> *"All possible measures must be rapidly undertaken to bring the tragic war in Ukraine to an end and create a permanently secure sovereign Ukraine, and secure peace and prosperity in Europe and the world.*
>
> *In 2014, before Russia annexed Crimea and the separatists established*

themselves in the Donbas region, I foresaw serious problems. I contacted Ban Ki-moon, the UK Foreign and Commonwealth Office, EU, NATO, US State Department and the Ukrainian prime minister, Arseniy Yatsenyuk, as well as the Russian Embassy in London. All had reservations about my proposals, but rather surprisingly Russia replied positively.

I proposed setting up a high-level conference with the objective of stabilising the situation and, with Ukraine's agreement, effectively "Finlandising" Ukraine. In 1939, following a short war between Finland and the Soviet Union, Finland became a secure, politically neutral sovereign state.

NATO and the EU would not offer membership to Ukraine, and Ukraine would remain a sovereign state with no political affiliation either to the West or Russia. Gas supplies from Russia would be secured. Economically Ukraine would be secured by grants from both the West and Russia.

In January 2022, before Russia recognised the breakaway East Ukraine as sovereign states and invaded Ukraine, I again contacted all the above interested parties, apart from Russia, but I received no significant responses.

Now we all, including Ukraine, NATO, EU, UK, USA, UN and Russia must immediately call a high-level meeting of all interested parties.

Any agreement will require compromises by all parties, Ukraine and the West must agree that NATO and the EU will admit no additional states, and Russia must agree to withdraw all troops from Ukrainian territory, now and in the future.

All interested parties will undertake irrevocably to ensure Ukraine's social, political and economic future, including fuel supplies. All interested parties will give grants to rebuild Ukraine and secure its economic future stability."

In light of the worsening situation in Ukraine, with increasingly ruthless actions by the Russian troops and increasing destruction of Ukrainian towns and cities caused by bombing and shelling, I wrote again some days later.

"My apologies for writing to you again, but sadly the situation in your country, Ukraine, worsens daily in terms of losses of your brave young men, women and children and destruction of many parts of your cities.

I fully understand that you do not trust the Russians, and that any agreement with Russia would necessitate them obtaining some of their objectives, but an agreement, such as I propose, underwritten by the West (USA, EU, UK, NATO, UN), as well as Russia, could not in any sense be construed as a surrender.

Basically, the proposal is that Ukraine approach US, EU, UK, NATO, UN and Russia and request them to set up a high-level meeting.

It will require Ukraine to accept that membership of NATO and EU will never be possible, due to Russia's intransigence. But Ukraine would remain an independent, sovereign state, with its future irrevocably secured and underwritten by the West and Russia. Economically all these parties must donate significant grants to assist the rebuilding of Ukraine and to secure its financial future. Gas and oil supplies from Russia will be insured. Most importantly Ukraine, Europe and all the world could look forward to a peaceful and productive future.

I ask you to give serious consideration to this proposal."

Shortly afterwards President Zelensky announced that Ukraine would not be seeking to become a NATO member.

My final letter stated:

"*Following the remarkable achievements of Ukrainian soldiers, there possibly will be an acknowledgement by Russia that definitive 'peace' talks should begin.*

Certainly, the main sticking point will be Russia's annexation of Crimea and the Donbas.

If one looks again at the situation following the 1939 war between Finland and the Soviet Union, an agreement was reached which entailed Finland losing 10 per cent of its territory. However, the result was that Finland for the last 80 years has remained secure, sovereign and financially viable.

Although it will be very difficult for Ukraine and the Ukrainian people to accept, the only way Ukraine can achieve a sound, secure and prosperous future will be to accept that sadly Crimea and parts of the Donbas will remain under Russian rule.

The longer the war continues the greater will be the loss of Ukrainian lives and the greater will be the destruction of your cities, towns and villages and the Ukrainian economy."

That had been the relatively easy part of my planned approach; now, I felt, was the time to contact President Putin.

This would need to be written in Russian and required a very different approach. I am very appreciative of Martin Dewhurst's excellent correction and amendment of my poor written Russian.

"Уважаемый Президент Путин

Чтобы победить в битвах на Украине, Россия должна быть готова потерять много солдат и боевой техники. При этом они разрушат и разорят Украину.

Россия останется с территориями, которые потребуют непрерывной охраны в течение многих лет, вероятно, порядка 250 000 военнослужащих, постоянно находящихся там, с высоким риском партизанских кампаний.

У Украины будет мало промышленности, он потеряет большую часть своих сельскохозяйственных ресурсов и будет постоянно истощать российскую экономику.

Международные санкции будут по-прежнему применяться, что нанесет дополнительный ущерб российской экономике с риском возможных волнений среди населения России.

Россия будет нести ответственность за 40-миллионное украинское население, которое будет злым, отказываться от сотрудничества и искать способы причинить серьезные проблемы России и русским.

Какой кошмар.

Искренне Ваш

Доктор Харальд Липман

Почетный профессор Российской медицинской академии непрерывного профессионального образования

Ранее старший медицинский советник Министерства иностранных дел и по делам Содружества Великобритании."

"Dear President Putin

In order to win the battles in Ukraine, Russia must be prepared to lose many soldiers and much military equipment. In the process they will destroy and impoverish Ukraine.

Russia will be left with territories which will require continuous policing for many years, probably in the order of 250,000 troops permanently based there, with a high risk of guerrilla campaigns.

Ukraine will have little industry, will have lost much of its agricultural resources and will be a continuous drain on the Russian economy.

International sanctions will continue to be enforced causing further damage to the Russian economy with the risk of possible unrest amongst the Russian population.

FINALE

> *Russia will be responsible for the 40 million Ukrainian population, which will be angry, uncooperative and seeking ways of causing serious problems for Russia and Russians.*
>
> *What a nightmare.*
> *Yours faithfully*
> *Dr Harald Lipman*
>
> *Honorary Professor of the Russian Medical Academy of Continuous Professional Education*
> *Formerly Senior Medical Adviser Foreign & Commonwealth Office UK"*

I received an acknowledgement from the Administrative Office of the President of the Russian Federation.

My follow up letter took a different approach.

> "*Dear President Putin*
>
> *May I respectfully make a suggestion.*
>
> *If Russia were now to propose an immediate ceasefire in Ukraine and call for an urgent meeting with Ukraine, the whole world would welcome their statesmanship and recognise how wise, powerful and influential Russia is internationally.*
>
> *This humanitarian act would save many Russian and Ukrainian lives and the economies of Russia and the world could start to normalise.*"

President Putin had by then publicly acknowledged that attempting to occupy and control the whole of a ravished Ukraine would be extremely difficult and he decided to concentrate on extending the areas Russia already occupied in the south and east.

In April I sent my final, letter to Vladimir Putin.

> "*Dear President Putin!*
>
> *Allow me, please, to make you a modest offer!*
> *If now Russia offered an immediate ceasefire by both sides in Ukraine, and also offered an urgent meeting with the President of Ukraine, the whole world*

would welcome your statesmanship and would recognise how wise, powerful and influential Russia is at the international level.

This humanitarian act would save many lives of both Russians and Ukrainians, and, by the way, the economy of both Russia and the whole world could begin to normalise."

*

Religious leaders from across the world, including the former Archbishop of Canterbury Rowan Williams, the Minister General of the Franciscan Friars, Archbishop Nikitas Lulias of the Greek Orthodox Church in Great Britain, Rabbi Jonathan Wittenberg of the New North London Synagogue and Muslim, Hindu and Buddhist leaders from a number of other countries travelled to Ukraine "to demonstrate solidarity and friendship with those affected by the war".

*

I decided to write to Rowan Williams, suggesting that an interfaith group might consider making a visit to Moscow to meet President Putin and Patriarch Kirill, head of the Russian Orthodox Church, to discuss how to end the tragic war.

Letters proposing this visit were also sent to Archbishop of Canterbury Justin Welby, Pope Francis, the Dalai Lama, the Chief Rabbi of the UK and leaders of other religious faiths – Hindu, Sunni and Shia Islam and Shinto.

During a sermon delivered in Moscow, Patriarch Kirill had portrayed the invasion of Ukraine as part of a "metaphysical" struggle against a decadent west – a civilisation deemed to have capitulated to materialism, moral relativism, globalisation and the promotion of homosexuality. Having become a vassal of the sinful west, Ukraine must be saved and restored to "Holy Rus."

In view of the Patriarch's expressed views, none of the religious leaders were prepared to speak with him.

*

All involved parties in Russia, Ukraine and the West, in light of the ruthless and inhumane Russian behaviour, were intent on escalating the war, and the likelihood of a negotiated peace seemed to be fast disappearing.

I realised there was nothing further I could do to stop the war.

FINALE

*

A Russian Chair

I was informed, some months before the Russian invasion of Ukraine, that in recognition of my work over the years to assist health care in the Russian Federation, I would be awarded the honorary title of Professor in the Russian Medical Academy Faculty of Postgraduate Education – РОССИЙСКАЯ МЕДИЦИНСКАЯ АКАДЕМИЯ ПОСЛЕДИПЛОМНОГО ОБРАЗОВАНИЯ. In light of the coronavirus pandemic, the award ceremony was temporarily postponed until November 2021.

I was invited to give my inaugural talk by Zoom on 23 November 2021 and had prepared a talk in Russian. Unfortunately, due to technical problems, I was unable to personally give the talk, but Alan Asmanov kindly spoke on my behalf.

Epilogue

***A Russian colleague, Inflation UK 2023, Prigozhin, Navalny,
Donald Trump re-elected, Butterflies of the world***

Thirty-five years had passed since we'd first placed a foot on Russian soil in 1983. The world had moved on, but, perhaps surprisingly, still continued to spin on its axis. So far, mankind, sometimes by the skin of its teeth, had managed to survive.

Russia in many ways was now a different country, and yet one didn't need to scratch too hard to find that little had changed. Many older people still harked back nostalgically to the days of Communism, when if they kept their heads down and their noses clean, life had been more secure than the present time. Or so they thought.

Others accepted Putin's present-day received opinion, and harked back even further to the days of Peter the Great, when perhaps Tsarist Russia had been at the zenith of its power.

Russian nationalism had remained a powerful influence during many different and varied political regimes. The age-old question still remained unsolved of whether Russia should be influenced by turning to the West or should look at its own internal strengths and look eastwards.

The younger generation, possibly influenced by easy access to social media, held different beliefs and thought in different terms from that of earlier generations.

Perhaps in some ways, at least in the field of health care, we had played some small part in helping Russia and the Russians progress in their onwards and upwards aspirations to improve their health care system and reduce early mortality from heart disease and stroke.

*

Russian colleague

In September 2022, I received a very disturbing email from a Russian doctor I had known for many years. Conscription into the army of 300,000 Russian men had been announced and in order to avoid it, he and his family had left Russia.

We had to find some way to help them, as their lives had been completely turned upside down. He would prefer, if possible, to bring the family to live in the UK and practise as a doctor.

EPILOGUE

Having approached many people, including some of our scholars and members of the Foreign Office, eventually Roderic Lyne suggested contacting CARA, the Council for Assisting Refugee Academics. A CARA Fellowship would cover travel to the UK, academic tuition fees and annual subsistence for a year. When finally it was awarded to him, the family all came to stay with us in London.

*

Inflation UK 2023

Soaring inflation. Widespread industrial action. *Top Gun* in the cinema. Kate Bush at number one in the charts. You can be forgiven for thinking we've returned to the 1980s!

In March 2023, the UK's annual inflation rate was 10.1 per cent.

Pandemic-related supply shortages were a major factor. As the global economy recovered from its pandemic-related recession, there was increased demand for products and materials.

At the same time, it shut down factories and ports, creating havoc along finely tuned global supply chains. The inevitable result was a sizable increase in the prices of affected goods.

The conflict in Ukraine also led to higher commodity prices, from energy to agricultural goods and metals.

Energy was a big part of the story. Britain's high rate of energy inflation reflects its heavy reliance on gas for power generation and home heating, as well as the poor energy efficiency of its housing stock.

By far the biggest drivers of inflation were soaring food, fuel and energy prices, clothing and vehicles. Putting all this together, around 80 per cent of inflation was due to global shortages and the jump in prices of goods set on global markets, such as oil.

Five pounds (US$6.21) in Britain in 2023 would only go as far as four pounds did in 2019 – a rate of inflation unmatched by other Western European countries over the same period.

The Bank of England was worried that high inflation might cause a lasting increase in wage demands and business pricing strategies, exacerbated by a post-pandemic reduction in the labour force and trade and jobs market problems caused by Brexit.

In Germany, the currency, the euro, became known as "the teuro", a pun on *teuer* (expensive).

*

Prigozhin

In June 2023 Yevgeny Prigozhin, leader of the private mercenary army, known as the Wagner group, made a short-lived unsuccessful coup against the Russian army. Although ostensibly pardoned by President Putin, two months later he died in a plane crash.

*

Alexei Navalny

Following the death in prison of Alexei Navalny the Trustees of the Great Britain-Russia Society stated:

Alexei Navalny – who was the leading critic in Russia of the Putin regime and the war against Ukraine, even from his prison cell – was a man of outstanding courage and driven by great moral clarity in his leadership of the opposition.

A brilliant communicator and campaigner, he was a valiant promoter of freedom, democracy and the rule of law. Fearless in his exposure of corruption at all levels, and the complete antithesis of Putin, Alexei Navalny represented the very best of Russia.

Alexei's death has deprived the Russian opposition of its best-known and bravest figure, And his death, for which (whatever its precise immediate causes) Putin and his regime are wholly responsible, is a tragedy for the Russian people. The loss to the world of this true hero of our time at the early age of 47 will be deeply mourned by civilised people everywhere.

Since his return to Moscow in January 2021 after a bungled attempt to poison him with Novichok in August 2020, Alexei Navalny had been incarcerated in increasingly cruel, degrading and inhuman conditions in maximum security prisons.

*

In a chaotic world with wars raging in Europe, the Middle East and several other countries, Donald Trump was elected President ot the USA by a significant majority of American voters. In light of his known ludicrous and 'top of the head' decisions, one must be very concerned about their potentially disastrous worldwide effects.

*

Let us paraphrase Marx's well-worn phrase, *пролетаріи всѣхъ странъ, соединяйтесь! вам нечего терять, кроме своих цепей* – "*Workers of the world, unite. You have nothing to lose but your chains.*"

"*Butterflies of the world, unite. You have nothing to lose but your lepidopterists.*"

Index

A
Abraham, Adolphe, 183
Abramovich, Roman, 175
Adamishin, Anatoly, 93, 94, 96
Alexeeva, Zhenya, 200, 201, 231
Amish, The, 112
Angel, Phillip, 71, 76
Angel, Liz, 93, 94
Annan, Kofi, 117, 174
Arkhangelsk Oblast, Introduction
Arnisson-Newgass, Paul, 3
Aung San Suu Kyi, 23

B
Ban Ki-moon, 233, 264, 265, 306
Balkan States, pp 132, 133, 160
Barlow, Sheila, 63, 64, 69, 70, 73, 75, 145
Beale, Marcus, 216, 222, 240
Bering, Vitu, Introduction
BESO (British Executive Services Overseas), 13, 14, 75
Blair, Tony, 110, 120, 132, 152, 201, 215, 271
Bloomberg, Michael, 211
Bond, Kingsmill, 13, 73, 75, 92, 93, 105,
Boyde, Dicky, 19, 102
Boytsov, Sergei, 230, 233, 249, 266
British Museum, 60
Bruce Lockhart, Robert, Introduction
Braithwaite, Introduction, Sir Rodric, 200, 297
Braithwaite, Jill, Introduction, 4, 209, 297
British Embassy, Introduction, 7, 15, 40, 54, 58, 80, 88, 92, 133, 210, 253, 259, 274, 298
Bulgakov, Mikhail, 300
Burgess, Guy, 2
Buzaev, Igor, 246, 293

C
Caplan, Aby, 130
Carpenter, Hugh, 9, 76
Cartledge, Sir Bryan, 6, 7, 15, 56, 58, 100,
Cartledge, Ruth, 56
Chalidze, Vera, Introduction
Chalstrey, Sir John, 58, 96

INDEX

Chan, Professor Margaret, 231, 231, 233
Cherepov, Yuri, 10
Chilcot Enquiry, 215
Christ's College Cambridge 189, 190
Collyer, Sarah, 13
Cook, Kate, Introduction
Coomaraswamy, Tara, 213-215
Covid 19, 302-4, 172, 189,
Cox, Lady Caroline, 7, 15, 54. 55, 88, 90, 91, 94, 150, 151, 152, 157, 162, 197, 256
Cox, Murray, 88, 91
Crawford, Olga, 88, 138, 210, 259, 297

D
Dalai Lama, 175, 17, 245, 310
Dale, Linda, 63, 69, 70, 73, 75
Davydova, Natalia, 227, 248, 251
de Laune, Gideon, 56
Dhaka, 22
Diamant, Françoise, 79
Diana Memorial Fund, 125, 138, 150
Diana Princess of Wales Tushinskaya Memorial Scholarships, 127, 139, 219, 222, 239, 300
Dmitrieva, Olga, 92, 128, 129, 179, 290
Dmitriev, Sacha, 92, 290
Duddington, Nataly, 2, 73, 93, 118, 297

E
Earl of Douglas, Archibald (Henry IV part 1), Prologue
ENRC (Eurasian National Resources Corporation), 217, 221, 223, 225, 227, 259, 266, 273, 274, 276, 288
Evans, Christine, 18

F
Family Centred Care, 10, 14, 61, 62, 70, 85, 104, 05, 130
Fall, Brian, 58, 88
Fasmer, Bente, 58, 88, 93, 94, 151, Acknowledgments
Fayed, Dodi, 117
Fenn, Nicholas, 22
Flavell, Bridget, 93, 105
Ford, Harrison, 56, 112
Foreign and Commonwealth Office, 35, 306
Fraser, Neil, 40, 45

G
Galimova, Rezida 210, 217, 228
Gates, Bill, 224, 227
Good Friday Agreement, 132

Gorbachev, Mikhail, 4, 5, 217, 239
Gorbacheva, Raisa, 161, 217, 222, 227, 229, 238, 239, 240, 253, 269
Great Exuma Island, 192-4
Guildhall, 58, 96, 98,

H
Hals, Ottar, 102, 103
Ham & High, 65, 272
Harkness Fellowship, 110
Harris, Peter, 139
Harris, Judy, 139
Harris, Jayne, 71, 75, 82
Hatch, Professor David, 6, 149
Hay, Barbara, 299
Henry IV (Shakespeare), Prologue
Homeopathy, 86
Hospital acquired infection, 10, 12, 14, 74, 84, 101, 105,
Hussein, Saddam, 1, 174

I
ICHARM Project, 185, 192, 196, 199, 201, 202, 204, 207, 218, 219, 220, 221, 227, 228, 231, 232, 233, 235, 239, 241, 245, 246, 248, 249, 259, 260, 261, 266, 275, 296, 302
IELTS (International English Language Testing System), 126, 239, 247, 277
Ivanov, Vadim, 9, 14, 71
International Date Line, 51
Isis, 237,
Ispolatovskaya, Emilia, 126, 130, 141, 142

J
Jephson, Patrick, 54, 88, 95
Johnson, Boris, 248, 283, 297,
Johnson, Sandra, 22
Jones, Kathryn, 71, 75, 82, 90, 145

K
Kaplan, Fanny, Introduction
Karamova, Irina, 220, 228, 229, 260
Kargopal, Introduction
Kebede, Enku, 8, 40, 45
Khamzina, Nurgul, 247
Kidd, Michael, 9, 61
Ki-moon, Ban, 233, 264, 265, 306
King's Fund, 8, 9, 17, 58
Know How Fund, 13, 64, 138
Kipling, Rudyard, 25
Kirby, James, 299

Kissinger, Henry, 95, 96, 122, 265
Koch, Tamar, Dr, 222, 246, 256
Kosigina, Margarita, 55
Khrushchev, Nikita, 302
Kurtianyk, Olga, 9, 62

L
Lebedev, Alexander, 217, 224, 225, 239, 253
Lebedev, Evgeny, 217
Lee Kwan Yu, 29
Leon, Dave, 196, 235, 265, 266
Leshkevitch, Ivan, 9, 10, 11, 21, 58, 60, 68, 125, 130
Lidstrom, Ing-Marie, 18, 103, 127
Lipman, Nahid, Dedication, Acknowledgements, Introduction, Prologue, 2, 8, 9, 14, 17, 18, 27, 28, 29, 34, 39, 40, 41, 44, 46, 47, 50, 51, 53, 55, 56, 67, 69, 70, 72, 74, 139, 140, 143, 144, 145, 146, 147, 148, 149, 150, 161, 162, 163, 165, 169, 170, 183, 189, 192, 193, 203, 207, 213, 218, 219, 229, 230, 231, 236, 239, 247, 248, 249, 252, 253, 261, 273, 286, 288, 290, 313
Lipman, Marc, 1, 36, 67, 69, 105, 106, 110, 111, 112, 180, 208, 209, 228, 243, 247, 278, 80 281, Acknowledgements
Lipman, Amanda, 17, 27, 29, 47, 67, 87, 105, 175, 185, 189, 203, 208, 209, 228, 233, 235-237
Litvinenko, Aleksandr, 167
Litvinov, Maxim, Introduction
Litvinov, Misha, Introduction
Lloyd Webber, Andrew, 27
Longrigg, Tony, 100
Lovett, Ken, 12, 185
Lovett, Susi, 185
Lubyanka, Introduction, 65
Lyne, Sir Roderic, 107, 177, 202, 215, 313
Lysenko, Trofim, 303

M
Maclean, Donald, 2
Maclean, Fitzroy, 133
MacQueen, Susan, 6, 58, 70, 84, 93, 102, 149, 161, 259
Mad Cow Disease, 107
Major, John, 2
Mandalay, 24, 25
Mansion House, 96, 97
McDermott, Frank, 38
McKenzie, Sheila, 9, 62
McWilliams, Sir Francis, 55
McMillan, Charles, 36
Marquez, Patricio, 198, 233
Meakin, Richard, 222, 246
Mendis, Shanti 207, 230, 256

Minina, Marina, 63
Morey, Tony, 151
Morel, Agni, 151
Mossoviet, 6
Mok, Quen, 161, 184, 259, 274
Murphy, Mary, 105, 211
Murrell, Kathy, Introduction, 7, 8, 21
Murrell, Geoff, 7, 8

N
Navalny, Alexei, 314
Nehru, Jawaharlal, 133
Naigovzina, Nelli, 9, 10, 11, 55, 62, 185, 199, 210, 220
Nicholls, Michael, 6, 19, 58, 102, 135 138, 152, 161, 187, 188, 190, 293

O
ODA (Official Development Assistance), 34, 35, 43, 45,
Oganov, Raphael, 199, 200, 230, 248, 249
Osmanov, Ismail, 161, 177, 196, 216, 238, 248, 281

P
Paediatric Nursing School, 62, 64, 66, 68, 72, 73, 75, 81, 82, 101, 102, 105, 129, 130, 145
Paediatric Nurse Teacher Training, 128
Pagan (Burma), 24, 25
Pankin, Boris, 55
Pasternak, Boris, 69
Patriarch Kirill
Pavlov, Yuri
Pectopah (cat), 17, 27, 28, 67, 77
Peart, Michael, 22
Pemba, Norbu, 102
Pemba, Tsewang, 19, 102, 241, 242
Peters, Gordon, 9
Pinewood Corporation, 95
Princess Diana, 54-59, 72, 75, 87-96, 117-123, 219, 237, 288
Pushka, Pekka, 230
Putin, Vladimir, 104, 124, 198, 230, 233, 245, 247, 253, 264, 286, 296, 298, 304, 307-310, 315

Q
Queen Elizabeth II, Introduction, 35, 47, 120

R
Raisa Gorbachev Foundation, Introduction, 161, 216-7, 222, 229, 239, 240, 253
Raisa Gorbacheva Institute, 217, 269
Ransome, Arthur, Introduction,
Ratford, Sir David, 100, 104, 106, 152, 161, 231

INDEX

Ray, Inessa, 128, 129, 141, 167, 177, 228, 297, 300
Reid, Norma, 299
Rezayev, Sergei, 64, 73
Rezayev, Masha, 73
Romanyuk, Galina, 12, 55, 62, 71, 92
Romanyuk, Sergei, 8
Rosenthal, Joe, 222, 228, 246
Rutherford, Margaret, Introduction

S

Saunders, Hannah, 101
Scales, Prunella, 94
Sinatra, Frank, 291
Singapore, 1, 27, 29-30
Skorobogatova, Olga, 9, 15, 62, 64, 66,6, 75, 76, 90, 105
Skorvotsova, Veronika 203, 220, 221, 235, 248
Skripal, Sergei, 295
Solzhenitsyn, Aleksandr, 65
St Dorothy's Hostel, 186, 217, 235, 256, 288, 293
St Helena, 166
Szombati, ZsaZsa, 143
South Africa, 113-116, 166
Streisand, Barbra, 81
Sutherland, Jeanne, 286
Sutherland, Sir Iain, 286

T

Thakin Aung San, 23
Totma, Introduction
Trotsky, Leon, 238, 302
Trump, Donald, 286, 314
Turing, Alan, 24
Tushinskaya Hospital, 10, 13, 14, 57, 62, 63, 64, 67, 81, 83, 85, 91, 91, 94, 130, 144-5, 151, 249, 253, 259, 271, 282, 283, 288, 293, 300
Tushinskaya Trust, 1, 6-7, 57, 81, 91, 95, 104, 125, 166, 177, 178, 179, 187, 213, 216, 217, 225, 236, 241, 248, 274, 293, 302

V

Vaganov, Sergei, 139, 148
Vas Dias, Susan, 61, 70, 85, 106
Vologda, Introduction
VSO (Voluntary Service Overseas), 33, 34, 43

W

Welby, Justin, 310
West, Timothy, 94

Williams, Col. Violet, 7
Williams, Rowan, 310
World Trade Centre, Moscow, 231, 232
World Trade Centre, New York, 157
Worshipful Society of Apothecaries, 55, 56, 148, 263
Wydell, Janet, 72, 82, 145
Wyse, Dr Richard, 184, 200, 228

Y
Yeltsin, Boris, 4, 49, 60, 79, 80, 104, 117, 124, 279

Z
Zelensky, Volodymyr, 305, 307
Zelinskaya, Dina, 10, 128, 129, 141, 142
Zyuganov, Gennadi, 104

Printed in Great Britain
by Amazon